AF643659

Vlad Naumescu

Modes of Religiosity in Eastern Christianity

Religious Processes and Social Change in Ukraine

LIT

Cover Photo: At Lake St Anna in western Ukraine, pilgrims seek healing by immersing themselves in the cold water provided by a miraculous spring (2003) (Photo: Vlad Naumescu).

This work was submitted in partial fulfilment of the requirements for the Degree of Doctor of Philosophy at the Faculty of Philosophy of the Martin Luther University, Halle-Wittenberg.

Zugl.: Halle-Wittenberg, Univ., Diss., 2006

∞

Gedruckt auf alterungsbeständigem Werkdruckpapier entsprechend
ANSI Z3948 DIN ISO 9706

Bibliographic information published by the Deutsche Nationalbibliothek
The Deutsche Nationalbibliothek lists this publication in the Deutsche Nationalbibliografie; detailed bibliographic data are available in the Internet at http://dnb.d-nb.de.

ISBN 978-3-8258-9908-0

A catalogue record for this book is available from the British Library

© LIT VERLAG Dr. W. Hopf Berlin 2007

Auslieferung/Verlagskontakt:
Fresnostr. 2 48159 Münster
Tel. +49 (0)251–62 03 20 Fax +49 (0)251–23 19 72
e-Mail: lit@lit-verlag.de http://www.lit-verlag.de

Distributed in the UK by: Global Book Marketing, 99B Wallis Rd, London, E9 5LN
Phone: +44 (0) 20 8533 5800 – Fax: +44 (0) 1600 775 663
http://www.centralbooks.co.uk/acatalog/search.html

Distributed in North America by:

Transaction Publishers
New Brunswick (U.S.A.) and London (U.K.)

Transaction Publishers
Rutgers University
35 Berrue Circle
Piscataway, NJ 08854

Phone: +1 (732) 445 - 2280
Fax: + 1 (732) 445 - 3138
for orders (U. S. only):
toll free (888) 999 - 6778
e-mail:
orders@transactionspub.com

Modes of Religiosity in Eastern Christianity

Religious Processes and Social Change in Ukraine

In this book Vlad Naumescu explores religious phenomena in contemporary western Ukraine (historic eastern Galicia), focusing on the Greek Catholic Church and its transformations under socialism and postsocialism. Beyond the details of this particular case, he addresses more general questions about the role of religion in Ukrainian society and about patterns of reproduction and change in eastern Christianity, the dominant religious tradition in eastern Europe. Naumescu's processual model, based on the 'modes of religiosity' theory developed by Harvey Whitehouse, pays close attention to variation in ritual transmission in order to reveal a dialectic between imagistic and doctrinal religiosity. When analysed through the modes theory, eastern Christianity is seen to be a tradition in equilibrium, drawing constantly on both modes in order to maintain its vitality and the commitment of its believers.

The plural religious landscape of Ukraine contrasts with the religious monopolies characteristic of most postsocialist countries. This pluralism is usually seen in terms of a 'marketplace' of religions, but Naumescu argues that western Ukraine has a single 'Orthodox imaginary' that encompasses the majority of the competing churches. The roots of this imaginary lie in the local tradition of practice and belief, which is the result of an original synthesis of eastern and western Christianity, the two great traditions that meet in this region. By connecting to this Orthodox imaginary, local people transcend the newly established confessional borders and have no difficulty moving between churches, taking their devotional practices with them.

Naumescu observes the emergence of religious plurality and the everyday experience of diversity in two principal field sites: Sykhiv, a suburb of L'viv largely constructed in the Godless era of socialism, and Shchirets, formerly a multicultural Galician town and now a Ukrainian village. Cases from these sites, and the example of the traditionalist movement in the Ukrainian Greek Catholic Church more generally, illustrate the uneasy passage from imagistic to doctrinal in the local tradition. The alternative structures and imagistic practices developed by Greek Catholics while they were repressed during the Soviet era have gradually been routinized to form the doctrinal core of the re-established church. The redefinition of religious orthodoxy depends on the 'recovery of memory' of the church's underground existence and on the standardization of the rite. Both processes are part of the establishment of a new ecclesiastical hierarchy and its demarcation from alternative sources of authority.

In his later chapters Naumescu contrasts the routinized religious practices of his urban and rural sites with the excursions into spirituality that some believers make to sites of imagistic religiosity. Apparition sites and a monastic community famed for its exorcism rituals show how people formulate collective and personal responses to social changes and express them in a religious idiom. Ritual performances generate an imaginary that permeates the lived reality of monks and pilgrims, who are not passive recipients of 'divine agency' but concrete agents of change. Naumescu thus argues that religion does more than merely accommodate to social change through specific mechanisms of the imagistic mode; this eastern Christian tradition is itself a potential source of social transformation.

Halle Studies in the Anthropology of Eurasia

General Editors:

Chris Hann, Richard Rottenburg, Burkhard Schnepel

Volume 15

LIT

Contents

List of Illustrations

Maps

Plates

(all photographs taken by Vlad Naumescu and Klára Trencsényi, 2003-2005)

Preface

Thanks to the work of historians such as John-Paul Himka and Paul Robert Magocsi, the complex history of the church nowadays known officially as the Ukrainian Catholic Church of the Byzantine Rite and the role played by its outstanding twentieth-century metropolitan, Andrei Sheptytskyi, are well known far beyond the western Ukrainian homeland. This region is largely congruent with the territory known as eastern Galicia in the time of the Habsburg Empire. Although it falls outside today's European Union, an identification with the West and with Europe lingers strongly, especially among the inhabitants of L'viv. The church still popularly referred to as Greek Catholic has been a key agent in sustaining that orientation, before, during, and after the socialist interlude.

Although Ukraine falls entirely within the traditional territory of eastern Christianity, its contemporary religious landscape is fragmented. This pluralism is a result not only of the Union of Brest, which gave birth to Greek Catholicism more than 400 years ago, but also of several more recent splits that have divided the Orthodox churches. The postsocialist state has refrained from identifying with any one church and permitted a large degree of religious pluralism; indeed, it is possible that this religious fragmentation has contributed to the continuing weakness of the state. It might appear that 'supply-side' models of the kind developed by sociologists of religion to explain the outcomes of denominational competition in North America are relevant to this case. As Catherine Wanner has shown, Jehovah's Witnesses, Pentecostalists, and other evangelical Christians have made considerable inroads in Ukraine in recent years. However, Vlad Naumescu argues in this book that most people in western Ukraine have greater difficulty accommodating such converts in their 'religious imaginary' than they do the adherents of other eastern Christian churches and even Roman Catholics. Greek Catholics are included in an 'Orthodox imaginary' that sets limits to the toleration of new faiths in the country and to the value of a market model in the analysis of religious choices.

The re-emergence of the Greek Catholics in the 1990s, after more than four decades in the 'catacombs', is a dramatic story. Naumescu tells it well, concentrating on two main field sites, the L'viv suburb of Sykhiv and the nearby village of Shchirets. The former was supposed to be an exemplar of socialist secular urban planning, but in fact it was the scene of a lively Greek Catholic underground religious life before 1990, tellingly evoked here through the oral reminiscences of participants. Naumescu shows how Greek Catholics were able to re-enter the public sphere in the nationalist climate after 1990, although strong competition from other denominations prevented them from establishing a monopoly. Conflicts developed within Greek

Catholic ranks as the church consolidated itself organizationally. The suffering of the past was duly commemorated, but the charismatic appeal of the ex-underground priests gradually gave way to more routinized structures of authority and standardized rites as the church reconstructed its formal hierarchy with the help of many new arrivals from the West.

Naumescu's second principal field site was the multiconfessional village of Shchirets. Again he provides a detailed account of contemporary religious behaviour, making use of survey methods that remain relatively uncommon in socio-cultural anthropology. As in Sykhiv we see certain tensions: some villagers are dissatisfied with the religious services available locally and pursue a wider range of spiritual activities outside their community. One of these supplementary channels is provided by the resurgence of monastic activity, exemplified by the Basilian monastic community at the remote village of Kolodiivka, near Ternopil. The splinter group of monks who pioneered this community were pursuing *communitas* in Victor Turner's sense. The main secret of their attraction for large numbers of pilgrims was their dramatic rituals for expelling evil spirits. Eventually the spreading fame of the exorcism rituals helped to accentuate divisions within the community. When Naumescu revisited the monastery a year after completing his fieldwork he found that the precarious balance established by the founding group of monks under its charismatic abbot had been lost; several monks had come to find this religious imaginary unacceptable and left the monastery.

Naumescu's diverse ethnographic materials are integrated by a strong theoretical argument. Although cognitive approaches have been widely applied in recent years in the anthropology of religion, this is the first systematic application of such an approach to any eastern Christian tradition. Naumescu draws primarily on the influential model of Harvey Whitehouse, with its sharp opposition between the doctrinal and imagistic modes of religiosity (corresponding to semantic and episodic memory, respectively). What makes eastern Christianity distinctive is not the way in which a 'great tradition' interacts with a 'little tradition' but a unique equilibrium between the two modes. At the same time, Naumescu rejects stereotypical views of the conservatism of Orthodoxy in favour of a processual model that emphasizes a continuing dialectic between the two modes of religiosity, understood as ideal types. This balance is dynamic: it changes primarily as a result of acts of individual creativity, which in turn are shaped by the wider social context.

Naumescu further develops the application of the cognitive model through a contrastive account of apparitions at Seredne during the Soviet era and similar phenomena at Lishnia in the post-Soviet years. Under socialism, religious repression was countered by a welter of visionary experiences in the Ukrainian countryside, which the authorities could never bring under control. Especially among Greek Catholics, a radical rejection of Soviet authority was coupled with a pro-nationalist stance. Although the emphasis upon national unity has continued in the postsocialist years, the context is now quite different. Sites such as Lishnia, known locally as 'the new Fatima', continue to multiply and to attract organized pilgrims in ways that were impossible before. Some clergy, however, have reservations about the spread of such 'foolishness'. The travelling priests who support the apparition sites are in a sense the successors to the underground priests of the socialist era, the purveyors of an imagistic mode that nowadays rubs up uneasily against the newly consolidated institutional strength of the doctrinal mode. Finally, conventional sociological models of causality are turned around as Naumescu argues that religious imaginaries can be the causes as well as the consequences of social change.

Given the social uncertainties of the years following the collapse of socialism, it is hardly surprising that the imagistic mode has provided a continuous motor for dynamic renewal and at times has appeared to dominate the religious imaginary in western Ukraine. Whitehouse's concepts help us to make sense of otherwise puzzling patterns in popular religion, such as the exorcisms at Kolodiivka, and also of tensions in ecclesiastical politics such as those between priests who made their reputations in the underground and the new cohorts who have assumed power in the course of recent institutionalization. But Naumescu advances a more general thesis. Imagistic practices, present in all religious traditions (especially in times of social instability) and crucial to their renewal, are in the case of eastern Christianity more readily integrated into the mainstream of doctrine as well as practice. Whitehouse's model needs modification because the 'tedium effect' becomes an unnecessary condition for change in the religious tradition and the dynamic interaction of the two modes is often determined by religious politics. The more general point is that greater attention needs to paid to the particular historical conditions and social forces at play when applying the cognitive model to different religious traditions.

While specialists in religion will appreciate this study for its sustained application of a cognitivist model to eastern Christianity, others will value the light it sheds on multiple dimensions of contemporary social life in a large country where little anthropological research has been undertaken to date. Naumescu argues persuasively that the study of religion yields rich insights into multiple facets of postsocialist transformations and individual coping strategies. Inevitably some questions arise as a result of the author's multiple ambitions. Does the contestation surrounding the exorcism rituals at the monastery in Kolodiivka exemplify the *longue durée* interplay of two modes of religiosity in one strand of a world religion, or are these events better viewed as ephemeral products of 'the transition' in Ukraine? What remains of the general ambitions of the cognitive approach if it needs major modification in this case? (The modifications would presumably have to be much greater in the case of religions lacking a textual tradition altogether.) How exactly does the balance of doctrinal and imagistic in eastern Christianity differ from that found in other religious traditions, such as the popular Catholicism of the Mediterranean region or indeed the neighbouring variety in postsocialist Poland? Can the observable differences be attributed largely to the weaker institutional structures and less centralized authority of the eastern tradition, or do they have deeper roots in theology? How far can these postsocialist patterns be fruitfully compared with innovative religious imaginaries in other 'postcolonial' contexts?

These are just a few of the exciting questions Vlad Naumescu raises in this monograph. He himself begins to answer them with references to comparative materials from Catholic Europe, and it seems to me that it might prove fruitful to extend the comparisons much farther, at least to the other world religions. Meanwhile readers will welcome the present volume as a major contribution to the ongoing cognitivist debates and also to the emerging 'anthropology of Christianity', within which eastern traditions have so far been almost completely neglected.

Chris Hann

Halle/Saale, September 2007

Acknowledgements

This book is the result of a three-year doctoral thesis project developed under the auspices of the Max Planck Institute for Social Anthropology (MPISA), Halle/Saale, Germany. During that time, many people aided me in various ways. First, I am grateful to the people in Ukraine who accepted me in the beginning and helped me throughout my stay: the families among whom I lived in Shchirets and Kolodiivka; my closest collaborators, Volodia, Taras, and Natallia; and the wonderful people at the Ukrainian Catholic University who provided continual support for my work and from whom I learned a great deal. I thank Arseny and Roman, former monks in the Kolodiivka monastery, and Father Ruslan and the other priests and parishioners in Shchirets and Sykhiv who had confidence in my research and offered much of their time for my work. I am grateful for the help of Jaroslav Hrytsak and Viktor Susak, and I thank the latter's students in the sociology department at Ivan Franko National University for helping with research in Sykhiv in 2003–2004.

In Halle, I am grateful to my supervisor, Chris Hann, whose constant support and close interest in the subject helped me formulate my argument and achieve something I would not previously have thought possible. In the writing-up stage I received valuable comments and endless encouragement from my colleagues at MPISA, for which I am extremely grateful. Richard Rottenburg's comments and the inspiring discussions during his seminar at the Institute of Anthropology, Halle University, greatly improved my analysis. I want also to thank Berit Westwood and Anke Brüning for their technical support and Jane Kepp for her excellent editorial work. Some of the inspiration for this research came from lectures and conferences I attended in Halle. In particular, the conference on eastern Christianities organized at MPISA in September 2006 proved an excellent occasion for making my ideas known and receiving valuable feedback.

Finally, I thank my wife, Klara, for the wonderful way in which she accompanied me in this journey, and for Daniel.

Note on Transliteration

The Ukrainian transliteration used in this book follows the US Library of Congress system, without diacritical marks. All translations from Ukrainian are mine.

Chapter 1
Introduction

In this book I describe the evolution of a local variant of eastern Christianity in order to expose the interplay of religion and social change in western Ukraine. Following Ukraine's postsocialist religious revival, religion re-emerged into the public sphere to a remarkable degree. Although this was something new for central and eastern Ukraine, it was nothing startling for the western part, which had preserved its religious tradition throughout the Soviet period. I look at the processes that generated western Ukraine's present-day pluralism, searching for patterns of religious development. I examine expressions of local religiosity, modes of transmission of religious knowledge, and the creation and reproduction of confessional identities in the making of churches.

I have focused this book mainly on the religious dimension of social life because the people with whom I worked were intensely preoccupied with religious issues. Their devotion and attachment to the spiritual world were stronger than one usually finds in modern Western societies. Observing these people, I understood that religion was a major force fuelling social transformation, even though it had remained a peripheral subjcct in the anthropological literature on postsocialism. In addition to discussing the role of religion in postsocialist Ukraine, I use the case of the local religious tradition to address more general questions about patterns of reproduction and change in eastern Christianity, the largest religious tradition in this part of Europe.

My work bridges two bodies of anthropological literature: postsocialist studies and the anthropology of religion. Anthropologists have largely ignored associations between the two fields and have kept postsocialist studies regionally focused, with no substantial input into the anthropology of religion. The approach I take builds more than a purely ethnographic account of religious life in western Ukraine. I examine postsocialist religious phenomena in a comparative perspective, but I also engage with sociological models – tentative explanations of postsocialist religiosity – as well as historical accounts and theologically informed arguments. The guiding theoretical frame is based on theories of ritual transmission recently proposed in cognitive studies of religion. I weave together various concepts and ideas in an effort to explain the complex phenomenon of religious life in western Ukraine.

To lay out the theoretical frame of the book, I start in this chapter from an oscillation I observed in my field sites between different forms of religious practice that constituted the local tradition. Following a line of thought in anthropological studies that focuses on ritual transmission, I introduce the 'modes of religiosity' theory (Whitehouse 1995, 2000, 2004), which proposes two sets of psychological and socio-political features corresponding to two modes of religious transmission, the doctrinal and the imagistic. The doctrinal mode encompasses frequent, routinized rituals with standardized messages and little personal involvement, whereas the imagistic mode involves sporadic, small-scale rituals triggering intense emotions and spontaneous exegetical reflection. The interaction between the modes determines the evolution of the religious tradition. Imagistic rituals channel individual creativity and innovation (religious revelation) into the religious tradition in culturally accepted forms. When analysed through the frame of the modes theory, eastern Christianity appears to be a tradition in equilibrium, drawing on both modes in order to stay alive and maintain motivation in its subjects. In the last part of this chapter I discuss the role of Greek Catholics in the postsocialist context and review the relevant regional literature on the subject.

In chapter 2 I offer a brief historical analysis to illustrate the development of a syncretic religious tradition in eastern Galicia, which sits at the intersection of two great traditions, eastern and western Christianity. I follow the transformations of the local religious tradition from its golden period in Kievan Rus through the multiculturality of Austrian Galicia to the Soviet repression and the religious revival of the 1980s. When observed over such a long span, religious institutions appear as ambiguous constructs, maintaining flexible borders and fluctuating in conjunction with political transformations.

The processes that led to the splitting of the Orthodox Church and the formation of several eastern Christian churches in Ukraine in the early 1990s are of particular interest for understanding the present-day plurality of churches there. The case of 'fragmented Orthodoxy' and the dynamism of Ukrainian religious life independent of state and nation caused social scientists to propose different explanatory models to account for the relatively smooth achievement of religious pluralism in postsocialist Ukraine. Positioning my work against some of these explanations, I argue that the basis for practising pluralism in western Ukraine is the 'Orthodox imaginary', which encompasses a large part of the emerging churches. By connecting to this representation, people go beyond the borders of confessional differentiation and manage to transport their practices to a diversity of churches. This conclusion is reflected in the ethnographic case presented in the subsequent chapter.

In chapter 3 I examine the macro-processes described in the previous chapter through a case study of the local 'making of churches'. The case of Sykhiv, a Soviet suburb of L'viv, reveals the mechanisms that generated the 'making' process and the way religious pluralism came about as a grassroots development. With six religious groups emerging in the first part of the 1990s, all closely positioned around the same square, Sykhiv is an excellent illustration of the metaphor 'religious marketplace'. The emergence of religious plurality in Sykhiv had its roots in the socialist period, when two parallel forms of religious practice existed: a formal practice connected to the official church and an informal one linked to the 'underground' (*pidpilnyi*) church. The religious revival of the 1990s generated a redefinition of spaces and institutions in which Greek Catholics spread out in the district, profiting from the temporary conjuncture of national ideals and a particular religious identity. The making of churches was characterized by successive divisions and structural instability, reflecting the social unrest of the postsocialist period. Behind this, however, lay a shared base of practices and beliefs that belonged to the local religious tradition. The sociological survey data I discuss in chapter 3 reveal patterns that sustained the unity rather than the partitioning of the local community. The everyday experience of diversity in Sykhiv proves the actual functioning of the Orthodox imaginary.

In chapter 4 I move a step farther into the making of churches, engaging with the institutionalization that began in the second part of the 1990s. An analysis of the traditionalist movement in the Ukrainian Greek Catholic Church shows how the emerging church attempted to consolidate its hierarchical structure and redefine orthodoxy within church tradition. The role of the underground church in the re-establishment of the Ukrainian Greek Catholic Church was crucial, but the revived church pushed aside the controversial figures of the underground, marginalizing them. Competing groups contested and claimed authority over the church, but one group succeeded in imposing its vision. The 'recovery of memory' involved the objectification of individual memories into an official church history that created an image of the 'martyr church'. This standardization of the collective memory of the underground supported the establishment of the church's authority and solidified its separation from alternative sources of authority emerging from the underground. The 'purification of the rite' affected local religious practices adapted to the underground experience, which had to be transformed again into standardized church ritual and differentiated from the practices of 'other eastern churches'. I observe the apparently divergent trends within the Ukrainian Greek Catholic Church, between 'modernists' and 'traditionalists', or 'easterners' and 'westerners', which shape the evolution of the religious tradition.

I use chapter 5 to expose the patterns of religious life in western Ukraine by analysing 'ordinary' and 'extraordinary' rituals and expressions of rural religiosity. Developing the chapter around the routinized religious practices of the village, I describe church-related rituals and domestic devotion. Village religiosity became the main preserver of religious life during Soviet times, and while adapting to difficult conditions, it managed to preserve the local tradition. Since the religious sphere has been reorganized, more choices have appeared, yet people do not see them as such. The case of the village of Shchirets also supports the argument that people connect to an Orthodox imaginary, the basis of which is the rite, language, and beliefs shared by eastern churches. The rituals I describe maintain the continuity of religious practice and the doctrinal aspect of the local tradition. The household survey data I present underscore the sense of routine that characterizes local practice, a monotony from which people escape by searching for alternative sources of religious experience, usually outside the village community. Chapter 5 is built in direct contrast to the following ones, which are dedicated to 'excursions into spirituality' – to sites of religious practice alternative to those that form the routine of church life.

In Chapter 6 I bring together the making of churches and the dynamic provoked by the interaction of the modes of religiosity to analyse the short life story of a monastic community. This splinter group emerged from a troublesome monastic order by redefining tradition around Orthodox ideals and cultivating an imagistic ritual. The story of the splinter group illustrates one possible scenario of the modes theory: the separation, attempted institutionalization, and subsequent disintegration of a community because of a clash between two modes. The first part of the chapter revolves around the setting up of the monastery, the pursuit of an ideal, and the creation of the new community united around the exorcism ritual. This imagistic practice maintained the cohesion and motivation of the group while generating a particular imaginary based on the cosmology of the ritual. In the second part of the chapter I deal with exorcism and the religious imaginary that formed around the ritual. The strength of the imaginary deriving from the ritual permeated the lived reality of monks and pilgrims in concrete ways. The tendency of one group to reinforce the imagistic mode, counter to the common practice of drawing on both types of rituals, led to the splitting of the monastery. This case illustrates the social dynamics resulting from the conflicting interaction of the modes of religiosity when manipulated by religious experts.

Chapter 7 is focused on the religious imaginaries produced through rituals of the imagistic type. Such extraordinary expressions of religiosity are equal in importance to the ordinary aspects of religious practice described in chapter 5. Religious apparitions are particular occasions on which people formulate collective responses to social changes and express them in a religious idiom. I analyse variations in the contents of the religious tradition and their relation to changing social conditions. By comparing apparitions – one related to Soviet repression and others to the postsocialist revival – I expose changes in the form and contents of these visions as responses to specific social conditions. Minor inputs from believers are mediated through the ritual, generating new interpretations that are later incorporated into the religious tradition and become common practice. As the cases analysed in this chapter show, religion is a potential source of social change, empowering certain persons to act and modify social patterns. For that reason, an investigation of the patterns of transmission of religious knowledge and variation in the contents of religious imaginaries can reveal the role of religion in accommodating social changes, particularly those specific to the postsocialist period in Eastern Europe.

1.1 Theoretical Context

The individual's relation to religion has been a recurrent theme in anthropology. The religious experience, with its individual and collective dimensions, lends itself well to enquiry; on the one hand, individual experience forms the basis for religion, and on the other, religion plays a primary role in accomplishing certain social functions. Whether or not the individual is seen as the locus of religious experience depends on the anthropological and philosophical tradition from which a scholar comes. Anthropologists have studied religion through various theoretical approaches, from phenomenology to psychoanalysis and, more recently, cognitive theories. Such a multiplicity of theoretical inputs has inspired anthropologists to move beyond an exclusive focus on the sociological processes involved in religion and towards comprehending mechanisms of individual religiosity. Within the anthropology of religion, a growing body of literature dealing with both local and global religions contends that an appreciation of psychological processes is crucial to a proper understanding of religious phenomena.

The study of religion, rather than having an explicit singular focus, has revolved recently around different ideas and assumptions about the nature and origin of religion and the social functions or psychological mechanisms involved in belief. Melford Spiro (1999: 140) stressed that the approach taken in studying religion is shaped by the aims of the researcher:

> Many studies of religion, however, are concerned not with the explanation of religion, but with the role of religion in the explanation of society. Here, the explanatory task is to discover the contribution which religion, taken as the independent variable, makes to societal integration, by its satisfaction of sociological wants. We seriously err, however, in mistaking an explanation of society for an explanation of religion, which, in effect, means confusing the sociological functions of religion with the bases for its performance.

Spiro noted that an adequate explanation of the nature and persistence of religion in society requires both psychological and sociological variables. In line with Spiro, Clifford Geertz (1966) called for an enlargement of the theoretical frame of anthropological studies of religion to include the insights provided by other disciplines. He argued that the tendency to remain exclusively within the canonical intellectual traditions of Durkheim, Weber, Freud, and Malinowski had stymied theoretical advances in the anthropology of religion.

This plea for the inclusion of other disciplines in the anthropological study of religion has been heeded by anthropologists taking a cognitivist approach to culture and religion. In recent years, cognitive anthropologists have worked out some of the most interesting and far-reaching theories of religion precisely because of the innovative ways in which they have linked psychological findings about brain function with anthropological theories of social processes. Cognitive anthropologists have investigated several dimensions of religion: the origins and evolution of religious beliefs; modes of religious consciousness; self and cognition in religious experience; religious transmission; and ritual and cognition, among others.[1] The assumptions cognitive anthropologists tend to make, derived from recent advances in neuropsychology and developmental psychology, have sometimes strayed far from the narrow path of the canonical anthropological tradition and thus have been met with skepticism.[2] Even so, these theoretical advances offer promising and powerful explanatory frameworks for anthropologists interested in exploring social phenomena beyond established paradigms.

---

[1] Armin Geertz (2004) provides a helpful overview of the religious domains covered by cognitive studies of religion.

[2] For instance, most introductory texts to the anthropology of religion fail to take cognitive approaches into consideration (Bowie 2000; Morris 1987). This lukewarm reception may stem from the fact that, all too often, writers who appropriate cognitive models do so blindly and to the detriment of recognizing the importance of the social in cognition (see Geertz 2004: 354).

I began my research in Ukraine focusing on social processes related to religious institutionalization. I distinguish two defining elements in the process of institutionalization: a normative patterning of action and an embedding of patterned actions in formal structures that achieve a certain degree of autonomy, being tied to no particular actor or situation (Zucker 1987). Churches are typical religious institutions, yet Ukrainian churches cannot be analysed as such in a diachronic perspective, because under socialism they were repressed and destroyed. Religious structures had to be radically transformed in order to survive. The postsocialist revival saw a second transformation, one of informal religious structures back into religious institutions. I refer to religious institutionalization as the process whereby religious life is standardized and normative patterns of action are re-established in order to ensure the re-creation and reproduction of religious structures.

But my intention in conducting this study was to go beyond the social dynamics involved in religious institutionalization. I was interested in individual religiosity and in elements of religious experience lying outside the bounds of routinized practice – that is, in 'personal religion' (James 2003).[3] In trying to account for the forms of religiosity I observed in western Ukraine, I found myself vacillating between social and psychological explanations. However, my project was set from the beginning as an ethnographic approach to religious life, and after observing a wide range of religious experiences and rituals, I came in the end to a categorization of local ritual practices. I could distinguish roughly two types of religious events: routinized practices to which people attended sporadically and perfunctorily, and long-awaited 'excursions into spirituality' involving forms of devotion that triggered strong emotions.[4]

The sorts of religious dynamics I observed in western Ukraine have been described at length in the anthropological literature, usually through universalistic models such as Weber's classic model of tension between charisma and routinization (Weber 1963). Charismatic authority brings innovation and intense emotions but eventually undergoes routinization and recedes with the development of institutional structures. Victor Turner's (1995) seminal approach to religion and society offered another dualistic

---

[3] William James (2003) has argued that only the firsthand, individual experience of religion is authentic, and churches play at best a secondary role by transmitting and communicating the 'revelation'. He contends that in order to investigate religion, one should go to the effervescent believer and not to the second-hand believer, who learns about this original religious experience only through its social transmission as 'dull habit' (James 2003: 335).

[4] I include the *rites de passage* (e.g. baptisms, weddings, funerals) in the first category, that of routinized rituals, because of their standardized ritual forms. Even when they trigger strong emotions, these are not necessarily related to the religious aspect or meaning of the rite.

model based on the dynamic of structure and *communitas*. In this approach, structure is conceived of as a stable hierarchical system based on established patterns of social interaction, whereas communitas represents all that opposes structure – the creative, spontaneous, primordial side of humanity (Turner 1996).

Ernest Gellner's (1981) famous analysis of the political dynamics in Muslim societies similarly followed the 'pendulum swing' between two 'syndromes' corresponding to distinct forms of ritual action. Gellner introduced a new aspect related to technologies of codification: orality versus literacy. His 'syndrome P' encompassed literacy and predominated in political centres (urban life), whereas 'syndrome C' was set in the rural periphery, which recurrently took over the centre to renew the political elite. Even closer to the paradigmatic change produced by literacy, Jack Goody's (1986) differentiation between literate and non-literate societies underscored the role of literacy in determining cultural and religious transformations. By providing the basis for the creation of a doctrinal core, literacy facilitated the construction and transmission of universal religious traditions.

Drawing on the work of his predecessors, Harvey Whitehouse argued that they were right to distinguish between two types of religious expression but wrong to do so in terms of literacy versus orality. Shifting the focus from technologies of codification to cognition, Whitehouse argued that the crucial distinction was created by the codification of religious experience in memory: the distinction was between autobiographical and semantic memory (Whitehouse 1995, 2000). Aware that he was adding yet another dichotomy to the strand of universalistic models, Whitehouse highlighted the explanatory limits of previous models, arguing that a cognitive approach was better suited to answering questions about religious transmission and the evolution of religious traditions.[5]

The grounds on which Whitehouse created his dichotomous model of modes of religiosity were provided by recent cognitive approaches to religion and culture, informed by work in evolutionary psychology. His research has followed that of other cognitivists working within the paradigm of the 'epidemiology of representations', a 'selectionist' view of human cultural evolution (Sperber 1985). Pascal Boyer (1990) held that religious concepts that survive over time are those which, through specific processes of cultural

[5] Whitehouse introduced his theory in his monograph on the Pomio Kivung movement in Papua New Guinea (1995) and developed it further in *Arguments and Icons* (2000). For extensive reviews of the latter book, see Whitehouse (2002), Whitehouse and Laidlaw (2004), and Whitehouse and Martin (2004). Whitehouse's third book (2004) gave him a chance to elaborate the cognitive basis of his theory and thus to respond to some of its detractors. I do not attempt to summarize the debates surrounding the modes theory, because they are spread across various publications.

transmission, have better resisted erosion and disappearance. Various cognitive mechanisms, among which memory plays a crucial role, influence the selective transmission of cultural representations, thus becoming key explanatory principles in the evolution of religion – and, more generally, in cultural evolution. In a similar vein, the 'modes theory' shows how the ability of a religion to survive is directly related to the way in which its content is encoded in individual memory.

Whitehouse (1995) built his modes of religiosity theory on a rich ethnographic treatment of the Pomio Kivung religious movement in Papua New Guinea and broadened its scope by drawing on comparative material from the anthropological literature on religious transmission in Melanesia.[6] His fieldwork was focused on the relationship between two contrasting political-religious factions coexisting in the Pomio Kivung movement. He meticulously observed both the mainstream movement and a splinter group that emerged in the community he studied. By contrasting the two groups in terms of a series of variables, Whitehouse illuminated two modes of religiosity, which constituted the core of his theory (Whitehouse 1995).

The mainstream movement was based on an institutionalized system that functioned similarly in all Pomio Kivung communities. Such communities tended to be large-scale, centralized, and hierarchical, and their membership was diffuse. These social features corresponded to certain features that Whitehouse called psychological: verbalized doctrine, frequent ritual performances, and routinized practice. This complex of psychological and socio-political features formed Whitehouse's *doctrinal* mode of religiosity (Table 1.1). In contrast, the splinter group he observed promoted a religious experience specific to his second, *imagistic* mode of religiosity. The splinter group appeared as a small-scale, innovative, and cohesive community, but one difficult to spread. It moved away from the verbalized doctrine and standardized rituals of the mainstream group, instead cultivating non-verbal, highly emotional, imagistic rituals.

[6] The Pomio Kivung is a religious movement from East New Britain 'based around a mixture of millenarian, Christian, nationalist and 'cargo cult' ideas', with strong anti-missionary attitudes (Whitehouse 1995).

Table 1.1
Contrasting Modes of Religiosity

Variable	Doctrinal Mode	Imagistic Mode
Psychological features		
1. Transmissive frequency	High	Low
2. Level of arousal	Low	High
3. Principal memory system	Semantic schemas and implicit scripts	Episodic/flashbulb memory
4. Ritual meaning	Learned/acquired	Internally generated
5. Techniques of revelation	Rhetoric, logical integration, narrative	Iconicity, multivocality, multivalence
Socio-political features		
6. Social cohesion	Diffuse	Intense
7. Leadership type	Dynamic	Passive/absent
8. Inclusivity	Inclusive	Exclusive
9. Spread	Rapid, efficient	Slow, inefficient
10. Scale	Large-scale	Small-scale
11. Degree of uniformity	High	Low
12. Structure	Centralized	Non-centralized

Source: Whitehouse 2004: 74.

The differentiation between the imagistic and doctrinal modes that Whitehouse proposed by assembling two series of opposing variables differs insignificantly from Turner's (1995) contrast between communitas and structure. Yet Whitehouse's insight was that the two modes of religiosity corresponded to the functional separation of memory in two different mechanisms of memory retention, the semantic and the episodic (Whitehouse 1995, 2000, 2004). Imagistic rituals such as rites of initiation in Papua New Guinea trigger intense emotions and unique experiences, which are stored in one's episodic memory. Routinized, doctrinal rituals such as those run by Christian missionaries constitute not new, vivid experiences but predictable, tedious moments. Therefore they match already existing mental schemas and so join one's semantic memory.[7]

[7] According to this model, the cognitive system, when receiving new information, searches for a suitable schema on the basis of which to anchor appropriate responses. Familiar, routinized events quickly find their way into semantic knowledge. Events that violate existing schemas set off a search for relevant schemas based on any possible similarities that might make sense of the experience. If the attempt fails, the event is encoded into an entirely new,

Whitehouse emphasized the connections between psychological and social processes in a second book, *Arguments and Icons* (2000), in which he illustrated how the different modes of transmission of religious experience affected patterns of social cohesion in Melanesia. On the basis of differentiation in ritual transmission, he argued that Christianity and local religious cults corresponded to two different modes of religiosity. Melanesian religions were based exclusively on the imagistic mode, using analogic coding through non-verbal imagery in rarely performed rituals within a particular community.[8] Christianity, on the other hand, was transmitted through a doctrinal mode of religiosity, in formalized rituals using language and text, which were more easily spread by religious specialists. The two religious systems, Whitehouse argued, came into conflict in Papua New Guinea when Christian missionaries began to suppress Melanesian imagistic practices and replace them with doctrinal rituals.[9] Eventually this altercation led to a change in indigenous people's patterns of social relations and community formation. This opened a space in which an 'imagined community' (Anderson 1991) could be constructed and thus provided a basis for local nationalist movements.[10]

The case of Melanesian Christianization offers an ideal model of the way the interaction of modes of religiosity determines the evolution of religious tradition. In reality the two modes are not so clearly differentiated; rather, they appear as ideal types, or 'attractor positions' (Whitehouse 2004: 75), in any religion. Mainstream Christianity tends to be doctrinal, but it also maintains, to a certain extent, imagistic practices.[11] Usually the imagistic and

---

'particular' schema, forming vivid and detailed memories of unique events (Whitehouse 2000: 196).

[8] In Whitehouse's view, influenced by an evolutionary paradigm, the imagistic mode is older than the doctrinal one. See his discussion 'The Imagistic Mode in the Upper Palaeolithic' (Whitehouse 2000: 161–168).

[9] 'Consequently, the meeting of religious traditions of Melanesian and European origin amounted to a confrontation between two starkly opposed styles of codification, transmission, and political association' (Whitehouse 2000: 16).

[10] Whitehouse suggested that the move from the imagistic mode of religiosity to the doctrinal facilitated the formation of incipient nationalist movements in indigenous communities. Thus he could argue against the mainstream literature on millenary cults by maintaining that the relationship between millenarianism and nationalism was not, as widely supposed, related to the content of an ideology but was linked more fundamentally to the mode of transmission.

[11] In some countries, such as Spain (Christian 1989), Greece (Stewart 1991), and Malta (Mitchell 1997), Christianity offers a vivid imaginal relation with divinity, expressed in the devotional culture known as popular religion.

doctrinal modes exist together in one religion, and their specific interaction determines certain features of that religious tradition.[12]

The most interesting implication of the modes theory for the anthropology of religion is that the interaction of the two modes seems to generate the dynamics of evolution of any religious tradition. In religions operating primarily in the doctrinal mode, people tend to lose interest and motivation and begin looking for novel forms of religious practice. This may lead to a separation of these novelty seekers from the mainstream community as the splinter group reinterprets dogma and modifies ritual. The imagistic mode that emerges counters the 'tedium effect' of routinized practice. This renewal and innovation of the religious message increases motivation and reinvigorates a religion that has become too doctrinal.

Because the modes theory could be generalized into a universal theory of religious transmission, several commentators have set out to test it for other religious traditions and to formulate further models of interaction (Whitehouse 2002, 2004: 157–163; Severi 2004; Whitehouse and Laidlaw 2004).[13] Ted Vial (2004: 155) used the forms of interaction offered by the modes theory to look at different movements within Christianity. He provided several additional scenarios, one of which occurs when a splinter group emerges and is *not* later reabsorbed but creates a competitive and apparently hostile religious system, thus reinforcing people's commitment to the mainstream group. An example is the Counter-Reformation as a reaction to Protestantism. A second pattern is represented by revivalist movements, which are encouraged by the mainstream doctrinal tradition for the purpose of strengthening and reviving faith, as in the Great Awakening in colonial North America.

Another scenario, which corresponds better to the circumstances I observed in western Ukraine, is the 'equilibrium' position. It appears in a religious tradition when one mode of religiosity is not enforced over another, so that people remain integrated in the tradition and splinter groups tend not to develop. In such cases the practice of both doctrinal and imagistic modes could correspond to the continuity and change of the religious tradition. I believe eastern Christianity represents just such a case of equilibrium. It is

---

[12] Some reviewers have argued that the inevitable co-existence of the two modes in almost all religions reveals Whitehouse's dichotomy to be artificial (see Whitehouse and Laidlaw 2004).

[13] See especially the chapters in Whitehouse and Laidlaw 2004 by John Peel, Brian Malley, David Shankland, James Laidlaw, and Leo Howe, who apply the theory retrospectively to their own field material, with interesting comparative results. One could undertake empirical testing of the theory in the field situation, but only when data collection is shaped according to the theory's variables.

precisely the balance between the two modes of religiosity that has driven the evolution of the eastern Christian tradition over the centuries.

In order to discuss the dynamics of a religious tradition, one must understand its functioning. Anthropologists, especially anthropologists of religion, have tended to use the notion of tradition in a non-reflexive manner. Tradition is said to give value to the past and to stand in opposition to a modern, present orientation, as in 'modern' versus 'traditional'. Boyer (1990) discussed the problematic treatment of tradition in anthropology, arguing that theorists of tradition had focused on intellectual constructions (worldviews, conceptions, beliefs) while ignoring the most visible aspect of tradition: that any tradition is a cluster of repeated events. For him tradition was a type of human interaction, and ritual, a repetitive act of communication. Boyer attempted to move beyond the hollow constructions anthropologists usually took as 'tradition' and to avoid the 'Great Divide' models that polarized tradition and modernity. Instead he focused on 'traditional interactions', which one could investigate in 'traditional societies' as well as in modern ones.

Fredrik Barth (1987), in his analysis of the Baktaman religious tradition, put a similar emphasis on ritual as communicative acts performed in specific, recurring situations. He not only considered the persistence and repetitiveness of specific social interactions but also looked at the innovation that arose through such interactions. He operated with 'traditions of knowledge', looking at the modalities of communication embedded in local social organization. His focus was on the variety of ideas that formed the content of tradition, on their modalities of expression, on the patterns of distribution within communities and between communities, and on the processes of (re)production – altogether, that is, on processes of creativity, transmission, and change within traditions of knowledge.

I refer to Barth's work because his approach influenced Whitehouse's theory, particularly with respect to the imagistic mode of religiosity. Whitehouse discussed 'modes of transmission' and 'frequency'; Barth analysed 'patterns of reproduction'. But whereas Whitehouse's modes theory eschewed discussion of the content of any particular religion, Barth analysed knowledge in relation to transmission by describing the variety of ideas that make up a religious tradition and the modalities in which those ideas are expressed (the process termed 'codification' in Whitehouse's model). The notion of revelation appears in the modes theory as an important part of the mechanism of transmission because it provides participants with a motivation to repeat the ritual. Revelation appears as 'the act or an instance of revealing, especially the supposed disclosure of knowledge to humankind by a divine or supernatural agency' (Whitehouse 2000: 19). Each mode of religiosity is supposedly supported by different means of revelation: the doctrinal by intellectual persuasion, using rhetoric, logical integration, and narrative, and the imagistic by 'spontaneous exegetical reflection' (Whitehouse 1995: 197, 2000). Boyer, commenting on Whitehouse's theory, disagreed with the use of revelation, 'considering it a confusing concept, devoid of any scientific value' (Boyer in Whitehouse 2002: 11). He claimed that revelation was irrelevant to ritual and could not constitute the motivational basis for the repetition of ritual. People did not expect revelation in exchange for performing rituals. Instead, they repeated certain rituals because the action itself alleviated 'the ill-defined danger or some potential cost in not reproducing these occurrences' (Boyer in Whitehouse 2002: 12).

I retain revelation as a useful concept that refers to the 'message' or 'content of the doctrine' (Peel 2004: 12). The revelatory potential of certain rituals can be found in the participants' search for meaning in the ritual – in theological terms, exegesis. Each mode of religiosity makes possible a different type of exegesis. In the doctrinal mode, exegesis appeals to rational understanding and logical communication. The meaning of the ritual is intrinsic to the ritual performance itself, which, once created, is perpetuated by the religious authority. Participants seldom have the chance to elaborate an individual exegesis, and if they do, the result is amended by the respective authority. Therefore the exegesis present in the doctrinal mode assures the accurate transmission of the religious message, securing the continuity of the religious tradition.

Whitehouse argued that in imagistic rituals, the interpretation of the message is dependent on participants through an individual process of spontaneous exegetical reflection. Such rituals use analogic imagery as a privileged means of codification (Barth 1987). Analogic codification is essentially iconic, based on concrete metaphors that trigger multiple connotations, which often have a strong emotional or sensual character. The space of the ritual is favourable to the use of metaphor as a means of codification, offering a broad variety of multivocal and multivalent symbols and acts, which facilitates the transmission of knowledge.[14] The ritual space creates the possibility of transferring representations between the subjective imagery and the collective imaginary by way of two processes: subjectification and objectification (Obeyesekere 1981). In Gananath Obeyesekere's terms, subjectification is 'the process whereby cultural patterns and symbolic systems are put back into the melting pot of consciousness and refashioned

[14] The idea originates in Turner's work on symbols (Turner 1967). Multivocality is a regular feature of symbols, each having, as it were, a fan or spectrum of referents (Turner 1967: 50). Thus there is no necessary contradiction among the alternative imageries moving in a medium that offers a wide range of metaphors and associations.

to create a culturally tolerated set of images that . . . [are] designated subjective imagery' (1981: 170). The reverse process, objectification, is the process by which personal meanings and deep motivations are canalized into public culture (1981: 136).[15]

Imagistic rituals have the potential to channel individual creativity and innovation into collective representations. In order to correlate the theological understanding of revelation with the vocabulary of the modes theory, I consider that understanding synonymous with the spontaneous exegetical reflection that takes place in imagistic rituals, rather than synonymous with doctrinal exegesis, which comes closer to interpretation. The idea is not novel but can be traced back to various anthropological accounts, starting with Victor Turner's approach to ritual as a process that takes participants from one psychological and social state to a new and sometimes original condition (Turner 1995). Other researchers (Ortner 1999; Kapferer 2003, 2005) have also pointed out that certain rituals that I would call imagistic (following Whitehouse) make possible the expression of novel human potentialities in culturally acceptable forms. One might argue, then, that whereas the doctrinal mode assures the reproduction of a religious tradition, the imagistic brings to it innovation and change.

1.2 Eastern Christianity

In order to analyse patterns of religious life in western Ukraine, I use the modes of religiosity theory as I examine the local religious tradition. One of my main arguments is that in spite of recent confessional differentiations within the Orthodox tradition, which gave rise to a variety of denominations, people in western Ukraine relate to a 'community of practice' based on a common religious tradition acknowledged as Orthodox. The particularities of eastern Christianity become evident when one looks at the theological understanding of tradition, church, and revelation as it developed in the history of Christianity (Schmemann 1977; Pelikan 1989; Fairbairn 2002).[16]

One of the main historical differences between branches of Christianity is the effect of the Reformation and Counter-Reformation, which shaped

[15] Obeyesekere brought together Weber's definition of culture and the Freudian 'unconscious motivation' to show how personal symbols (cultural symbols whose primary significance and meaning lie in the personal experience of individuals) are integrated in collective phenomena such as ritual practice.

[16] 'Eastern Christianity' refers to the common tradition that includes eastern Orthodoxies and 'Uniate' churches, those Orthodox churches that united with Rome. When using 'Orthodox' I refer mainly to the Orthodoxy that claims its roots in early Kievan Rus and later separated into various patriarchates either independent or united with Rome, Moscow, or Constantinople.

the contemporary tradition of western Christianity (Fairbairn 2002). Orthodoxy, which did not undergo a similar process, stands out for its variety of local traditions and decentralized structures of authority. Orthodox theologians undertook to explain how such diversity could be consistent with a putatively coherent, universal image of Orthodoxy. Although Orthodox churches are spread across the world and shaped by local cultures, they share a firm view both of what Orthodoxy is about and of what it means to belong to this imagined community. Thus, an important theological discussion emerged about what constituted the unifying factor of Orthodoxy in the absence of a unique institution, doctrine, or tradition like that found in the Roman Catholic Church. Theologians concluded that in Orthodoxy, tradition was neither local nor universal. Vladimir Lossky, one of the most influential twentieth-century Orthodox theologians, proposed a differentiation between 'traditions', which represent local forms, and 'Tradition' as revelation.

Although it is necessary to distinguish between what is transmitted (the oral and written traditions) and the unique mode in which the faithful believe this transmission is received from God (Tradition as the principle of Christian knowledge), it is impossible to separate these two aspects of religiosity entirely. Hence the ambivalence of the term 'tradition', which designates simultaneously the multiplicity of local Orthodox traditions emanating from religious practice and the divinely inspired Tradition revealed to the church (Lossky 1985: 155).

For Lossky, the plurality of traditions emerged naturally over time, beginning with the apostles, the first transmitters of the original message. Different traditions developed in forms articulated in 'written and spoken Word and through images and symbols' (Lossky 1985: 155). The Orthodox tradition drew on a number of equally important sources of inspiration: the writings of church fathers, the decrees of ecumenical and local councils, the divine liturgy, canonical prescriptions, the architecture and iconography of the church, and devotional practices (Lossky 1985: 143). Most Orthodox sources originated in particular historical contexts as parts of local practices and particular understandings of religion, but over time they became part of the common Orthodox heritage.

This process of formation of Orthodoxy means that 'tradition' cannot be reduced to religious practice over time, yet unlike Catholic doctrine, it also represents more than the teachings of a set of authoritative texts abstracted from religious life. In Orthodoxy, doctrine belongs to tradition only as a limited manifestation expressed in a particular context and time. Dogmas, the bases of doctrine, were formulated when the church was challenged and had to 'speak' in order to fix a certain aspect of its religious practice. Throughout the history of Christianity, dogmas have appeared mostly as responses to explicit, 'heretical' challenges to accepted religious knowledge.[17]

Differences between understandings of doctrine in the Catholic and Orthodox traditions also appear because of their respective interpretations of the relationship between written text (represented by scripture) and oral tradition. Orthodoxy did not propound a clear separation between scripture and tradition, whereas both post-Reformation Catholicism and Protestantism did. Orthodox theology considers the Orthodox tradition (*paradosis*) a source of revelation together with scripture, but post-Counter-Reformation Catholicism and Protestantism separated the two elements, claiming the pre-eminence of the written text over the oral tradition.[18] According to patristic understanding, which Lossky followed closely, scripture and Tradition were 'two modalities of one and the same fullness of Revelation communicated to the Church' (Lossky 1985: 143).[19] Dogma and doctrine could not replace revelation as a source of religious knowledge (as was the case in the Catholic Church), and revelation was not an invitation to break completely with dogma (as in the case of heresies). In Orthodoxy, Tradition and dogma coexist in symbiotic relation: they are, respectively, the faculty of knowing the truth in the Holy Spirit and the rule of faith kept by the church.

Most germane to my discussion of eastern Christianity is the strong emphasis Orthodox theologians and historians place on the modes of transmission of revelation. Orthodoxy understands revelation to be, in its simplest form, 'practising the sacraments' (Lossky 1985: 144; Pelikan 1989: 262–265). The modes of transmission correspond concretely to oral preaching, representing the Tradition, and written text, or scripture. Eastern Christianity supports both modes as complementary forms of religious knowledge. This particularity came about over time in response to the dichotomies constructed around visible differences between eastern and western Christian religiosity. Iconography is one of the keys to understanding eastern Orthodoxy and its forms of religiosity, which function alongside 'the Scripture as source of 'true practice'' (Fairbairn 2002: 158). Anthony Ugolnik (1989) contended that distinct cultural inheritances had produced a tendency in the western tradition to distil meaning from text, whereas in the eastern tradition meaning was sought in images. He opposed 'word' to 'image', each the

[17] In eastern Orthodoxy, theological teachings emerged as dogma in response to Latin influence and theology (Pelikan 1974; Schmemann 1977: 324–330).

[18] The Greek word *paradosis* is translated as 'tradition' in Latin-derived vocabularies (from Latin *traditio*). It means both 'tradition' in a modern sense and 'Tradition' as the entire post-scriptural church experience, which is accepted as normative. The Catholic Church uses the same word, tradition. The Russian equivalent is *predanie,* and the Ukrainian is *tradytsia.*

[19] Patristic understanding is that of the church fathers, the early theologians, and writers about Christianity from the first five centuries before the schism and separation of churches.

essential characteristic of the respective Christian tradition, assuming that they represented equally valid ways of looking at faith in their own contexts (Ugolnik 1989: 42–86).

One way to understand such cultural differences between eastern and western Christianity is to consider their different conceptions of authority. In comparison with Catholicism and its doctrine of papal primacy, Orthodoxy developed more diffuse forms of authority. The Orthodox tradition, rooted in revelation, is liberated from worldly authority. On the one hand, the permissive character of Orthodoxy, with its loose frames, encouraged the development of a variety of traditions; on the other, Tradition had the role of authenticating and validating variegated innovations and of rejecting routinization (Lossky 1985: 157). By considering revelation to be the main engine in the production of religious knowledge, and by making tradition its theological basis, Orthodoxy was able to escape centralized structures of authority and to contain the possible emergence of a hierarchical institution that might seek to establish its authority over revelation.

Indeed, Orthodoxy is understood by its members as a 'living faith', which means that the primary source of renewal lies in the 'experience of the divine'. In Orthodox understanding the church becomes a community of people experiencing the divine, united around liturgical practice – the concept of *sobornost*, identifying the church with the 'community of sacraments'. Again the accent is placed on the collective dimension of religious experience, which forms the church as a community of worship rather than as a hierarchical structure based on distinctive patterns of authority.[20]

The various sources of authority in eastern Christianity – apostles, early church fathers, bishops, mystics, and laypeople – are intimately connected in what constitutes the 'whole church'. Authority evolves in a relational framework that connects each of these diverse sources. Eastern theologians consider the problem of authority to be very different in Orthodoxy and in the West because of a different hierarchical structuring of the sources of knowledge. A direct consequence of the Orthodox model of authority is that the borders between practical and doctrinal religion become blurred, making the application of classical anthropological models unlikely.

Earlier anthropological work on religious traditions, using Robert Redfield's model of great and little traditions (Badone 1990: 6), divided popular from elite religion. In this view the orthodox religion belongs to an

[20] Eastern Christianity sees the expression of church unity neither in the fellowship of local churches (as in much of Protestantism) nor in the presence of a single church structure (as in Roman Catholicism and some branches of Protestantism), but primarily in the liturgy and the sacraments. 'Nicolas Zemov states that the Orthodox see the church primarily as a worshiping community' (Fairbairn 2002: 26).

elite group of church and laypeople who maintain a theological culture, while the masses remain unorthodox in their devotions and insensitive to novelty. William Christian (1989) and later Charles Stewart (1991) argued that the two spheres 'religion as practised' and 'religion as prescribed' were autonomous and yet interacted (Christian 1989: 178). Stewart, studying Greek Orthodoxy, followed Christian's line of thought, assuming that great and little traditions could be found in Orthodoxy in the same way they existed in western Christianity. Yet Christian, working on Spanish Catholicism, employed a diffusionist perspective, arguing that what was considered 'religion as practised', or the little tradition, was often the great tradition as it had taken root in a particular place and time and remained locally unchanged despite overall changes to the great tradition.[21] In Orthodox Christianity the tendency is rather towards change initiated from the bottom up, as popular reflexivity and practice actually create and shape theological knowledge. Here the distinction between popular and official religion is hardly visible, and authority is predicated on popular religiosity to the extent that sainthood tends to emerge popularly, only later to be confirmed by the church (Kokosalakis 1995: 443).

In Greece, Stewart wrote, Orthodox people had a cohesive vision of Orthodoxy and did not see such divisions within the local tradition. Both great and little traditions shared a common base of symbols, conceptions, and ritual forms that produced the overall Orthodox framework (Stewart 1991: 7). Ellen Badone commented on the fact that Orthodox believers tended to focus on ritual practice, or on 'practising the sacraments', rather than on the meaning of the ritual. The emphasis on ritual performance left space for a plurality of interpretations that might conceal discrepancies between doctrinal and popular readings.

The Orthodox participant, regardless of background, also worked within open frames of interpretation. As Stewart remarked, Orthodoxies resulting from different processes of syncretic formation tended to encompass extraneous beliefs and practices present in local cultures. This attribute stemmed from the simplicity of the Orthodox 'salvation idiom' (Obeyesekere 1981: 22), a term that denotes a basic structure of a religion grounded in the few essential features recognized by all its members. Stewart identified the salvation idiom of Orthodoxy as a 'hierarchical, monotheistic arrangement, with God at its pinnacle in heaven, the Devil at its nadir in hell, and humanity living in the world in between. The narrative of Christ's birth,

---

[21] Christian's 1989 book is an example of such dynamics. Another is the case of the traditionalist movement in the Catholic Church, to which Badone refers in her introduction to an edited volume on religious orthodoxy and popular faith (Badone 1990: 19–20). I refer to a similar traditionalist movement in Ukraine in chapter 4.

death, and resurrection then provides the model for human movement on this landscape' (Stewart 1991: 11). As long as a form of religious expression stays within this salvation idiom, it remains within the confines of the Orthodox tradition. In Orthodoxy, local interpretations may deviate to a certain extent from this basic representation without causing a splinter in the mainstream tradition. This is the case with the *exotica,* local representations of the devil, that have been accommodated over time in the Greek Orthodox tradition (Stewart 1991: 141).

The doctrinal core of the Orthodox tradition is visible in its literate theological tradition, similar to that of Catholicism or Protestantism. At first glance Orthodoxy seems more rigid than the other Christian traditions, because of its pattern of faith transmitted unchanged through time (Ware 1980: 318). Orthodoxy is conservative in the sense that 'Church doctrine has been remarkably insulated from change' (Stewart 1991: 140), and its essential features have been less affected by historical transformations in the world at large. Orthodox theology makes a clear point that the progress of tradition comes through accumulation, not through refutation or complete renewal. Nevertheless, to survive and remain a relevant worldview for its adherents, Orthodoxy should still give answers to concrete questions related to life, salvation, and society and should maintain considerable levels of motivation and participation. Thus, what is perceived as a static, unchanged Orthodox tradition contains inner means of change. I argue that the accent put on orthopraxy rather than on the orthodoxy of theological interpretations makes Orthodoxy more open to change and innovation.

My approach, focused on processes of reproduction and change, is intended to illuminate Orthodoxy as a living tradition, or *paradosis* in theological terms (Lossky 1985). In this view, the present variety of religious expressions in Orthodoxy can be seen as the result of the interaction of different modes of transmission, doctrinal and imagistic, within a single religious tradition. Looking at religious practice, one can distinguish socio-political features that correspond to the doctrinal mode: diffuse cohesion of the community, inclusive assemblies, the imagined community of Orthodoxy, and a certain degree of uniformity in practice and beliefs (the salvation idiom). In chapter 5 I describe rituals that involve psychological features present in the doctrinal mode, such as low levels of emotional arousal, passive participation, a non-reflexive understanding of the meaning incorporated into the ritual performance (liturgical exegesis), and frequent repetition of rituals. In contrast, I underscore features belonging to the imagistic mode: the lack of orthodoxy and doctrinal authority, the intense social cohesion of certain groups evolving from the underground period of the church, the flexibility of church structures, the central role of mystical revelation, and the diversity of imagistic practices.

Iconography is among the forms of religious expression that reflect Orthodoxy's special blending of the doctrinal and the imagistic.[22] Icons are non-verbal forms of communication that offer a vehicle for the transmission of religious messages. 'Icons over the centuries became essential carriers of the Orthodox tradition in the sense that they communicate and express the patristic theology at a popular level' (Kokosalakis 1995: 443). They transmit theological and ritual significance but also connect directly to individuals in the least mediated way. Orthodox icons connect the realm of the transcendent with the material world but also have spiritual power attached to them, an idea reinforced by theology as well as common religious practice (Hanganu n.d.). Iconography as a specific form of religious expression is imagistic, not because it is image based but because of its open exegetical potential. Icons are 'condensed symbols' (Turner 1967), characterized by multivocality and the ability to produce strong emotional responses in viewers.[23]

Monasticism, a case I develop in chapter 6, takes a particular form in Orthodoxy. Monasteries are perceived as islands of spirituality separated from the mundane world. The evangelical spirit of renunciation that ruled the life of the early Christian Church remained an attribute of monasticism rather than of the whole church. When the church became a 'community of this world', being absorbed into the mundane world, monastic life emerged as the route to the ideal 'community of God' (Schmemann 1977: 106, 134).[24] The proximity of the divine as experienced in monastic life made Orthodox monasteries essential centres of revelation. Mystics, visionaries, and charismatic personalities emerged from such 'spiritual places', adding their revelations to the life of the church without falling outside common tradition (Evdokimov 1999). For such actors, revelation usually appeared as a response to the strong doctrinal tendencies manifested in the church at a certain point, and their imagistic practices became central to the Orthodox

---

[22] Iconography is an essential part of the eastern Christian tradition and thus deserves a thorough analysis from the perspective of the cognitive theory of religion, particularly from the perspective of theories explaining religious transmission.

[23] Turner took the concept from Edward Sapir, who defined icons as 'highly condensed forms of substitutive behaviour for direct expression, allowing for the ready release of emotional tension in conscious and unconscious form' (Turner 1967: 29).

[24] Schmemann saw monasticism as the transmitter of the social and moral ideal of Christianity, which, unlike in the official church, remained uncorrupted. The ideal of monasticism does not correspond to real monasteries, which remain in the world as much as any other religious institution. Yet monasteries retain their role as custodians and, at the same time, innovators of the religious tradition.

tradition. They could perform successfully outside church structures, blurring the distinction between consecrated and lay.[25]

Another interesting factor common to Catholicism and Orthodoxy is visionary phenomena. Anthropologists have long regarded apparitions as one of humans' favourite means of expressing collective responses to social and political tensions (Christian 1989; Zimdars-Swartz 1991; Bax 1995; Matter 2001; Valtchinova 2004).[26] During the Soviet years, apparitions regularly manifested in western Ukraine and served to mobilize national and religious feelings.[27] The visions constituted a means of empowerment for activists opposing the regime (Markus 1989; Bociurkiw 1993). Such unorthodox phenomena deepened the breach between the community of believers and the official church. Believers, freed to improvise so that they might sidestep official restrictions, opted for 'practical adaptability' (Shlikhta 2004b) and considerably altered ritual forms. Religious rituals came to provide an answer to Soviet repression and control and thus mediated social changes. The modification of both life-cycle and sacramental rituals took place throughout the Soviet period and in the early postsocialist days. Restrictions placed on religious activity triggered a proliferation of imagistic practices, which increased motivation and fortified the community of practice. With the traditional parish community destroyed by Soviet policies, a new type of relationship developed between clergy and believers, out of which new forms of collective practice emerged (Shlikhta 2004b: 202). Thus, under the Soviet regime the imagistic mode of religiosity was better suited as a successful engine of religious transmission. This predilection for the imagistic had direct consequences for the postsocialist institutionalization of churches discussed in chapter 4.

The movement from one mode of religiosity to another as a response to socio-political change is not specific to socialist or postsocialist countries. Parallels can surely be drawn with the postcolonial context, in which ambivalent feelings towards change have been expressed through increases in

---

[25] In a short description of the historical development of the Russian Orthodox tradition, Schmemann recalled how such dynamics emerged in the sixteenth and seventeenth centuries: 'In this era of state 'obligation', fixed pattern of life, and static, oppressive 'sacralness' there matured in Russia the type of the wanderer, the tramp, the eternal searcher after the Spirit and the truth, free with the freedom of complete abnegation, but achieving unity with nature and men' (Schmemann 1977: 322).

[26] Scholars of modern Christianity, notably Sandra Zimdars-Swartz (1991) and William Christian Jr (1984, 1987), have explained the twentieth-century rise in apparitions of the Virgin Mary as part of a phenomenon of response to social and political tensions, especially the threats of Communism and nuclear war.

[27] This has continued to be the case since 1990, as new apparition sites appear all over western Ukraine. I discuss this further in chapter 7.

imagistic practices. Following the literature on the role of religion in post-colonial contexts, Clough and Mitchell (2001: 5) argued that the transformation in religious expression was connected to modernization: 'The proliferation of images of excess and evil is seen as part of a resistance to or accommodation of the economic processes introduced by colonialism – capitalism, market economics, money, new forms of accumulation. These become the objects of a resistive or responsive (re)enchantment of people's life-worlds that runs counter to received wisdom concerning the rationalizing disenchantment brought about by capitalism.'

Religion becomes, then, a field of action with the power to transform social reality. Religious discourse attracts members, alters religious beliefs, and changes social patterns. Such approaches acknowledge the local, individual agency expressed in 'the action of individuals 'with strength' to carve out human domains of religious influence' (Michael Taussig, quoted in Clough and Mitchell 2001: 240). Clough and Mitchell (2001: 240) remarked that unfolding modernization in Malta engendered a social fluidity that empowered the religious imagination. Individual creativity was expressed in culturally accepted forms (visions and dreams), which were mediated by local authorities (priests, healers, witches). Discussing the intensification of imagistic activity, Clough admitted that traditional social institutions tried to control and sometimes suppress it (Clough and Mitchell 2001: 244). Imagistic activity in Maltese Catholicism remained at the margins of institutional religion. It rarely entered mainstream practice and never made its way into doctrine, instead being condemned as an unorthodox expression of religiosity. Such practices have greater effects on mainstream Orthodoxy, as I show in chapters 6 and 7.

The term 'imaginary' became common in the social sciences with the work of theorists such as Cornelius Castoriadis, Benedict Anderson, and Charles Taylor. Although for some it seems to replace out-of-fashion anthropological concepts such as 'culture' and 'cultural beliefs' or 'cultural models' (Strauss 2006), I believe 'social imaginary' grasps well a dimension of reality that lies between individual and society. My understanding of the religious imaginary draws on Taylor's (2004) exploration of social imaginaries. He understands the social imaginary as a co-constructed way in which people see their social existence in relation to others and to the norms and images that underlie social expectations. It is an 'ensemble of imaginings that enable our practices by making sense of them' (Taylor 2004: 165).

The social imaginary is a result of human imagination and relates to the ways in which people construct images of the world they live in. It includes the ways in which people imagine their existence in relation to those around them, but also their awareness of the world in terms of what they expect and what is expected from them (Taylor 2004: 24). This normative aspect of the social imaginary implies a certain compliance of the individual to social norms. The social imaginary enables people to interact with one another, shaping their views of themselves and others, while all the time they are transformed by their experience and reflection on the world.

Thinking of Western societies, Taylor wrote about the concomitant existence of various modern forms of social imaginaries: economy, public sphere, and polity. These are made possible by the post-Durkheimian dispensation in which the sacred has been separated from political allegiances (Taylor 2002: 96) and people choose the religion of their preference, the one that inspires and fulfils them most. In an 'enchanted world' the religious imaginary was probably the only way people imagined reality, but with the detachment of social life from the transcendent – Weber's (1963) 'disenchantment of the world' – religion became one among several dimensions of the modern social imaginary. Contemporary religious imaginaries contain collective responses to recent transformations articulated in the religious idiom.[28] In this context religious institutions act as restrictive frames for innovation and individual creativity through their regulation of revelation and their reproduction of orthodoxy.

1.3 Postsocialism and Religion: The Case of Ukraine

Ethnographies of religious phenomena are still lacking among studies of postsocialism. An overview of postsocialist themes in the anthropological literature shows that religion is underrepresented (Hann 2002b; Rogers 2005). When religion does appear, it is mostly in connection with national and ethnic identities, a line of thought that extends earlier anthropological studies of socialism (Hann 1985; Verdery 1991). The postsocialist emergence of religion is considered 'in the context of a general loss of faith in socialism as an ideological system' (Hann, Humphrey, and Verdery 2002: 6). Religion becomes, then, an ideology that was initially to be replaced by the socialist system of beliefs. With the fall of socialism, understandably, the reverse was expected.

Scholars of socialism, whose studies still form the foundation of postsocialist approaches to religion, considered ritual an important topic. During the socialist era, anthropologists were preoccupied with understanding the relationship between religion and socialist ideology, which they could

[28] The religious imaginary is not the only means of expressing individual and collective responses to social transformations, and eastern Christianity is not the only religious tradition undergoing such processes of change. My purpose, however, is to look at the way religion, particularly eastern Christianity, deals with such transformations, and so my argument is limited to this particular case.

achieve effectively through detailed ritual analyses. The socialist state created secular rituals as alternatives to religious ones, appropriating and imitating religious rituals as a means of enacting and reproducing its ideology (Lane 1981; Kideckel 1983). Religious rituals and spaces appeared to anthropologists of the time as 'forms of resistance', means of preserving local identity and memory, which socialism tried to erase (Kligman 1988; see Naumescu 2004). Gail Kligman's (1988) study of Greek Catholic peasants in Ieud, Transylvania, offers an example of the way the socialist state relied especially on the religious elements of the national identity to construct a socialist 'tradition' and of the way peasants used tradition to resist ideology.

Ina Vogelsang (2004: 158) argued that in Ukraine, religious and socialist ideology and practice functioned in parallel throughout the Soviet and post-Soviet periods. She acknowledged, together with Chris Hann (1993), that Soviet ideology penetrated people's lives to such an extent that for some it became a belief. Yet to Vogelsang it was evident that people's understanding of religion was of a different, if not directly opposing, belief system from that promoted by the state, and people could draw on both systems at once. Public rituals encouraged by all the socialist states remained central features of social life after the fall of socialism but became increasingly religious in their outward appearance. Rituals were used as means of legitimating national ideologies and emerging political authorities (Gal 1989) but furthermore became sites of contestation in the postsocialist context (Wanner 1998; Verdery 1999).

Everywhere in Eastern Europe and the former Soviet bloc, postsocialist transformations brought disruptions of the social sphere. The failure of the socialist economic and welfare system, the transition to open markets, and the uncertainties of everyday life challenged people's sense of the world. The resurgence of religion in the public sphere in 1989–1990 was part of the social changes that came to be called postsocialist transformations. Sociologists of religion have investigated the religious revival, often employing economic terms grounded in the rational choice approach to account for religious phenomena.[29] In the social sciences it became increasingly common to apply the term 'market' to religious life after socialism (Rogers 2005: 10). The main reason for such comparisons was that they drew a contrast between the apparent absence of religion under socialism and the increased manifestation of religion after its collapse.[30]

---

[29] Pankhurst (1994) offered an overview of the general sociological models of religion that had been applied to the postsocialist context, counting seven most often used models.

[30] A second sense would be that of the associations between religion, economic transformation, and the new emerging markets, an area to which anthropologists have contributed significantly since the end of socialism (see Caldwell 2005; Creed 2002).

Scholars from various social science disciplines seem to have found in Ukraine an ideal case on which to experiment with theoretical models. In recent years an extensive literature engaging with theories of nationalism, nation-building, ethno-linguistic identities, regionalism, and religion has emerged from political science, sociology, and history. Little of this scholarship is based on empirical data, and even studies that do take this step tend to rely on large surveys and national censuses rather than on in-depth studies (Markus 1995; Hrytsak 2000; Razumkov Centre 2004).[31]

Notions such as 'religious market' and 'marketplace of religions', which were initially used to describe religious life in the United States, are currently employed in many descriptions of postsocialist religious life.[32] Among formerly socialist countries, Ukraine is seen as 'one of the most active and competitive 'religious marketplaces' in Eurasia' (Casanova 1998: 95). It is also considered 'a model of religious pluralism' (Wanner 2004: 736) because of its smooth achievement of a religiously diverse society. An extensive sociological literature has emerged to account for this, and several interpretations have been proposed to explain Ukrainian religious pluralism. Sociological accounts of Ukrainian pluralism have usually been determined by the market model (Mitrokhin 2001; Borowik 2002), but many authors also underscore the relation between politics and the state in shaping the religious sphere (Tataryn 2001; Plokhy 2002; Boeckh 2003; Krindach 2003; Yurash 2005b).

By far the most frequent subject in these studies is that of 'fragmented Orthodoxy', set in the larger context of Ukrainian religious revival. In chapter 2 I discuss the splintering of the 'Soviet' Ukrainian Orthodox Church, which led to the formation of four major postsocialist churches that share the same religious tradition: the Ukrainian Orthodox Autocephalous Church (UOAC), the Ukrainian Orthodox Church associated with the Kyiv Patriarchate (UOC-KP), the Ukrainian Orthodox Church associated with the Moscow Patriarchate (UOC-MP), and the Ukrainian Greek Catholic Church (UGCC). In Ukrainian studies, this fragmentation is presented as an institutional reorganization determined by religious politics in relation to the new state and to nation-building (D'Anieri, Kravchuk, and Kuzio 1991; Sysyn

---

[31] Such theoretical contributions to Ukrainian studies reach far beyond the scope of this book, and I mention them further only when they are particularly relevant for the religious dimension.

[32] Set in the rational choice paradigm, this sociological model tried to explain the diversity of religious life in American cities in relation to high rates of church attendance and religious commitment. In such an environment the existence of unregulated religious economies determines competition among religious groups, which, as a result, produces higher levels of religious commitment. The degree of competition is determined by the number of religious organizations and the level of state regulation (Finke and Stark 1996).

1993; Bociurkiw 1995; Markus 1995; Wilson 2000; Fagan and Shchipkov 2001; Plokhy 2002; Krindach 2003; Yurash 2005b).

Among the authors of these studies, only a handful deeply probe the connection between religion and nationalism (Senyk 2002; Yelensky 2005). Some take over the secularization thesis and emphasize that Ukraine, unlike most other postsocialist countries, has achieved a separation between state and religious institutions (Mitrokhin 2001; Yelensky 2005). Others discuss the 'privatization of religion' as religion becomes more an individual search for spirituality detached from religious authority (Borowik and Babi'nski 1997; Borowik 2002). A recurring theme throughout these works is that of interconfessional relations between Orthodox Christians and Greek Catholics, considered an important factor in contemporary religious dynamics.

Two of the main theories in the general sociology of religion that have been applied to Ukraine have recently been amended for the postsocialist context. Sociologists remarked that classical secularization theory had failed to offer a universal explanation. The religious boom in Eastern Europe and other parts of the world showed that secularization, rather than being a universal trajectory, applied narrowly to Western Europe and to a secularist intellectual project emerging from there (Berger 2001).[33]

Steve Bruce (1999) and later Paul Froese (2004) revised the supply-side market model of religious pluralism to apply to the postsocialist context. They considered that for Eastern Europe, pluralism and increased competition could not explain higher levels of religiosity. Instead, intense religiosity in the postsocialist context was caused by post-1989 religious monopolies – religious groups that dominated a religious market through a combination of state support and state regulation of minority religious groups (Froese 2004: 61). The market-like model would work for a religious society in which ethno-religious identities were weak and people lacked strong institutional commitments, as in the American case (Bruce 1999: 274). Throughout Eastern Europe, connections between nation and religion and between ethnic and religious identities remained strong and prevented market mechanisms from coming into play to regulate the religious sphere.

Focusing on Ukraine, José Casanova (1998) showed that the link between ethno-linguistic and religious identities was not so straightforward and that in this aspect postsocialist Ukraine might be a singular case. He drew an interesting comparison with the American case, starting from the premise that the religious circumstances of Ukraine came closest to the denominational situation present in the United States. The denominational model

---

[33] Some attempts have been made, however, to reconsider and expand the secularization thesis in order to account for more general phenomena, including the religious fervour of Latin America and Eastern Europe.

applies to a society that, like the American one, is based on a civic model incorporating religious values – a 'civil religion', in Robert Bellah's term (1980).[34] The outcome of Casanova's argument was that religious life in Ukraine had the potential to become an open market of religions based on fair competition, similar to that of the United States (Casanova 1998: 97).

This concerted effort by sociologists of religion to explain religious life in Ukraine has not been ignored by anthropologists, and some of the sociologists' terminology has been incorporated in the anthropological literature on postsocialism. Anthropologists have adopted concepts such as 'marketplace of religions' and 'religious pluralism' without questioning their application and the theoretical frame in which the terms originated.[35] In chapter 2 I discuss some of these sociologically informed interpretations, dismissing the market model as unsuited for explaining Ukrainian religious dynamics. I describe the mechanisms at work in Ukrainian religious pluralism and how the community of practice generates an Orthodox imaginary that transcends confessional differentiations and institutional commitments.

The first anthropological studies of postsocialist Ukraine also dealt with nation-building and the emergence of a national culture corresponding to the new Ukrainian state. Catherine Wanner (1998) and Adryana Petryna (2002) wrote ethnographies of the new nation, examining cases in which people became 'subjects' and 'patients' of the state. By means of multi-sited field research, they explored patterns of interaction between the state and individuals and extrapolated those patterns to the level of national processes. Other recent researchers have shown interest in the interplay of memory, history, and local identity in postsocialist narratives. This is a common theme in ethnographies of place, such as those set in Odessa (Richardson 2000), Simferopol (Vogelsang 1996), and the region of the Tatar minority in Crimea (Uehling 2004). Such localized ethnographies contextualize recurrent themes regarding regional identities and local interpretations of national history and collective memory. Religion does not play a significant role in these works, appearing at most as an additional attribute of local identity (Uehling 2004) or as a manipulated symbol of national ideology (Wanner 1998).

Very recently, interest has been growing in conversion and the boom of new religious movements throughout the postsocialist world. Wanner (2003, 2004), for example, explored the new wave of evangelical Protestantism in Ukraine. She showed how a global religion had been adapted to the

[34] 'Civil religion' represents a set of cultural symbols, beliefs, and practices that draw connections between a nation and some conceptions of the sacred (see chapter 2).

[35] There have been a few recent exceptions; see Pelkmans 2006 for a discussion of the usage of 'market' in studies of postsocialist religion.

local Ukrainian context through a dialectical process of accommodation and change of traditional practice. The arrival of evangelicalism, with its novel forms of religious expression, altered the traditional ties between religious and national or group identities and facilitated the emergence of new social networks to replace those that had failed with the demise of socialism. The 'new morality' proposed by charismatic Protestantism allowed people to re-create themselves as 'better' persons through personal conversion (Wanner 2003). In this sense my interest in eastern Christian churches complements well her approach to Protestant churches, and together they create a nearly full picture of religious life in contemporary Ukraine.

1.4 Greek Catholics

'Contestation' has been a favourite theme in postsocialist studies, and Greek Catholics emerged as a subject of interest precisely because of their troublesome presence in the postsocialist scene. Greek Catholics are Christians of eastern rite who 'belong' to the Roman Catholic Church. The Greek Catholic churches, also known as Uniate churches, emerged and developed in Central and Eastern Europe in the sixteenth through eighteenth centuries from local Orthodox churches that recognized the pope's authority and accepted Florentine doctrine while retaining the Byzantine tradition with its eastern liturgical rite. The controversies surrounding the emergence and later development of Uniate churches produced a significant historical literature, mostly concentrated on three topics: the emergence of Greek Catholic churches in the context of Polish or Habsburg Catholicization policies (Gudziak 1998); the active role of Greek Catholic clergy in nation-building in the eighteenth and nineteenth centuries, culminating in the birth of nation-states in Central Europe (Hvat 1984; Himka 1986, 1999); and the peculiar situation of the underground, or 'catacomb', Greek Catholic Church during socialist times.[36]

Not only historians studied Greek Catholics during socialism; some anthropologists also took note of the continued survival of Greek Catholicism as a religious identity linked to religious practice and local tradition (Hann 1985; Kligman 1988). But only with the end of socialism did Greek Catholicism start to receive more attention from anthropologists working in postsocialist contexts. Chris Hann, interested in the presence of Ukrainian Greek Catholics in south-eastern Poland, reflected on their case in a series of

[36] The experience of the Greek Catholic community during Soviet times is discussed in historical works focused on religion under socialism (see Fletcher 1981; Markus 1989; Ramet 1987; Zugger 2001). Several valuable works dealing with the suppression and clandestine survival of Greek Catholic communities have recently become available, and new archival material and oral history projects provide the empirical material for some of these works (Bociurkiw 1996; Bourdeaux 1995; Hosking 1991; Pelikan 1990).

articles published beginning in the early 1990s. Caught in a conflict with the nationalist Roman Catholic Polish majority over church property, Greek Catholics in Przemyśl, Poland, became Hann's illustrative case for discussions of theories of nationalism (Hann 1993, 1998a), ethnic identity, and intolerance versus liberal values and civil society (Hann 1998b, 1999, 2002a, 2005). The case of Greek Catholics provided an argument against essentializing theories such as Samuel Huntington's 'clash of civilizations' (Hann 2000d) and opened a space for discussion of the possible application of 'civil religion' as a model of tolerance in postsocialist societies (Hann 2000c, 2003b). By looking at eastern and western Christian influences on the Greek Catholic tradition, Hann showed that it offered an opportunity for researchers to appreciate its original syncretism and continuous crossing of cultural boundaries (Hann 2003b).

Katherine Verdery used the case of 'moving dead bodies' to illustrate how the postsocialist context determined a redefinition of almost everything, from social relations to moral values, as part of 'a reordering of people's entire meaningful worlds' (Verdery 1999: 35). The reburial of a Romanian Greek Catholic bishop gave her the opportunity to discuss symbolic property, legitimation, and politics of commemoration in the resurgent Romanian Greek Catholic Church. Greek Catholics appeared as a group contesting the religious monopoly of the Orthodox Church and established relations between nation and religion in Romania. The issues Verdery raised reappeared in other articles in which, through different case studies, scholars analysed the contested presence of Greek Catholics in postsocialist Romania (Iordachi 1999; Dorondel 2002; Zerilli 2002; Mahieu 2004).

Most of the studies mentioned here analyse discourses of elites, often in relation to an illustrative case study that happens to be highly politicized and conflictual. They devote primary attention to the way Greek Catholicism has been reworked at the official level by elites who came to form the church hierarchy, while paying little attention to religious practices and the way religion has been redefined for the far greater number of 'ordinary' people. One good example to the contrary, based on long-term fieldwork and rich ethnographic evidence, is a doctoral thesis by Stephanie Mahieu, who investigated the revival and institutionalization of the Romanian Greek Catholic Church since 1989 (Mahieu 2003; see also Mahieu 2004). Based on multi-sited ethnography in Transylvanian Greek Catholic communities, Mahieu's work offers a rich historical and theological background and constitutes a valuable monograph on the Romanian Greek Catholic Church.

Mahieu emphasized the paradoxical situation of Romanian Greek Catholics as deriving from historical circumstances related to the massive, intolerant presence of Romanian Orthodoxy, which continued to be a nuisance for Greek Catholics even into the present. She described the motivations driving those who struggled to revive a vanishing church, as well as what inspired people to rejoin the resurrected church. She stressed that the 'multi-attendance' of churches and what sociologists describe as the marketplace of religions were both related to the syncretic regional religious tradition, which allowed for a multiplicity of approaches to God, as valued by the local culture. In many respects I deal with the making of churches in the first part of this book in a manner similar to Mahieu's. Together, her study and mine offer a comparative perspective on the early processes of religious revival and institutionalization of Greek Catholic churches in Ukraine and Romania.

The works I have mentioned share a failure to deconstruct Greek Catholic identity, maintaining an image of a cohesive group united around tradition, ethnic or national identity, and collective memory. Some of these studies note the syncretism of Greek Catholic practice, which combines Latin and Byzantine rituals and devotions, but they do not explore it in any depth.[37] Trying to maintain their distinctiveness within the broader Catholic Church but fearing reabsorbtion into the Orthodox world, Greek Catholics stress both the differences between the two Christian traditions and their unifying characteristics. They cherish the supreme authority of the pope and their Catholic affiliation while retaining the 'true tradition' of eastern Christianity. The Greek Catholic tradition cannot be separated from its two component sources, but its existence is a matter of balancing these two tendencies, a dynamic I examine in chapter 4.

Contrary to previous studies focused on confessional identities, institutions, and discourses, I concentrate my work on the 'community of believers' by observing the tradition of knowledge and practice a community shares. This allows me to witness the way Greek Catholic and Orthodox Christianity are conjectural identities grounded in a single religious tradition. Rather than being a study of Greek Catholics or Orthodox Christians, this book is about a particular religious tradition that is the product of specific processes of syncretic formation.

1.5 Field Settings

My initial research project was focused on the postsocialist religious revival and aimed at comparing the development of the Ukrainian Greek Catholic

---

[37] However, see Hann's detailed discussion of the influence of western and eastern Christianity on Greek Catholic Church music (Hann 2003b) and the syncretism of the Greek Catholic tradition in Galicia (Hann 2005). See also Mahieu's (2005) analysis of liturgical changes in the Hungarian Greek Catholic Church.

Church (UGCC) and the Romanian Greek Catholic Church (RGCC). The Greek Catholic community in Romania had fewer than 300,000 members in 2002, concentrated mostly in the north-western part of the country, in Transylvania.[38] In Bucharest, the city where I worked, there were six parishes and fewer than 300 churchgoers. The UGCC, on the other hand, claimed more than three million members, ten eparchies in Ukraine, and several others around the world.[39] The historical trajectories of the two churches were for a long time similar, from their inception to their dissolution and hiatus under the socialist regime and finally to their surprising revival in 1989. Since then, the Ukrainian church has successfully grown into an established national church, whereas the Romanian church seems to face a continuing struggling for acceptance. This discrepancy pointed toward some significant differences in both the internal dynamics of the two churches and the socio-political circumstances of the two countries, aspects I wanted to investigate. The choice of western Ukraine for my field research was obvious, for this region was a stronghold of Ukrainian Greek Catholicism, just as Transylvania was for Romanian Greek Catholics.[40] L'viv has been western Ukraine's historical capital, the main centre of Ukrainian Greek Catholics, and, since 1988, the centre of the UGCC's revival.

During the first month of my stay in Ukraine in 2003, I was often told that the religious enthusiasm of the revival was gone and people were becoming less interested in religion. After the spectacular religious revival of the early 1990s, a period of stabilization followed from 1995 onward, in which churches underwent institutionalization (Krindatch 2003; Yurash 2005a). My work was structured around two objectives: to investigate the processes that led to the so-called revival, which accounted for the present religious situation, and to explore current religious dynamics and patterns of religious expression.

My first field site was the village of Shchirets, thirty kilometres south of L'viv, which I chose with the help of a student at the Ukrainian Catholic University whose family came from the village. At the turn of the twentieth

---

[38] This church appeared through a union of the Orthodox Church in Transylvania with Rome in 1700. With the formation of the Romanian state it spread into southern Romania. It remains a regional church, however, gathering its strength mostly from Transylvania and Maramures. The 2002 census counted 191,556 Greek Catholics in Romania, around 1 percent of the population (www.recensamant.ro). The Romanian Greek Catholic Church itself claimed to have more than 500,000 members.

[39] For an overview of the structure, dioceses, and membership of the UGCC, see www.ugcc.org.ua/eng/ugcc_structure/.

[40] By western Ukraine I refer to what was once the Austrian province of Galicia, or eastern Galicia (Halychyna), which now comprises the oblasts of L'viv, Ternopil, and Ivano-Frankivsk (see Magocsi 1983: xv).

century it had been a small Galician town with a mixed population of 1,607 Jews and 1,205 Catholics, both Polish and Ukrainian speakers. Most of the Ukrainian population in the area, 1,354 people, lived in Ostryv, a village immediately north of Shchirets, which later merged with the town.[41] The end of this multicultural environment in Galicia came with the two world wars.[42] War and ethnic cleansing left few survivors in the town, and most of them were displaced to Poland after 1945.[43] In this exchange of population, Ukrainians from western Galicia (*pereselentsi*), now south-eastern Poland, were brought to the nearly deserted villages of Soviet western Ukraine. These dramatic events destroyed what might have emerged as a 'community of memory' (Irwin-Zarecka 1994) in the village. Even today the absence of collective expressions of remembrance of past events is striking.[44]

Officially, Shchirets had 5,500 inhabitants and 1,200 households in 2004, but with recent migration, many people had left the village for long periods of time to work in Spain, Italy, Poland, and Russia.[45] Most village inhabitants worked in industry and services in Shchirets and L'viv, commuting daily to the city. The large industry built during Soviet times fell apart in the 1990s, drastically reducing possibilities for employment in the village.[46]

---

[41] As was the case all over eastern Galicia, Ukrainians lived predominantly in villages while Jews and Poles lived mainly in towns (Himka 1988). These settlements keep their names today: Lany grew to become a village in itself, and Ostryv became part of Shchirets in 1945. Kolonia (Rosenberg), a former German settlement, was included in the southeast part of Shchirets (there were 16 German families at the beginning of the twentieth century), while Pyd Hora and Turky became the new neighbourhoods for the newcomers of Soviet industrialization. The most recent neighbourhood, Filipine, grew from building by the nouveaux riches.

[42] The first war caused a massive decrease in population, which continued between 1918 and 1945 when the town came under the successive occupations of Polish (1918), Russian (from 1939), German (from 1941), and again Russian (1944) administrations.

[43] The Ukrainian and Polish populations were killed by each other's militias, and the entire Jewish population was deported to a concentration camp in Belzec in 1942.

[44] There are small commemorations to the Ukrainian partisans (UPA) in the village, but they engage only the few nostalgic villagers and war survivors rather than the entire community.

[45] Data obtained from the town hall registers in summer 2004. It would be difficult to get accurate data on the phenomenon of migration, because families are afraid of taxes and do not give information. During my household survey I was usually asked not to write down information about members of the family who were abroad, and in a few cases respondents refused to give information about this.

[46] During the Soviet period there were some ten factories and a collective farm in Shchirets. Now only three factories are open and partially functioning. During Soviet times the largest factory in the village, Sklozavod, employed up to 800 people from Shchirets and surrounding villages.

Some inhabitants became small farmers, producing mostly for home consumption and selling products at the markets in L'viv.[47]

Shchirets is a multiconfessional village with two churches, Greek Catholic and Roman Catholic, in the village centre and an Orthodox church on a nearby hill. At the time of my fieldwork, however, people's choices among the churches tended to be more locational than confessional. Most people attended either the Orthodox or the Greek Catholic church, depending on which part of the village they lived in. Two additional small groups were also active in local religious life: Jehovah's Witnesses, who had their own prayer house in the village, and Pentecostals, with fewer than ten to fifteen people attending services in L'viv each Sunday and no activity in Shchirets.

I intermittently lived and worked in the village throughout my stay in Ukraine from September 2003 to August 2004. The bulk of my research was conducted in two steps, in autumn 2003 and late spring 2004.

In autumn 2003 I also visited new Greek Catholic churches in L'viv, most of them huge, half-finished constructions situated in the suburbs.[48] The most important postsocialist church, though not the largest, was in the south of the city, in a satellite town called Sykhiv (Sykhivskyi *massyv*). This district incorporated a large territory with a mixture of socialist housing blocks and scattered village houses reminiscent of the villages around L'viv that disappeared to make space for massive industry. Sykhiv began to be built in the 1970s as a dormitory (*spalnyi raion*) for the heavily industrialized area.[49] It was among the last projects to be accomplished in the Soviet urbanization campaigns and in 2004 still had the appearance of an unfinished construction site. After 1990 it continued to develop rapidly, with new housing blocks, markets, and churches appearing every day. According to official statistics, the population in 2004 was 100,000 inhabitants, but population had decreased significantly in recent years because of work migration.[50]

---

[47] People received 0.5 hectare per person during the land reform but no technical equipment, and the land was usually spread among several locations, which made it difficult to use.

[48] These Soviet suburbs contrasted strongly with the old city centre, a UNESCO heritage site with beautiful architecture and impressive cathedrals dating from the sixteenth through the nineteenth centuries and built during the Polish and later Austro-Hungarian administrations.

[49] The old village, 'old' (*staryi*) Sykhiv, that gave the new quarter its name is still part of the administrative district created after 1990. There is also a 'new' Sykhiv, which is the Soviet-built area concentrated mainly on the large central square, Cervona Kalina. The administrative district of Sykhiv is much larger than both old and new Sykhiv; it includes several other smaller, adjacent districts. People tend to identify Sykhiv with new Sykhiv, so this is the space I refer to later when talking about Sykhiv.

[50] In Sykhiv, as in Shchirets, no statistics were available on the number of residents who were abroad. Parish priests in Sykhiv said that almost every family had at least one member abroad, but this was guesswork.

Sykhiv corresponded perfectly to the oft-used metaphor of the marketplace of religions. The great variety of churches present in one place was impressive, and all the more so because of their proximity. Before 1990 the central square of the district, the Cervona Kalina, was an empty field expected to host the regional party headquarters. In autumn 2003 six church buildings clustered around the square, one next to another, in different stages of construction. Greek Catholics had the newest, largest church, set in the best location. Opposite it, on the other side of the square, were two chapels belonging to Orthodox congregations – one the Ukrainian Orthodox Church of the Moscow Patriarchate and the other the Ukrainian Orthodox Church of the Kyiv Patriarchate. Farther aside was a large rectangular building with no identification signs, the centre of the Jehovah's Witnesses. Right behind the Greek Catholic church and closer to a forest stood a fifth, massive, still unfinished church belonging to the Pentecostal community. Behind this church, deep in the forest, was a small Roman Catholic chapel. Before 1990 there had been one church and a single Orthodox confession in Shchirets. In fewer than ten years the central square had been filled with churches, none similar to the others and yet all prosperous. For a researcher about to examine religious revival and interconfessional dynamics, Sykhiv was an ideal field site. I began to pay regular visits to these communities in November 2003 and continued to work in them up to September 2004.

Apart from Shchirets and Sykhiv, where I spent longer periods of time conducting systematic research, I made several trips to popular pilgrimage sites and monasteries. Usually I joined people from the parish in Sykhiv on their pilgrimages, trips motivated by family or personal problems but also providing escape from daily routine into the special moment of the pilgrimage. Sometimes entire families undertook such excursions on their own, but usually people chose to join pilgrimages organized by a religious entrepreneur or an agency. From September 2003 I regularly joined such excursions, prearranged by a woman who enjoyed travelling and guiding others through the pilgrimage experience. I thus learned about alternative sites of popular devotion. We visited holy springs in remote areas, miraculous lakes with healing powers, the newest places of apparitions of the Mother of God, and old apparition sites and monasteries. Some devotional places were integrated into official church practice; others were completely unorthodox, the focus of popular religiosity. There were both Greek Catholic and Orthodox sites, but most were attended by everybody, regardless of confessional belonging.

These sites took on their significance in the context of a religiosity that had its roots in underground religious practices dating to Soviet times. They were also connected with each other by priests, monks, and pilgrims who travelled between them. Most people who participated in these pilgrimages were regular churchgoers, members of their parish churches, and informed believers. Observing rituals in these remote places, I understood how the margins of institutionalized churches could serve as settings for the expression of both individual problems and collective anxieties in socially accepted forms. The religious practices associated with such sites were just as much as a part of the local religious tradition as church-observed rituals. Participants found these excursions important for their spiritual well-being, because some of the powerful spiritual aura (*sylna molytva*) of the place was believed to be transmitted to the pilgrims.

Among the pilgrimage sites I visited was one that I decided to explore in greater depth. This was a new monastery in Ternopil oblast, 200 kilometres from L'viv. The monastic community was situated in the village of Kolodiivka, fifty kilometres from the oblast centre. From Easter to November, large numbers of pilgrims flocked to the village every week, with the biggest crowds gathering on the last Tuesday of every month.[51] The monastery and its village became my third field site, and I returned there every month until September 2004.

Engaging with a third field site was a challenge, but it soon became a rewarding experience. The bulk of my research in Sykhiv and Shchirets was already completed at that time, but it included little about personal religion. The type of religiosity practised by monks and pilgrims in Kolodiivka was of a different sort from the routine practice I observed in the other two sites. Having previously lived in other monasteries for short periods of time, I could understand how monastic life in Kolodiivka was being easily accepted in this community. Such swift assimilation would have been impossible in other Orthodox monasteries, but here the monks were young and enthusiastic about communal life and their spiritual ideals. The monastery had been opened in 1995 by a group of young Greek Catholic monks gathered around a charismatic priest who settled in Kolodiivka to try to establish an ideal community that followed the eastern monastic tradition.

The monks' very idealism, however, held the seeds of discord in the community. The monks regularly performed public exorcisms, which were part of the attraction the place held for believers. I had to accept these exorcism rituals as part of the religious practice I was researching. In time I understood the symbolic processes at work in the ritual and the constitutive power the ritual had for monks and pilgrims. But I also learned of conflicting views within the community regarding the practice of exorcism, a clash that was part of a larger problem regarding religious practice in the monastery. Because of differences of opinions, the community's cohesion was quickly

[51] Monks set this special date for pilgrims and organize a full spiritual program during the day.

eroding. Upon my return to the monastery in summer 2005 I found that some of the monks I knew had left.

Multi-sited ethnography means that the specificity of each location determines the approach to the field, and methods of investigation may alternate from one site to another. In Sykhiv and Shchirets I had to combine methods of data gathering in order to investigate the particularities of each church community within the broader multiconfessional context. This resulted in a variety of data that had to be analysed through both quantitative and qualitative methods and later integrated into a cohesive argument. In Shchirets I conducted a series of interviews with priests, covering their involvement in the religious revival, the building of the parish, liturgical practice, relations with other religious groups, hierarchical authority, and their life stories. I talked to the village intellectuals, primarily teachers but also journalists, local authorities, and small entrepreneurs. Our discussions focused on the history of the village, its social and political situation, and its religious life. My interlocutors had been involved in the religious revival of the village and were prominent members of the Greek Catholic and Orthodox communities.

To acquire systematic data that would allow for generalizations beyond my limited observations, I designed a household survey, which I conducted in Shchirets between May and July 2004. Half the interviews included direct questions about religious beliefs and practices, confessional differentiation and inter-confessional relations, church-related expenses, and church community. The other half included demographic and economic questions regarding the household; in these I also elicited political opinions.[52] The general questions of the survey inquired into religious life from 1990 onwards and the development of the multiconfessional community. I collected data on ritual practices, measuring frequencies of individual and family participation in collective rituals and private devotions. I also followed the process of confessional differentiation, looking for patterns by analysing situations in which such differentiation was enforced and situations in which it was transcended.

In Sykhiv I worked with similar questions in mind, hoping to uncover a story of religious revival in a Soviet *microraion* where no public form of religiosity was available before 1990. Instead of focusing on a single community, the Greek Catholic parish, as initially planned, I decided to continue working with all six religious groups. I interviewed priests and other religious leader from each parish and attended services and community meet-

---

[52] My fieldwork preceded the presidential elections in Ukraine in November 2004, which led to the 'orange revolution'. Yushchenko's victory was largely supported in my field sites and throughout western Ukraine.

ings. Thus I became acquainted with each group and interviewed people who were active in the community. I expanded from my original interviews in each religious community by utilizing a snowball sample in which I moved from one interviewee to another. After conducting more than thirty in-depth interviews, I recognized that no matter how many additional ones I might conduct, it would be difficult to obtain the larger picture by that means in a district of more than 100,000 people and more than six religious communities. Organizing a survey seemed a more efficient method, and with the help of the sociology faculty in L'viv, in spring 2004 I conducted a large survey focused exclusively on Sykhiv.

In the first stage of the research, I had explored through interviews the 'making of churches' – the organizing and institutionalizing of religious communities in Sykhiv. In contrast, the survey was designed to investigate the religious options of Sykhiv residents. I was interested in discovering whether a clear confessional identity existed among churchgoers and, if so, how that identity was connected to non-religious factors (social, political, economic, educational, and so forth). Because most residents had moved to Sykhiv fewer than twenty years before, and before 1990 there was no church to attend in the district, each family at some point had made the choice of attending one of the new churches or none.

In order to connect this research to my earlier work in Shchirets, I tracked similar questions in my urban survey: confessional differences, collective and individual religious practices, frequency of ritual performance, levels of tolerance, strength of institutional affiliation, and modes of transmission of religious knowledge. The last set of questions was intended to gather information about the demographic, economic, and social backgrounds of the interviewees.

The Sykhiv sample included 312 respondents, divided according to criteria compatible with the multiconfessional profile of the district: Pentecostal, Jehovah's Witness, Roman Catholic, Greek Catholic, Orthodox Moscow Patriarchate, Orthodox Kyiv Patriarchate, and Orthodox Autocephalous. Each confessional group in the sample was proportionate to the size of the religious community as estimated during the first stage of the research.[53] For this reason the sample disproportionately favoured Greek Catholics, but

[53] Depending on its religious tradition, each church had a different approach to the meaning of 'community', as was also the case with property, church buildings, rituals, and so forth. Roman Catholics, Pentecostals, and Greek Catholics had ready-made lists of their members. Jehovah's Witnesses initially refused to cooperate but eventually allowed me limited access. The Orthodox churches had no form of membership, but priests had a clear idea of the size of the community according to donations and Sunday offerings.

in doing so it reflected the preponderance of Greek Catholics in the district, as well as in L'viv and western Ukraine.[54]

My work in the Kolodiivka monastery concluded my long-term observations and empirical data on urban and rural religiosity. As in the other two cases, I was interested in following the short history of this monastic community as a representative case for postsocialist religious dynamics. I did not wish to produce an ethnography of the monastery but to compare the religious practice surrounding this site with that of the other two places. The different modes of religiosity employed in the three settings were by now evident. The interviews I conducted and the life stories of monks and pilgrims I recorded focused more on individual beliefs and devotions, the pursuit of a personal spiritual model, and interaction with the divine. I examined the rituals closely to learn more about their role in the community. Furthermore, I was interested in the mediation between individual beliefs and the collective imaginary that served as a backdrop to the ritual, observing how much freedom and creative input individual agents retained in these imagistic rituals. The observations I made during my stay in Kolodiivka became good material for a comparison of religious practices there and in Shchirets.

The results of multi-sited research are difficult to gather into a single argument. Yet an impression formed in the field is always a good starting point for analysis. While still in Ukraine I perceived a certain rhythm to religious life, which was reflected in my choice of sites. Accompanying my informants to common Sunday liturgies in the village and later to monasteries and places of Marian apparitions, I learned about their need to alternate between regular church activity and special, more personal devotion. Such excursions into spirituality had long-term effects on people's lives and religious beliefs and practices. The impression of a special rhythm of religious life remained with me when I began to consider the theoretical possibilities for dealing with such diverse material. The monastic experience and the specific practices surrounding apparition sites made me consider them as

---

[54] The Greek Catholic parish had 3,000 visitors on typical Sundays and around 8,000 for special celebrations. The Roman Catholic, UOAC, and UOC-MP churches each counted approximately 50 regular members, with turnouts of up to 300 on special occasions. The UOC-KP, Pentecostals, and Jehovah's Witnesses each had some 300 to 500 regular participants and as many as 1,000 for special events.

a distinct mode of religiosity. The idea grew to become a frame of analysis for the whole fieldwork experience, integrating these spaces of religious practice into a unified view of the local religious tradition.

Map 1. Western Ukraine (formerly eastern Galicia): research fieldsites.

Chapter 2
The Ukrainian Orthodox Imaginary

'Ukraine means borderland' is a common opening remark in studies of the country (Rudnytsky and Rudnytsky 1987; Magocsi 1996; Wanner 1998). Historians analysing Ukrainian territories, especially the western part of present-day Ukraine, portray them as spaces of ambiguity at the crossroads of cultures and religious traditions. Several works reveal the persistence of identity-related dilemmas in this territory: 'What makes this historical comparison interesting today is the permanence of plurality in the formation of Ukrainian identity and the reactualization of the problem of searching for Ukrainian identity somewhere between Occident and Orient' (Boyko 2004b: 66, my translation).

Ukrainian Christianity shares a similar image of unsettledness, of being a 'religion of the margins' (Boyko 2004), a middle-of-the-road construction between the Orthodox and the Latin world.[55] This common perception, which connects a territory with its religious tradition, is captured in the oft-used phrase, 'Ukraine, between east and west' (Sevcenko 1996; Wilson 2000b). In this formula, 'west' is a reference to Europe, either western or Catholic. 'East' stands for at least two historical realms: eastern Christianity, the religious tradition, which since the Christianization of Kievan Rus has evolved into one of the main Christian traditions in the world; and the population of Eastern Slavs that settled in these territories centuries ago (Rudnytsky and Rudnytsky 1987). The Kievan principality was Christianized in 988 by way of Byzantium. The arrival of Byzantine missionaries led to a Byzantine influence on the local religious tradition and culture that continued up to the fifteenth century. This period is today considered the great era of Slavic Orthodoxy. Unlike its inspirational model, Byzantium, the Kievan Rus state maintained a separation between political and ecclesiastical

---

[55] Boyko (2004) introduced the concept of 'margins' (*une religion des confines*) to build an historical model explaining floating religious identities in past and present Ukraine. Wanner (1998) portrayed Ukraine as a 'borderland' in the introduction to her book on the making of the modern Ukrainian nation.

authority, which left the church free to follow its Christian ideals independent of worldly matters.[56]

What is now known as western Ukraine was in medieval times an independent Eastern Slavic principality, the principality of Halych, which in the thirteenth century became the kingdom of Galicia and Lodomeria (Halychyna i Volodymyria) under Hungarian authority. Starting in the 1340s the region came under Polish rule, which continued from 1569, under the Polish-Lithuanian Commonwealth, until the first partition of Poland in 1572, when it was annexed by the Austro-Hungarian Empire. Even before Polish and Lithuanian rule, the vast Kiev Metropolitanate, which included this region, had lost its importance, having been torn apart by Moscow and Vilnius, emerging centres of political and religious power. The shift in the balance of power towards Russia coincided with the Russian Orthodox Church's rejection of the Union of Florence in 1439.[57] The old Kiev Metropolitanate thus split for the first time into a Ruthenian (Kievan) Orthodox Church and a Russian Orthodox Church.[58] The Kiev Metropolitanate remained in union with Constantinople, ruling over the Ukrainian and Belorussian territories (then part of the Grand Duchy of Lithuania and the kingdom of Poland), while the Moscow Metropolitanate emerged as an autocephalous church.[59]

The two metropolitanates, Moscow and Kiev, continued down separate paths, both subjected to an acculturation in which the religious tradition was suffused with local culture. For both churches, however, the Kievan Rus period remained the golden age of Slavic Orthodoxy, because of its flourishing of religious and cultural life.[60] The autocephaly of the Moscow church led to closer contacts between church and state. The metropolitanate soon became dependent on the authority of the Russian princes, and a nationalization of the Russian church began, which led in the end to the proclamation of

---

[56] Byzantium followed Justinian's model of 'symphony': two authorities derive from God – the priesthood, which is in charge of divine matters, and the empire, which is in charge of earthly matters – and the two are strongly connected (Rudnytsky and Rudnytsky 1987: 151).

[57] The Council of Florence (1431–1439) was the first successful attempt to discuss and reconcile the schism between eastern and western churches that took place in 1054. The union itself failed, but its four main theological points (including *filioque*) were taken over by later unions in the sixteenth and seventeenth centuries.

[58] The older name for Eastern Slavs living in Belarus and western Ukraine (including Transcarpathia), was 'Ruthenians'. They became 'Ukrainians' over the course of the nineteenth-century nationalist movements, which first created a Ukrainian identity in the nineteenth century. The term 'Ruthenian' has been preserved into contemporary times and refers to an ethnic group that considers itself 'Rusyn'.

[59] The Russian church became autocephalous in 1448. Soon after, the Russian Metropolitanate changed its name from 'Kiev and all Rus' to 'Moscow and all Rus' (Sysyn 1990: 5).

[60] 'The Kievan period is more and more acknowledged to have been perhaps the purest and most versatile of all periods of Russian religion' (Schmemann 1977: 295).

the patriarchate in 1589. This model, developed in Russia, in which secular power and religious power are strongly connected, survives today in the state-church partnerships that remain dominant in most Orthodox countries of Eastern Europe.

The Kievan church, for its part, struggled to keep together its subjects, who were now part of two separate Catholic states. The church was increasingly disadvantaged vis-à-vis the Roman Catholic Church. During this period the Polish state supported the Roman Catholic Church, and so it was able to organize dioceses in Galicia in direct competition with the Kievan church. The situation changed in the fifteenth century, when the Polish state found that it was in its interest to integrate the Orthodox nobility and guarantee equal rights to the Orthodox Church (Himka 2005: 24). The Protestant Reformation altered the balance by weakening the position of Catholics, but the Orthodox Church did not benefit from this change. The Reformation made converts among both Catholics and Orthodox Christians, and although the Counter-Reformation was putatively aimed at containing Protestantism, in reality it directed significant effort towards converting the Orthodox.

The religious transformations of the sixteenth and seventeenth centuries challenged the theology and practice of Orthodoxy. It was at this time that a significant western Christian influence entered the church, bringing remarkable innovations to Orthodoxy. It was also this period that saw the momentous achievement of the Union of Brest in 1596. The union joined Orthodox Ukrainians with the Roman Catholic Church, and out of this arrangement emerged the Greek Catholic Church, then known as the Ruthenian Uniate Church. From 1596 onwards, further attempts were made to unite the Eastern Orthodox Church with Rome, but they did not have the lasting effect of the Union of Brest.

The union brought about a new institutional division within the Kiev Metropolitanate: Ruthenians divided into two churches, one that accepted the union and papal authority and another that rejected the union, holding to the Orthodox tradition and the vague authority of Constantinople. Each of the new churches considered itself to be the successor to the Kievan Rus tradition, just as the Ruthenian and Russian Orthodox Churches had claimed after their earlier separation. The Union of Brest brought Orthodox bishops to the territories of the Polish-Lithuanian Commonwealth, under the jurisdiction of the pope. Orthodox bishops accepted the Florentine points as proclaimed by the Council of Florence and in return were able to preserve the eastern Byzantine rite in the Uniate Church. Thus, after the founding of the Uniate Church, no visible changes took place in local religious practice. This made the unification easier for the mass of believers, but it also facilitated later fluctuations in the memberships of entire dioceses and parishes between the Uniate and Orthodox Churches.

The Orthodox Church went through a short period of crisis immediately after the union, but it soon re-established its institutional structures and underwent complete reformation under Metropolitan Peter Mohyla. The Latin influence was felt in both churches, which adopted theological and liturgical reforms inspired by the western Polish tradition predominant at the time. During the sixteenth and seventeenth centuries the two rites, Catholic and Byzantine, coexisted peacefully, embodying the confessional plurality of the region. But cultural and religious diversity was not limited to the Catholic and Orthodox Churches. Western Galicia was also inhabited by Jews, Muslims, Armenian Gregorians, and Protestants, groups that represented a more distant 'other' for eastern Christians than did Catholics of Latin rite. The local eastern Christian tradition developed in interaction with the other Christian traditions, and exchanges took place continually among these sundry denominations.

The local religious tradition was challenged and stimulated in this polyphonous atmosphere. It absorbed and adapted influences from western Christianity while conserving its Byzantine past and its connections to the Slavic Orthodox world. This long-term process led to the emergence of new religious forms and the development of a particular syncretism of religious tradition that persists into present times.[61] Many contemporary religious movements in Ukraine find their precedents in these formative years.

The Kiev Metropolitanate was transferred from the jurisdiction of the Constantinople Patriarchate to that of Moscow in the late seventeenth century. By that time the Moscow and Kiev Metropolitanates had gone through very different experiences, which widened the distance between the two churches. This bifurcation favoured the development of distinctive religious traditions in Russia and Ukraine, and it inspired and ultimately justified the formation of autonomous Ukrainian churches in the twentieth century.

In the post-union period of religious effervescence during the sixteenth and seventeenth centuries, Galicia remained a stronghold of Orthodoxy. It accepted the Union of Brest only later, towards the turn of the eighteenth century, when Galicia was incorporated into the Austro-Hungarian Empire (1772). During this time the province consisted of a much larger territory than the present-day region, including parts of south-eastern Poland, up to Krakow. Austrian authorities favoured the Uniate Church –

---

[61] Although both Orthodox and Uniate Ukrainians underwent periodic movements to diminish Latin and western Christian influences, the westernization of the sixteenth and seventeenth centuries was so deeply embedded in religious tradition that it could not be uprooted (Sysyn 1990: 11).

renamed the Greek Catholic Church at the time – over both the Roman Catholic Church, which was considered too close to the Polish nobility, and the Orthodox Church, which was seen as an emissary of the Russian Empire.[62] It was then that the Greek Catholic Church was first given status equal to that of the Roman Catholic Church, and L'viv became the seat of the metropolitan.

Benefiting from state support and various reforms, the Greek Catholic clergy and laity were able to improve their socio-economic status in the province, and a Ruthenian elite developed that had not formerly existed. The expansion of the Greek Catholic Church in Galicia counterbalanced the bleak situation of the church in the Ukrainian territories that were incorporated into the Russian Empire after the 1793 partition of Poland. There, the Russian church and state began to destroy the union and forced Uniate dioceses to 'return' to Orthodoxy.[63] In fewer than 100 years the Greek Catholic church was whittled down to embrace a much smaller territory, namely, the Habsburg-controlled Ukrainian territory of Galicia.

Over the course of the nineteenth century, in the absence of a secular, educated elite, the newly formed Greek Catholic elite initiated nationalization, investing all its energies in creating a national consciousness among the Ukrainian people (Himka 1991: 55). Beginning as a cultural movement, the 'national awakening' later became a political matter promoted by the Greek Catholic Church.[64] In the nineteenth century, priests were considered the most important mediators between the national movement and the peasantry, and because of the pastoral work of Greek Catholic clergy, the message reached a large mass of believers (Himka 1988: 130).

Concurrent with the inception of the national movement, an easternizing trend arose within the Greek Catholic Church, spearheaded by people who considered the church to be excessively Latinized and thus Polish. These people looked towards Russian Orthodoxy as an alternative model. The construction of Ukrainian national identity was never straightforward

---

[62] Before Habsburg rule the church was known as 'Uniate', from the union with Rome, and the term had a pejorative connotation, implying the inferiority of Uniates to 'real' Roman Catholics. In 1774 Maria Teresa passed a decree replacing the name with 'Greek Catholic' (Himka 1988: 124 n. 129).

[63] From 1805, Russian authorities prohibited the election of a new Uniate metropolitan of Kiev, leaving the Uniate Church without a leader. Following intense attempts to purify the rite and other strong pressures, the dioceses of Kamianets and Volhynia converted to Orthodoxy in the first half of the nineteenth century. By mid-1870 the last Uniate diocese within the Russian Empire had become Russian Orthodox.

[64] 'The Greek Catholic Church supported *narodovstvo*, the Ukrainian national movement. Priests interpreted the national ideology, shaping it according to a pastoral-theological mould, and offered it to their parishioners (Himka 1988: 126).

but always reflected the intricate relations existing between religious identity and national identity. On one hand, the Ukrainian Orthodox tradition assumed an ambiguous role in nation-building, and on the other, the founding fathers of the Ukrainian nation maintained a circumspect distance from religion (Yelensky 2005: 152). The church itself was suffering an identity crisis and thus proved to be an imperfect vehicle for the creation of a national identity. Although Ukrainians believed the Orthodox faith they shared with Russians to be closer to the 'true' eastern tradition, they also perceived it as a tool of Russification. Yet they identified Catholicism with Polishness, the perpetual other for Ukrainians. This tension was reflected in the search for balance within the Greek Catholic Church, which moved between the extremes of Russophilia and Latinophilia.

The solution to this identity-related dilemma originated with Metropolitan Andrei Sheptytskyi, the most important personality of twentieth-century Greek Catholicism. Himself an easternizer, Sheptytskyi advocated a return to the eastern spirituality symbolized by Kievan Rus. He maintained, however, that this should be done while remaining part of the universal Catholic Church (Himka 1991: 61). The resolution he promoted brought the eastern tradition and the Catholic Church together in a creative expression of the union (Pelikan 1989). Having to deal with new tensions arising from an emergent secular intelligentsia that was nationalist and anti-clerical, Sheptytskyi also managed to put some distance between the Greek Catholic Church and the Ukrainian national movement.

With the First World War, Galicia changed rulership several times, alternating between the Austro-Hungarian and Russian Empires. The Russian authorities, persevering in their stance against Uniatism, tried to destroy the Greek Catholic Church and incorporate it into Russian Orthodoxy. The Habsburgs, on the other hand, re-established the church and backed its existence. In 1918, with the collapse of the Austro-Hungarian Empire, western Ukrainians managed to organize themselves into an independent state, the Western Ukrainian National Republic. It survived for less than a year. Poland took control of western Galicia, and the rest of the country became the Soviet Socialist Republic of Ukraine. The Greek Catholic Church fully supported the independent republic, but meanwhile a new Ukrainian church appeared out of the movement for autocephaly, ready to contest the Greek Catholic Church in its role as the 'national' church.[65]

The Ukrainian autocephalous movement arose out of national ideals and the Ukrainian revolution, which had sought an independent, national Orthodox church to match the new Ukrainian state. 'Autocephaly' became a

---

[65] At the turn of the twentieth century the Greek Catholic Church officially counted 1,854 parishes with almost three million believers in Galicia (Himka 1991: 59).

popular religious movement led by low clergy and members of the Ukrainian intelligentsia, who were at loggerheads with the Russian hierarchy in Ukraine. With the defeat of the Ukrainian Republic and the incorporation of eastern Ukraine into the Soviet Union in 1921, the autocephalous church became the only institutional carrier of the ideal of an independent Ukraine.

In the beginning, Soviet authorities allowed the autocephalous church to develop, aiming to use this grassroots movement against the official Orthodox Church. Its development culminated in the 1921 First All-Ukrainian Church Council (*sobor*), which established the hierarchy and lines of conduct of the new Ukrainian church.[66] The Ukrainian Autocephalous Orthodox Church that emerged from this council followed the Orthodox tradition but broke the canonical relation to Orthodoxy. Its new leaders 'nationalized' church life to a great extent. They empowered the laity by weakening the rigid distinctions between laity and clergy and by taking a more egalitarian and pragmatic approach to the Orthodox canons (Bociurkiw 1991: 242).[67]

This church was extremely successful in both the Soviet and Polish regions of Ukraine, reaching three million to six million faithful by the end of the 1920s. Not surprisingly, Soviet authorities, concerned with the amplitude of the movement, launched a campaign against it and staged a 'self-dissolution' of the church in January 1930. Later they allowed it to be replaced by a 'Ukrainian Orthodox Church' subordinated to the Moscow Patriarchate. The notion of autocephaly survived its institutional extinction, and during the German occupation the Ukrainian Autocephalous Orthodox Church was revived for a short time (1942–1943).[68]

After the third partition of Poland in 1939, Galicia was occupied by Soviet troops, and Soviet authorities initiated a similar campaign of persecution against the Greek Catholic Church. The occupation was too short to destroy the church; in 1941 Germans invaded Galicia and Soviet troops fled

---

[66] The First All-Ukrainian Church Council convened in Kiev in October 1921, gathering priests from all Ukrainian provinces, as well as Ukrainian intellectuals, but it had no bishop. In order to start the church, the *sobor* had to consecrate a bishop ad hoc. With this move it broke the apostolic succession and church canons (which state that only a bishop can consecrate another bishop), giving the other Orthodox churches a reason to declare its illegitimacy (Bociurkiw 1991: 243).

[67] The Ukrainian Autocephalous Orthodox Church had a relatively democratic structure, with self-government at all levels of the church, lay councils and brotherhoods, lay preaching, and married bishops. Bociurkiw (1991: 244) contended that the success of the church was based on its ideology, 'a revolutionary gospel that combined a revitalized Christian message with Ukrainian nationalism and social radicalism'.

[68] It also survived in the Ukrainian diaspora in the United States and Canada, where a large Ukrainian Orthodox Church, autocephalous and canonical, has developed since the 1920s.

east. The German occupation led to the extermination of the entire Jewish population of Galicia. Churches did not take part in pogroms, but otherwise their role in collaborating with the German administration is unclear (Himka 2005: 31).[69] Certain figures such as Metropolitan Sheptytskyi are considered to have been courageous opponents of the Nazi regime and the extermination of the Jews (Magocsi and Krawchuk 1989). The chaos of the war enabled nationalist partisan troops, both Polish and Ukrainian, to initiate guerrilla actions against civilians of the other ethnic group in Galician and Volhynian villages. The Ukrainian Insurgent Army (Ukrayinska Povstanska Armia), the military branch of the Organization of Ukrainian Nationalists, which was active from 1942 into the 1950s, and the Polish Home Army (Armia Krajowa) were together responsible for most of the ethnic cleansing that took place during these years. Both groups aimed to eliminate each other's compatriots from their respective territories.

With the end of the Second World War, eastern Galicia became part of the Ukrainian Soviet Socialist Republic, and the western side was incorporated into Poland. Galician multiculturalism was completely destroyed during the war and its immediate aftermath. With the Jewish population exterminated and the Polish population resettled in Poland, little was left of the region's historic religious pluralism. The Soviets shut down the Greek Catholic Church and 'reunited' it with the Orthodox Church in 1946. A vigorous anti-religion campaign that banned most religious activities discouraged religious practice, although it did not manage to obliterate every expression of religiosity. All religious groups were persecuted and reduced to remnants, but the Greek Catholic Church suffered most. Greek Catholic bishops were imprisoned; priests and monks who refused to sign the union with the Orthodox Church were arrested and deported to Siberia and Central Asia. Religious institutions were closed and church property confiscated, most of it being given to the new Ukrainian Orthodox Church affiliated with Moscow. Those who survived the persecution went underground and reorganized themselves into what came to be known as the 'catacomb' church.

The systematic repression of Greek Catholics forced both clergy and laity to adopt survival strategies. The majority of Greek Catholics formally moved into the Ukrainian Orthodox Church, which was allowed to continue operating. These 'converts' were left alone but remained objects of state suspicion. Priests and parishioners who 'signed' (*pidpysanyi*) formed a 'church within the church' (Markus 1989) as they continued to practise the rite as they knew it, considering themselves at heart to be eastern-rite Catholics. Because of this inconsistent and dangerous position, 'reunited' priests

---

[69] No study is available, for example, of relations between clergy and Ukrainian troops or partisans who helped the German army.

often had a dual identity (Keleher 1993: 73), and historians argue that most of them suffered a 'split in personality' (Shlikhta 2004b: 269).[70] Such was the case with Greek Catholics who did not go underground and were forced to choose between Orthodoxy and Catholicism when their church was banished.

Because of official restrictions, priests and the laity opted for 'practical adaptability' instead of 'dogmatic inflexibility', and this led to significant ritual modifications, the alteration of canonical rules, and the emergence of new forms of community life (Shlikhta 2004a: 198). The 'domestication' (Dragadze 1993) of religion allowed for a practice that was alternative to both state-sanctioned atheism and the rites of the Orthodox Church.[71] Indeed, two parallel churches were active throughout Soviet times: one an official church controlled by the state and the other a community of believers who practised a form of religiosity uniquely adapted to their circumstances. Maintaining the local religious tradition was also a form of resistance to Soviet authority, and anti-Soviet attitudes were important components of religious life in Galicia at the time.

After Khrushchev's anti-religion campaign of the late 1950s and early 1960s, Galicia became the region with the largest concentration of Orthodox Christians in the entire the Soviet Union. The Ukrainian Orthodox Church was officially subordinated to Moscow, but the Russian Orthodox Church found strength only in the large mass of Ukrainian believers and in Ukrainian church resources.[72] When Greek Catholics were forced to join Orthodoxy, they retained their parishes and priests and remained culturally and institutionally separate from the Russian Orthodox Church. The 'church within the church' maintained a clear religious and national character that became predominant in the Ukrainian Orthodox Church. A quiet Ukrainization of Orthodoxy took place in the region and later spread to the larger

[70] They also argue that this move was not really visible to the majority of laypeople, who lacked theological understanding and who, at least in the beginning, noticed no visible change in the everyday life of their church. However, given the tense political situation, laypeople were extremely aware of the changes taking place in all spheres, including the religious field. Their reactions were often expressed in a religious idiom, as in the case of the Penitents, discussed in chapter 7.

[71] 'Since the late 1950s, the conduct of illegal festive services was the established pattern of religious life, mainly in rural regions, wherever abandoned churches were suitable for services. When such a possibility did not exist, the faithful gathered for prayers or services on private premises' (Shlikhta 2004a: 230).

[72] The situation remained the same throughout the Soviet era, and on the eve of the collapse of the USSR there were about 4,000 Orthodox parishes in Ukraine – two-thirds of all Orthodox communities in the USSR (Yelensky 2005).

Orthodox Church.[73] This allowed the survival of the local religious tradition and of local networks within the Russian Orthodox Church, a factor that played an important role in the revival of Ukrainian churches in the late 1980s (Shlikhta 2004a; Yelensky 2005; Yurash 2005a).

This brief historical excursion into almost a millennium of Christianity in western Ukraine highlights the development of a local syncretic tradition, a result of the interaction of two great traditions, eastern and western Christianity. Christianity in Ukraine is a 'construction in between the Orthodox and the Latin worlds' (Wilson 2000: 243). This ambivalent position led to successive divisions of the church, from the splitting of the Kievan Rus church to repeated attempts at unification and the formation of an autocephalous church. This recurrent dilemma was embedded in conceptions of the Uniate Church, which borrowed from both traditions and proved to be a creative synthesis of the two. 'Throughout centuries one of the cornerstones of its identity has been the tension between the two orientations and the search for a living synthesis between the two traditions' (Gudziak 2000). Though characterized as an 'age-old tradition of ambiguity' (Boyko 2004: 40), the eastern Christian tradition of western Ukraine, aside from its borrowing of eastern and western elements, developed unique forms of religiosity expressed in church architecture, iconography, music, theology, and rite.

The history of Ukrainian Greek Catholics illustrates well the ambiguity of peripheries, for over the course of 400 years this group was subject to incessant fluctuations and transformations evolving between the two poles, eastern and western. Ever since the downfall of Kievan Rus, the local church had remained at the peripheries of other churches. Catholicism had strongly influenced the local tradition and, through the Polish church, had attempted to 'convert' the region. But for Ukrainians, the Catholic Church, tied to Polish people, always constituted the other in opposition to which they defined themselves. Orthodoxy, on the other hand, was the seed from which the local tradition developed, but the primary authority of the Russian Or-

---

[73] According to Yelensky (2005: 158), 'in the mid-1970s, thirteen out of sixteen Orthodox hierarchs in Ukraine were ethnic Ukrainians. Nine of the thirteen were western Ukrainians, and three were former Uniate priests. In 1966, for the first time after many years of exclusion, an ethnic Ukrainian, Archbishop Filaret (Denisenko), was appointed to the post of Kiev Exarch. The next year, former Greek Catholic Archbishop Nicolayi (Yurik) headed the L'viv and Ternopil Eparchy, the largest single eparchy of the Russian Orthodox Church (Bociurkiw 1977: 83), with more than 1,300 parishes out of approximately 6,000 parishes within the USSR borders. Natives from western Ukraine made up 50 percent all students in Leningrad theological schools . . . The Ukrainian bishops were the largest ethnic group within the Russian Orthodox Church . . ., and two ethnic Ukrainian metropolitans, Filaret (Denisenko) and Volodimir (Sabodan), had been contenders for the seat of the Moscow Patriarchate in the 1990 Russian Orthodox Church Local Council.'

thodox Church represented, paradoxically, the 'sameness' against which the Ukrainian church asserted its unique identity. The Ukrainian church neither was completely absorbed into the Russian church nor stood against it as an entirely separate entity. The main reason for this was the huge influence of Ukrainian churchmen on Russian Orthodoxy from the time of Kievan Rus until the Soviet period.

Over time, the Ukrainian religious tradition was able to accommodate frequent confessional changes marked by the balancing of political powers representing either Catholicism or Orthodoxy. Because people were connected to this local tradition rather than to one church or the other, they could adapt to such changes. Their adaptation resulted in a large degree of confessional mobility on the part of both elites and members of local communities, which also facilitated the forced incorporation of Greek Catholics into Orthodoxy under Soviet pressure and later the successful revival of Ukrainian churches during the glasnost period.

2.1 Religious Pluralism in Western Ukraine

The postsocialist transformations of Eastern Europe brought with them a redefinition of religion in the public sphere and in relation to the state. The bonds between traditional churches and national states, having developed during the nineteenth-century nation-building projects and having survived into the socialist period, were challenged in the postsocialist religious environment. The arrival of new religious groups and missionaries served to fill the 'spiritual void' left in the wake of failed socialist ideology. The mission of spiritual renewal, however, collided with the re-emergence of 'traditional' churches, which persisted in claiming privileged roles for themselves in the emerging democracies.[74]

Ukraine, like most other postsocialist states, now aspires to Western liberal models of governance, which dictate a strict separation between church and state and ask governments to protect people's freedom of religion. This freedom includes individual choice of religion and equal rights of worship and public expression for all religious groups. States that have tried to secure religious freedom have been subject to a tension between the desire to grant this right and the desire to favour certain religious identities that are part of the larger national identity (Hann 2000c; Plokhy 2002). Most states have, in the end, offered special status to the dominant church, giving it

[74] Calling a church 'traditional' carries political implications in the postsocialist context, so for Ukraine I use the emic terms while acknowledging that some churches perceived as 'new churches' (Pentecostals, for example) already have lengthy historical presences in Ukraine (Plokhy 2002; Wanner 2004).

rights denied to others in the name of a historical relationship. These churches, confirmed as 'national churches', could then dictate tolerance or, rather, intolerance towards other religious groups, replacing pluralism with religious monopoly. The differences between Russia and Ukraine are revealing in this context.[75]

In the broader postsocialist perspective, Ukraine makes an interesting case of the fairly smooth achievement of a religiously plural society. Two factors converged to create the premises for religious diversity there: an unregulated religious sphere and the absence of a single church corresponding to national ideals. Ukraine's transformation into 'a model of religious pluralism among formerly socialist societies' (Wanner 2004: 736) has provoked many discussions and been interpreted in a variety of ways, some of which I mentioned in the introduction. Later in this section I argue that Ukraine is not the paragon of religious pluralism it is generally understood to be. People have weak institutional commitments to churches, despite high levels of religious practice and manifest religiosity. They transcend recently built confessional borders within previously homogeneous Orthodoxy, transporting their practice and expectations to different churches as places of prayer. This leads to the acceptance and coexistence of religious groups imagined to be Orthodox or close to the Orthodox imaginary. The visible basis of the imagined community comes from the tradition of practice and knowledge that churches share. This imaginary becomes possible because of a separation of religious beliefs from political allegiances – what Charles Taylor called the post-Durkheimian dispensation, a third ideal type in the evolution of religion in society (Taylor 2002: 96).

In the postsocialist context, religious pluralism is usually seen as an existing or desirable characteristic of the religious sphere. The notion carries a certain ambiguity: it can refer either to the recognition of a variety of religious groups coexisting in a certain place or to an ideological position associated with a liberal view of religious diversity (Hamnett 1990: 7). In the postsocialist case, pluralism emerges as a direct consequence of the state's ideological failure and the introduction of liberal policies in a context lacking a religious monopoly. Its meaning shifts easily between 'circumstantial plurality' (Borowik 2002: 502) and 'expected pluralism' (Barker 1997; Casanova 1998; Wanner 2004). The first meaning applies when a large number of religious groups are active in one place, whereas the second presupposes a certain ideological substratum beneath the observed diversity.

The complex situation of Ukrainian pluralism in the postsocialist religious revival derives from the emergence of a large number of new religious

[75] For articles comparing Russia and Ukraine as opposing examples of the development of the religious sphere in relation to the state, see Krindach 2003, Plokhy 2002, and Tataryn 2001.

groups, the revival of traditional churches (a feature common to many post-socialist countries), and the fragmentation of Ukrainian Orthodoxy.[76] The last two developments had their roots in the history of Orthodoxy in Galicia prior to Soviet times.

Galicia had remained a stronghold of Ukrainian religiosity during the Soviet era, and religious transmission and practice continued in spite of widespread repression. In western Ukraine, church and popular religiosity provided a nucleus of resistance to Soviet religious politics. Political dissidents fought for human rights, including rights to religious freedom and native languages and culture, and advocated for the opening of churches. By the late 1970s religious activists had begun to seek out and cooperate with political dissidents. Like human rights activists, religious dissenters began to appeal to the Helsinki Accords, to which the Soviet Union was a signatory, asking for religious rights and freedoms (Dunn 1971: 188–189).

Thus, religious and political activists began to fight for their rights using the same discourse. Political dissidents marginalized by the state, moreover, could make use of the mobilizing potential and networks of religious activists to reach larger masses. A visible alliance emerged between the two activist groups, and the merger proved to be more successful in achieving the aims of both groups.[77] The active clergy and laity, meanwhile, used a combination of mysticism and anti-Soviet and nationalist discourses to mobilize people. One of the first public demands heard at the beginning of the glasnost period was the request for freedom of religious practice and legalization of the Greek Catholic Church.

The end of the 1980s brought further complications to the religious sphere. The Greek Catholic Church emerged from the underground in full shape, and with support from the Greek Catholic diaspora it moved quickly towards establishing an official structure. At first based on the informal networks of the catacomb church, it quickly gathered supporters among 'reunited' and younger Orthodox priests, their parishioners, and supporters

---

[76] Statistics on the number of religious organizations registered in Ukraine in 2005 can be obtained from Religious Information Service of Ukraine, www.risu.org.ua/eng/resources/statistics. There were 28,481 religious communities registered in January 2005. For a comprehensive article on the Ukrainian religious situation, analysing statistical data from 2001, see Krindatch 2003.

[77] Historians consider religious dissent in the Soviet Union a 'distinct sub-category of the larger phenomenon of political dissent, with which it shares a demand for the rule of law' (Bociurkiw, John, and Laux 1975: 58). At the same time, Soviet authorities saw 'religion as a political problem, religious doctrines as hostile ideologies and churches and sects as competing with the Communists for influence over society' (Bociurkiw, John, and Laux 1975: 58).

of Ukrainian independence who 'converted' to Greek Catholicism.[78] This posed a serious problem for the Orthodox Church, whose members were leaving for another church and, more importantly, whose Ukrainian identity was challenged by allegations that it was subordinate to Moscow.

The Orthodox response to the connection between Ukrainian nationalism and the Greek Catholic Church was a move towards autocephaly. The formation of an independent Ukrainian church separate from both Moscow and Rome looked, to Ukrainian nationalists already aspiring to an independent Ukrainian state, like the best solution. The Ukrainian Autocephalous Orthodox Church became the first official post-Soviet Ukrainian church, founded in Kyiv in May 1990 at an All-Ukrainian Church Council. The strongly nationalist, anti-Russian movement helped to create the two Ukrainian churches in a very short time, but it was unable to bring about a single, unified Ukrainian church. The competition between the two Ukrainian churches led to the splitting of many parishes and church communities into separate Autocephalous and Greek Catholic groups. This was the first in a series of splits that characterized this period.[79]

The new Ukrainian state encouraged collaboration between the two Orthodox churches, with the goal of merging them into a national Ukrainian church. But attempts to unite the Autocephalous Church, which was led by a celebrated diaspora figure, with the former Ukrainian branch of the Russian Orthodox Church, headed by a compromised patriarch, were unsuccessful. Divergences between the two Orthodox churches were reinforced by the attempts of a large group of pro–Russian Orthodox bishops and priests to reinforce ties with the Russian church. This group provoked a new split in the Ukrainian Orthodox Church when it declared its canonical unity with Moscow, 'freeing' the Ukrainian metropolitan from his duties and taking the name 'Ukrainian Orthodox Church–Moscow Patriarchate' in May 1992. Metropolitan Filaret, now relieved of his position, founded the third Orthodox church under the name 'Ukrainian Orthodox Church–Kievan Patriarchate' in June 1992. Altogether the former Ukrainian Orthodox Church splintered into four new churches: the Ukrainian Orthodox Church–Kiev Patriarchate (UOC-KP), the Ukrainian Orthodox Church–Moscow Patriarchate (UOC-MP), the Ukrainian Autocephalous Orthodox Church (UAOC),

---

[78] The highest-profile 'conversion', which signalled the beginning of the movement to take back churches, occurred in L'viv at the end of October 1989. It was then that one of the three priests at the Church of the Transfiguration, a church imbued with symbolism for western Ukrainians, announced that it would merge with the Greek Catholic Church.

[79] The story of the Orthodox splits and the early revival of Ukrainian churches has been told at length in several studies. Among them, see Bociurkiw 1995; D'Anieri, Kravchuk, and Kuzio 1999; Fagan and Shchipkov 2001; Krindatch 2003; Markus 1995; Plokhy 2002; Sysyn 1993; Wilson 2000.

and to a certain extent the Ukrainian Greek Catholic Church (UGCC), also called the Ukrainian Catholic Church of Eastern Rite. All of them legitimated their identities and traditions by reference to the Kievan Rus church of the tenth century.

The emergence of eastern churches in Ukraine involved confrontation and political battle, and their development came at the expense of the Russian Orthodox Church and its successor, the UOC-MP. The crucial aspect of this confessional dynamic was that the emerging eastern churches had to share the same resources: church buildings, parish communities, priests, and monasteries belonging to the former Orthodox Church of Soviet times.[80] Having to divide a common inheritance and redistribute church property among themselves, each church tried to differentiate itself from the others. The first to associate itself with the nationalist movement was the Greek Catholic Church, whose claim was supported by its martyrdom and the moral authority acquired during the underground period. Thus, the legalization and takeover of churches by Greek Catholics took place within the general Ukrainian nationalist movement. The UOAC and later the UOC-KP also appeared as candidates for a national church to serve an independent state, and they distanced themselves from the UGCC by emphasizing their Orthodoxy in opposition to the other's Catholicism (Jepsen 2005: 78). 'We want our church Ukrainian!' has been the most sensitive request of western Ukrainians throughout the years. The emergent UOC-MP claimed its legitimacy on the basis of the imagined community of Slavic Orthodoxy, over which Moscow was believed to be the rightful authority. These trajectories were not constant during this period, and the political, cultural, and ethnic characteristics of each church changed according to complicated inter-religious relations.

The way in which state authorities managed their relationship with the religious field contributed to the divisions among the eastern churches. The law on freedom of consciousness, adopted in 1991, and the new Ukrainian constitution, adopted in 1996, maintained a separation of church and state.[81] The state preferred to distance itself from the increasingly puzzling religious

---

[80] Official data recorded by the State Committee for Religious Affairs in 2005 list the UOC-MP as having 10,566 communities, the UOC-KP, 3,484, the UAOC, 1,172, and the UGCC, 3,386. Religious Information Service of Ukraine, www.risu.org.ua/eng/resources/statistics/org2005).

[81] The Law on Freedom of Conscience and Religion requires all religious organizations composed of more than ten persons eighteen years or older to register their articles and statutes as local or national organizations in order to obtain the status of 'judicial [or legal] entity'. This status is necessary to own property, carry out economic activities, and be considered for restitution of property. However, a significant number of unregistered religious communities are active in Ukraine.

situation and avoided following either the partnership or the protectionist model, unlike some other postsocialist countries. Yet in spite of what the law says, state officials have been drawn to intervene in church affairs, particularly at the local level (Plokhy 2002: 305). The first Ukrainian president, Leonid Kravchuk (1991–1994), insisted on the idea of 'plurality of faiths' (see Wilson: 234) but at the same time encouraged the formation of a Ukrainian Orthodox Church, which would come about through the nationalization of the existing Russian Orthodox Church. The creation of the Ukrainian Autocephalous Orthodox Church further complicated the religious situation, and the UOC-KP became the most convenient candidate for state support. Under the Kravchuk administration, the official relation between state and church was intermediated by an institution dating from Soviet times, the Committee for Religious Affairs. This group took steps to defend the Kiev Patriarchate against other denominations and, particularly, against its direct competitors, the Greek Catholic and Autocephalous Orthodox Churches.

The subsequent president, Leonid Kuchma (1994–2004), completely changed state policy towards religion. He closed the Committee for Religious Affairs but soon afterwards had to re-create it under the same name (Derzhkomreligij) in order to prevent conflicts like one that took place in Kyiv in 1995.[82] The Committee for Religious Affairs was responsible for registering religious organizations and implementing state policies in agreement with religious institutions. It maintained a national body with representatives in all regional centres of the country. During the Kuchma administration, the state backed the UOC-MP, which was closer to the political orientation of the country (Plokhy 2002: 306). From 1995 onwards, the general relationship between the state and churches, and between churches themselves, has been one of distant dialogue. A voluntary institution that gathered representatives of all national religious institutions was created in December 1996 at Kuchma's initiative. The All-Ukrainian Council of Churches and Religious Organizations is composed of leaders of sixteen religious groups. It has often been successful in offering a coherent, common position on important national issues such as legislation and religious education.

Somewhat independent of the evolution of state-church relations, the development of churches in the regions was determined by the ethnic and confessional features of 'particular *oblasti* and even *raiony*' (Mitrokhin 2001: 174). This came as a result of an arrangement that kept the registration

---

[82] In July 1995 the UOC-KP tried to bury its patriarch, Volodymyr (Romanchyuk), in St Sophia Church in Kyiv, which was a museum administered by the state. Church supporters fought with police in the streets but did not succeed in entering the church. The UOC-KP and UOC-MP still compete over this church, which represents a symbolic link to Kievan Rus.

of parishes and the distribution of land and property under the control of local authorities. In western Ukraine in 1990, local authorities tried to deal with increasing religious problems through democratic means. The city council of L'viv introduced local referenda at the town and village levels to determine which churches would receive which buildings, with the hope of stifling potential inter-confessional conflicts. The aim of the referenda was to determine how many adherents each church had in each locality where conflict had arisen. Where two or more church buildings existed, the majority confession was to receive the main building, and the minority, the less important building. If only one church building existed, it was to be given to the majority confession, but the majority would be obliged to provide material assistance to the losing minority so that it might obtain or build its own church. The churches, however, did not appreciate such democratic regulation, which was not achieving the expected results, and so the referendum procedure was terminated at the end of the year. Between 1991 and 1995, no more regulations were passed regarding the redistribution of property, and most situations were resolved by force within the local communities.[83]

Owing to regional peculiarities, any religious community, whether 'traditional' and 'non-traditional', was able to develop in an area only by working with local authorities. For this reason, as well as the historical and political factors discussed earlier, the four eastern churches today have a balanced regional distribution in Ukraine.[84] The Ukrainian Greek Catholic Church and the Ukrainian Autocephalous Orthodox Church are found predominantly in western Ukraine, which also has the heaviest concentration of religious communities. There, Greek Catholics, fully supported by local authorities, became a large majority in a short time and thus could shape the local religious environment. The UOC-MP predominates in the east and the south, while the UOC-KP is the dominant Orthodox church in the west. The two struggle for dominance in the central oblasts. The regional strengths of traditional churches are one of the causes of the contemporary 'balance of forces' in the religious sphere.

2.2 The Orthodox Imaginary of Western Ukraine

The relatively permissive legislation adopted in 1991 and the emergence of a fragmented Orthodoxy created the premises in Ukraine for the development

---

[83] At the peak of the inter-church confrontation, more than a thousand Ukrainian parishes were internally splintered as followers of the UGCC, the UOC-MP, the UOC-KP, and the UAOC were involved in open and frequently violent conflicts (Krindatch 2003: 69). After 1995 local authorities decided to take over the distribution of churches and land.

[84] See Markus 1995, Krindatch 2003, and Razumkov Centre 2004 for detailed discussions of the confessional distribution.

of an under-regulated religious sphere in which (unlike in Romania, Russia, and Poland) no single religious group was able to attain a monopoly. During the Soviet era, Ukraine was considered the 'Bible belt' of the socialist conglomerate, owing to the large number of Protestants living there.[85] Western Ukraine had a pre–World War I tradition of charismatic and evangelical Protestantism, which was strengthened during the inter-war period by missionaries from the diaspora and which lived on during the Soviet period in underground forms. The early 1990s saw a boom of Protestant missionary work and the establishment of Protestant communities throughout Ukraine.[86] In conjunction with the re-establishment of pre-existing religious traditions, a large number of non-traditional religious movements founded their own communities. The resulting religious pluralism, combined with a nominal commitment to Orthodoxy among large sectors of the population, has made Ukraine one of the world's most active and competitive religious marketplaces (Wanner 2003: 274).

The 'marketplace of religions' metaphor became a common marker of the religious context in the postsocialist literature. Like another frequently used concept with which it is usually associated – the concept of pluralism – the term 'market' holds a certain ambiguity. It can be a synonym for plurality; it can denote an ideological concept closely related to pluralism; and it can represent a sociological model of analysis (Pelkmans 2006). Using the sociological interpretation of the marketplace, researchers argue that the existence of unregulated religious economies engenders competition between religious groups, which produces greater religious commitment (Finke and Stark 1996).[87] The degree of competition is determined from the number of religious organizations and the level of state regulation. The status quo reached in Ukraine since the mid-1990s as a result of the balance of power among the eastern churches, and the stable relationship between these churches and the state, reflects the churches' fear of change. Any legislative modifications by which one church might win a dominant position over others would adversely affect the fragile equilibrium that has so far been preserved.

---

[85] 'Over half of the 1.5 million officially acknowledged Baptists and Pentecostals lived in Soviet Ukraine' (Wanner 2004: 732).

[86] By the mid-1990s, 3,600 Protestant communities were registered in Ukraine, and several unregistered groups functioned in parallel. Today there are more than 5,000 communities (Wanner: 742). 'Protestantism' here refers to charismatic and evangelical churches born out of the new wave of Protestantism. Reformation Protestantism has existed in Ukraine since the sixteenth century.

[87] Finke and Stark (1996) developed this analytical model on the basis of rational choice theory in order to explain church attendance in American cities. The model has since been tested in other parts of the world.

The 'supply-side' model, as the marketplace theory is also known, has been amended for the case of the postsocialist countries. Apparently, in such cases competition does not explain higher levels of religiosity (Bruce 1999; Froese 2004). According to the new interpretation, pluralism is not the cause of increased competition, as in the American case. Instead, post-1989 religious monopolies are thought to be responsible for intense religiosity.[88] The market model is applicable only to societies in which people do not have strong institutional commitments and where ethno-religious identities are not robust (Bruce 1999: 274).

Even in its amended form, the sociological model does not work for Ukraine. Historical and contemporary analyses of Ukrainian religion reveal that the religious sphere is far from being monopolized. Ukrainian identity to a certain extent intersects both Orthodox and Greek Catholic identities, but it does not associate itself with a particular confession. Political options do not depend on religious affiliation, though at a superficial level such tendencies can be noticed (Mitrokhin 2001: 183; Boyko 2004).

Moreover, western Ukraine has a long tradition of deep religiosity combined with weak commitment to religious institutions. Flexibility of confessional borders and ambiguity of religious belonging, rather than commitment determined along lines of religious competition, characterize western Ukraine. Competition among eastern churches in the postsocialist years has been limited mostly to religious politics, although to a certain extent it has also affected churchgoers. In the context of religious divisions, each community was obliged to define its position and its jurisdictional orientation by either confirming its traditional identity or switching to a new one (Yurash 2005a: 186). A process of self-identification among churchgoers took place between the 1980s and the mid-1990s, a time when people had to make religious choices.

Yet while religious elites with different political visions were competing with one another, ordinary people continued to carry their religious practices and beliefs from one church to another. They could do so because of their sense of belonging to a common tradition, an imagined community of practice that encompassed recently built differences. Many believers identified with the imagined community of eastern Orthodoxy and so avoided a forced choice of confession. Viktor Yelensky, a Ukrainian sociologist of religion, has contended that 'for many people, particularly in Central and Eastern Ukraine, belonging to Orthodoxy *in general,* but not to a specific Church, offers an opportunity to avoid painful dilemmas about their ultimate identity' (Yelensky 2005: 164). Other writers have also observed

---

[88] Certain religious groups are able to dominate the religious market through a combination of state support and state regulation of minority religious groups (Froese 2004: 61).

that a strong sense of Orthodoxy is part of Ukrainian culture (e.g. Borowik 2002). National identity is associated with a vague concept of eastern Orthodoxy that none of the four Ukrainian churches has so far been able to appropriate. This 'vague concept' is what I call the Orthodox imaginary.

Another sociologist of religion, José Casanova, took both secularization theory and the marketplace model further by proposing a denominational model for understanding the Ukrainian religious situation, which he considered similar to the American case. In his view, the political function of the community need not be based on a common religious foundation, either institutionalized or informal. The idea that animated this view when it was applied to Ukraine was that existing religious pluralism, including the divided Orthodoxy, and the absence of a national church created the foundation for a complete separation of religion and state. Therefore, religious life 'could be routinized into the normal institutional competition between religious firms competing on a more or less free and open religious market' (Casanova 1998: 97).

The denominational model denotes a society that, like the American one, is based on a civic model that incorporates religious values. Charles Taylor (2002) asserted that in the American case there was no need for one religion to be exclusively linked with the nation, because the nation itself was built as a religious project.[89] In this context, churches become denominations because they no longer attempt to enrol all members of a society the way national churches do. The loss of this ambition leads churches to transform themselves into 'affinity groups' (Taylor 2002: 73), accepting that there are other churches in the same space and that no single church will include all believers. The particularity of denomination-based pluralism is that it encompasses all religious groups without discriminating between them.

Such circumstances can be found in Ukraine, where the religious field is so fragmented that no single church houses all believers. Since Ukrainian independence, no single religious group has managed to position itself in close relation to the state and thus to become a national church. This has happened because no single religious institution became strong enough to dominate on a national level and thus to be a partner of the state in nation-building. Each of the four eastern Christian churches, however, still aspires to become national, and their visions incorporate the imagined community of the nation. Other religious groups previously not considered to be Ukrainian, and thus not potentially national, have also increased their influence in politics at the national level, showing ambitions beyond those of mere de-

[89] This corresponds to Robert Bellah's (1980) concept of American civil religion.

nominational groups.[90] Instead of existing as affinity groups, religious organizations attempt to incorporate large numbers of people, to speak in the name of Ukrainians as a whole, and to pursue a vision of becoming the national church.

In the climate of nation and church (re)building of the early 1990s, two Ukrainian churches had a chance to become national: the Autocephalous Orthodox and the Greek Catholic. After the socialist state collapsed, both churches became privileged carriers of moral values as religious discourse and practices provided a stage on which collective experiences of repression could be discussed and hopes of revival initiated.[91] Even if it had the potential, however, the UAOC did not have the resources to become the national church, and it seemed unconvincing. Most of its representatives were either too closely tied to past institutions of repression (as was the case with former Soviet Orthodox priests) or, having only recently returned after years of diaspora in the United States, were out of touch with common sentiment and experience. Greek Catholics, in contrast, had the experience of 'martyrdom' and pre-existing structures from the underground church. The UGCC was able to portray itself as the perfect embodiment of 'church and nation' and to rally western Ukrainians around both these flags. But with few Greek Catholics living outside of western Ukraine, the church's campaign went unrecognized in the rest of the country.[92] In the end, the Ukrainian national project remained separate from the religious enterprise.

The failure of the UGCC in this project has not been fully accepted in western Ukraine, and pluralism takes on a particular meaning there. One of the most active intellectuals in the Greek Catholic Church, Myroslav Marynovych, spoke to me about those who saw pluralism as 'the anomaly of plurality'. He said: 'The plurality of Ukrainian churches with Byzantine roots is seen by Ukrainian society not as confessional pluralism, which would eventually have to be tolerated, but as a schism, a temporary violation of the norm, which needs to be corrected . . . Many, especially among na-

---

[90] Plokhy (2002) and Wanner (2004) have discussed the growing role of Pentecostalism in Ukrainian politics. Wanner claims that as Protestant 'sects' gain greater acceptance, their status will shift to that of church.

[91] This was the case in other countries, such as Poland and Romania, where 'the sense of national domination and oppression, the sense of virtue in suffering and struggle, [was] deeply interwoven with religious belief and allegiance' (Taylor 2002: 78). The sense of belonging to a nation and to a specific confession were fused, and religious expression could channel and express for a while the moral and political experience of suffering.

[92] The Ukrainian Greek Catholic Church has tried to transcend its circumscribed regional influence and is spreading rapidly throughout central and eastern Ukraine, establishing new parishes and building churches in eastern Ukrainian cities.

tionalists, see the fragmentation of Ukraine's religious life not only as emblematic of broader societal fragmentation but as the cause of it.'[93]

This vision recognizes only 'traditional' churches – Orthodox and Greek Catholic, in particular – as legitimately Ukrainian. Members of these churches often describe their situation using words such as 'suffering' and 'division'. They stress their hope that the Orthodox and Greek Catholic Churches, which they perceive as 'ours', will someday be unified. This view of pluralism is in fact exclusive and ignores many religious groups that are nonetheless part of the religious sphere. Indeed, other observers of Ukrainian religious life have noted the discrepancy between 'plurality' and 'pluralism', believing that diversity in Ukraine has come about only as a circumstantial equilibrium that is not yet indicative of an overall atmosphere of religious tolerance (Yelensky 2005). Although the Orthodox imaginary seems to leave a space for religious pluralism, the church's achievement of its goal of becoming a single, national church would spell the certain end of this very pluralism. In this event, Orthodoxy might become the norm, and other, non-traditional religious groups might be marginalized and excluded.[94]

The imagined unity of Orthodoxy is reflected today in the general aspiration to create a unique Ukrainian patriarchate as a symbolic successor to Kievan Rus.[95] This objective is often implicit in laypeople's hopes for a national church and for Orthodox unity and is more explicitly pursued by the religious elites of all the eastern churches. In 2004 there was one patriarch in Ukraine: Filaret, head of the UOC-KP, who had the title 'Patriarch of Kiev and All Rus-Ukraine'. He was not recognized as such by the international community of Orthodox churches, and his church was still seen as unorthodox. In the early 1990s the UAOC also elected a local patriarch. Because the church aimed to be recognized by either Constantinople or the Orthodox Church in the United States, it later ceased ordaining patriarchs. Owing to a tradition inaugurated by Patriarch Slipyi in the 1960s, Lubomyr Husar, the

[93] From an interview with Myroslav Marynovych, vice-rector of the Ukrainian Catholic University and a civil society activist in L'viv.

[94] Other commentators on the Ukrainian situation have remarked upon the effects of the plurality of churches: 'The absence of a dominant confession with any realistic prospect of maintaining a spiritual monopoly in the religious life of Ukraine means that all religious organizations feel relatively at ease. As one of the leaders of a large Protestant congregation commented to me, 'Thank God this isn't Russia. For the time being the Orthodox are so busy arguing among themselves that they're not bothered about us'' (Mitrokhin 2001: 179).

[95] The problem of the Greek Catholic patriarchate in the Ukrainian religious context is discussed by Plokhy (1995), Fagan and Shchipkov (2001), and Boyko and Rousselet (2004).

head of the UGCC in 2004, was also addressed as patriarch, although he had not yet received official recognition as such.[96]

The struggles of eastern Christian churches to obtain patriarchate status are motivated by their desire to become 'national'. This desire is directly connected to the goal of acquiring legitimate autocephaly, recognized by the Orthodox world. Each church follows a different strategy for achieving its goal, and the process is complicated by their reliance on external centres of authority. Rome, Moscow, and Constantinople are all equally involved actors that, together with the Ukrainian state, can decide the result of this competition.

The two Ukrainian Orthodox churches that could arguably form a partnership, the UOC-KP and the UAOC, look towards Constantinople for formal recognition. Patriarch Filaret of the UOC-KP hoped that the state would move in this direction and endorse their unification. But beginning with the Kuchma administration and continuing under Yushchenko's, the state has maintained a policy of non-interference in church politics while encouraging the unification of the Ukrainian churches with the blessing of the Ecumenical Patriarchate in Constantinople. The UAOC looks to the Ukrainian Orthodox Church in diaspora as a church that might be able to introduce Ukrainian autocephaly into the community of Orthodox churches. Attempts by the UOC-MP to obtain autocephaly from the Moscow Patriarchate have been unsuccessful. However, the UOC-MP remains, for the time being, the only church that is recognized as part of the international community of Orthodox churches and that claims the entirety of Ukraine as its canonical territory. The UGCC has also moved towards obtaining patriarchate status, even considering a possible union with the other eastern Ukrainian churches for the establishment of an eastern Christian patriarchate in communion with Rome.[97]

Any of several possible scenarios regarding Orthodox unity and involving church politics and transnational religious networks could be realized in the future. Nevertheless, the political project of establishing a Ukrainian patriarchate echoes the imagined unity of western Ukrainian believers, who together form a unified community of practice.

---

[96] Josyf Slipyi, one of the most memorable figures of the twentieth-century Greek Catholic Church, repeatedly asked for patriarchal status for his church while in exile in Rome during the socialist years. The Vatican did not grant his request, but he nonetheless proclaimed himself patriarch of Kiev and Halych in 1974 (Plokhy 1995).

[97] This possibility represents the modern re-enactment of the sixteenth-century Kievan Rus metropolitanate.

2.3 Conclusion

Most Ukrainians share a common religious tradition that is the local synthesis of religious influences stemming from the country's location at the intersection of two great traditions, eastern and western Christianity. The local religious tradition initially developed in a multicultural environment, providing space for a plurality of religions – which would be destroyed in the twentieth century. In spite of attempts at differentiation, the eastern churches in Ukraine are perceived as similar by laypeople on the basis of the shared tradition uniting them. Several traits can be seen as common constitutive parts of the local religious tradition: a cult of Ukrainian saints, particular liturgical music, a liturgical language (which is Ukrainian but in its more orthodox forms can be Church Slavonic),[98] a Marian cult that combines Latin and Byzantine elements, the use of common ornaments, a particular architectural style, the use of religious flags, and a Galician iconographic style.

This historical ambiguity reflects the division embedded in Ukrainian religiosity, which is plural by default. When describing the religious sphere, most people hasten to associate it with the idea of religious pluralism as conceived within the frames of liberal doctrines. This ascribed pluralism is based on an observed religious diversity that has its roots in the region's unique history and has been facilitated since 1990 by the permissive legal frame and the lack of religious monopoly. Advocates of modernization interpret Ukrainian pluralism as a sign of thriving democratic exercise in which the secular state guarantees freedom of religion and equal rights for all religious groups. Sociologists view this diversity in terms of market-like competition, making sense of the Ukrainian case with reference to the American denominational model. Ukraine's actual religious composition and the concrete historical circumstances of its national formation forced Ukrainian nationalists to maintain a degree of deliberate distance from religious politics. Nation-building has over time moved away from attempts at forming linkages with particular confessional identities, instead embracing more secular relations between state and church. Nonetheless, religious organizations continue to pursue their national agendas, hoping to one day occupy a more privileged position vis-à-vis the state as national churches.

Today's Orthodox plurality in Ukraine derives from a specific historical process driven by changes in socio-political regimes and a series of arguments and disagreements within pre-existing and re-emerging religious institutions. The postsocialist plurality has developed and been shaped by the

[98] The liturgical language can be Church Slavonic in the same way Latin remains the spiritual or mystical language of the Catholic Church.

dynamic interaction of local ethnic and confessional formations, on the one hand, and majority religious groups and state authorities, on the other. The everyday experience of religious diversity is connected to less institutionalized forms of religious practice, which, instead of consolidating confessional boundaries, permeate them. People relate to this common, organic basis of local practice and belief and thus are able to transport practices and beliefs between churches by connecting to an Orthodox imaginary that affirms the existing religious plurality.

The observed diversity of the religious sphere, however, is not without limits to tolerance. New Protestant groups are peripheral to local religious traditions and have not yet been deeply incorporated into the local social imaginary. Religious pluralism does not abide today because of a deliberate, ideologically motivated practice and project of liberal tolerance issued from the top down. Instead, it is a contingent formation of the Orthodox social imaginary.

Chapter 3
Soviet Realities and the Post-Soviet Making of Churches

The first stage of religious development in western Ukraine after the fall of the socialist state, from 1990 to 1996, was a time of social, political, and religious unrest. Seen from a distance, postsocialist transformations brought with them a revival of religious life all over the Soviet bloc. In Ukraine, the first years of glasnost witnessed the revitalization of religious life, mostly in western towns of the Ukrainian SSR. These general changes involved specific processes such as the splintering of the Orthodox Church and the emergence of a large number of religious groups. Two interconnected processes unfolded: the 'making of churches' and a shift in the dominant mode of religiosity.

The making of churches split religious communities and swung priests, churchgoers, and entire parishes between churches, all as part of a larger reintegration of religious practice into the public sphere. The splintering of churches at all levels, from national institutions to small parishes, prompted the formation of new religious groups and became one of the main causes of the multiplication of churches that is commonly perceived as a religious revival. Changes in the dominant form of Ukrainian religiosity were directly connected to these social transformations. The improvised forms of religious practice that had survived the socialist anti-religion campaigns were gradually replaced with standardized forms of religious practice, closer to what I described earlier as the doctrinal mode of religiosity. One can see, then, a transformation of the social sphere and of religious institutions as part of the postsocialist transformation, side by side with more discrete modifications of the collective expression of religiosity.

In this chapter I analyse the emergence of religious plurality in a particular part of L'viv, the Sykhiv district (Sykhivskyi *massyv*). In spite of the marginal urbanity of the neighbourhood, it preserves a spatial unity and cultivates a distinct identity, that of the Sykhivian person (Sykhivianyn). Before the 1960s, the territory that now composes the neighbourhood was an ethnically mixed village, Sykhiv (Sichow). Like most villages surrounding

L'viv, Sykhiv was predominantly Polish, with 70 percent Polish Roman Catholics and fewer than 30 percent Ukrainians, who spoke both Polish and Ukrainian. On the whole, Ukrainians tended to be Greek Catholics.[99] The two churches in the village corresponded to its two ethnic groups: a Roman Catholic *kosciol* (a brick church) built in 1910 and named Blessed Mary, Queen of Poland – later changed by Greek Catholics to St Mykhail's, for the Archangel Michael – and a Greek Catholic wooden *tserkva* dating from 1648, named Blessed Trinity.[100] The two churches sat not far from each other, in the former centre of the village, and Blessed Trinity had its own cemetery nearby.

Plate 1. St Mykhail's church in old Sykhiv, originally Roman Catholic, then Orthodox, and now Greek Catholic.

The mixed composition of the village changed dramatically starting in 1939, when the village suffered the same fate as most others in Galicia. The com-

[99] There might have been some Jewish families, too, but there was no synagogue in the village, and villagers did not mention the presence of any Jews.

[100] In western Ukraine, *kosciol* refers to a Roman Catholic church, whereas a Greek Catholic church is referred to by the Ukrainian word *tserkva*. The two also represent different architectural types.

munity was split by inter-ethnic conflicts and destroyed by military and guerrilla attacks.[101] From 1941 until the end of the war, the battlefront moved through the village several times, causing many casualties, among which the death of the Greek Catholic priest Father Andrij Ishchak (1887–1941) is now the most commemorated.[102] Ishchak was killed in front of his own parishioners by Soviet soldiers retreating from L'viv in 1941. He was buried in the local cemetery, where his grave can be found today. On the occasion of a visit by the pope in 2001, he was made a 'martyr of the church', a symbolic recognition for the parish itself, part of a larger process of memory recovery discussed in the following chapter.

Plate 2. The wooden Church of the Blessed Trinity at the periphery of new Sykhiv.

---

[101] Of the thirty-eight Ukrainian families living in the village, half were killed during the war and the others left, seeking refuge in more distant villages.

[102] Ishchak's death was investigated in the early 1990s by the Institute for Church History of the Greek Catholic Church. The investigators interviewed the few survivors from the village, whose stories converged in their descriptions of his death. He was taken in the middle of the day from his house in the village by four men wearing uniforms (Russians) and was shot dead in some bushes not far from the church. People were afraid to retrieve his body and bury it, so it lay there for some time until the cantor of the church brought it to the cemetery. Institute for Church History (hereafter ICH), interviews with Sofia Ventyk and Maria Onysko, 2 July 1994 (see archival sources in bibliography).

After World War II, with the Polish residents resettled across the border, the Polish church, St Mykhail's, was taken over by Ukrainian Greek Catholics. Among them were many Ukrainian families resettled from western Galicia, now part of Poland. Between 1941 and 1946, three Greek Catholic priests successively headed the parish. Locals remembered Father Tarnavsky most clearly, because it was during his priesthood that Soviet authorities 'converted' the village church to Orthodoxy. The parish was by then ethnically homogeneous, but village residents were of mixed confessional backgrounds. Some of the resettled Ukrainians were Orthodox, and others, Greek Catholic like the remaining original villagers.[103] Irrespective of confession, all villagers attended the same church, which remained Ukrainian Greek Catholic until 1946.

The shift to Orthodoxy that year, following the forced reunification of the Greek Catholic Church with the Russian Orthodox Church, went relatively smoothly in the village, given the general repressive atmosphere of the time. This happened because the village priest signed the declaration of union (*pidpysanyi*) but did nothing to change the parish's religious practice. Sofia Ventyk, one of the villagers, remembered how, when she returned to the village after some time away, she noticed no change in the church services at first, and only later was told about the conversion: '[The union] was done in silence, and the priest didn't explain anything. Only the cantor told me: 'We became Orthodox!' And I asked: 'How?' He said: 'Look, everything is done in the Orthodox [way].' I couldn't ask during the liturgy how, who, and where . . . and people didn't learn about it. Afterwards they understood that it is Orthodoxy' (Institute for Church History [ICH], Sofia Ventyk, 2 July 1994).

Because neither the form of the ritual nor the priest was changed, people did not react to what was merely a change of name, from Greek Catholic to Orthodox. Priests such as Father Tarnavsky formally accepted Orthodoxy, with the tacit approval of their parishioners, but they continued to consider themselves Greek Catholic at heart. Villagers tended to approve of this purely formal gesture because of their interest in ensuring the continued presence of their priest and church.

When I asked about the implications of shifting confessions at that time, Hanna, an older woman from Sykhiv, underscored the similarities between the Orthodox and Greek Catholic confessions, which from her perspective were one and the same. Most of those who belonged to the old parish shared her explanation and supported the priest's decision to 'convert'. Hanna belonged to a group of Greek Catholic Ukrainians who had left

---

[103] Ukrainians were resettled from two main regions of eastern Poland, one of them Greek Catholic (Tomashevski *raion*) and the other Orthodox (Stanislavski *raion*).

Poland to be resettled in Sykhiv after the war. When the Greek Catholic church there became Orthodox, Hanna became nominally Orthodox, too. In 1991, when Greek Catholics took over the church, she chose to follow the old priest, who remained Orthodox. In 1993, when the Orthodox congregation split again, she supported the same priest, becoming a member of the church council of the Ukrainian Orthodox Church–Kiev Patriarchate (UOC-KP) parish in Sykhiv. Hanna thus changed confessions three times in her life, in 1946, 1991, and 1993. She told me:

> At the time [after 1946] there was only the Orthodox Church. I don't know who thinks about a church that it is Catholic or Orthodox . . . You enter a church and kneel to pray to God, so how do you pray: 'My Father, Greek Catholic', or do you say, 'My Father, Orthodox', or do you say [simply], 'Our Father'? The prayer cannot be changed, and the word 'Orthodox'; even the pope came here and said: 'And all you Orthodox Christians'. It is right to believe in Christ's faith . . . But if you are going to subordinate [*pidchyniatysia*] yourself to the pope, or to Kyiv or Moscow, that is your own business – who wants to [be subordinate to] whom . . . But nobody says a prayer other than the Creed, Our Father, Mother of God; [nobody] has the right to change these.

The former Roman Catholic church building, now St Mykhail's, accommodated the village community well, so it remained open as the parish church of Sykhiv throughout the Soviet period. The old, wooden, Greek Catholic *tserkva* was closed in 1953 and declared an architectural monument. During Soviet times there was always an Orthodox priest in the village, the first being the 'reunited' priest, Father Tarnavsky. He was followed by two older priests and, in the 1960s, by a third, named Kuzytski. Old Sykhivians remembered Kuzytski because his arrival in the parish coincided with the beginning of construction of the new district of Sykhiv in 1964.

In the early 1960s the intense industrialization that had started in L'viv reached Sykhiv, leaving its mark on the village. Heavy industry appeared on the outskirts of L'viv, and new factories surrounded the village and its environs.[104] The village was incorporated into the city's industrial zone, and the landscape to which Sykhivians were accustomed became completely reconfigured in only a couple of years. People from Sykhiv and other villages surrounding L'viv went to work in the factories, which employed primarily local labour. Under Soviet planning, L'viv became one of

---

[104] Among the notable factories built near the village were the autobus and automobile factory, ISKRA (*Izoliatornyi zavod*), Reaktyv (the chemical factory), Poliaron, LVK-48 (a transport repair factory), another tank repair factory, and the electric lamps factory (*Lampovyi zavod*).

the fastest-developing industrial cities of the entire Soviet Ukraine (Czaplicka 2002). The immediate effect was 'under-urbanization' (Szelenyi 1981), a process pervading the entirety of the socialist bloc and characterizing the urban fabric of the L'viv region.

Sykhiv illustrates how an area can be simultaneously highly industrialized yet relatively unurbanized. Soviet authorities, compelled by the need to accommodate the sudden influx of migrants into the city, erected dormitories next to the factories as a short-term solution. The long-term solution was to create an entirely new district in the vicinity of the industrial area. Sykhiv was annexed by L'viv through a Communist Party decree in 1960. As the industrial zone was being built, the first new housing blocks appeared around and in the village, with additional blocks radiating from the village into the fields. Villagers displaced by the new construction were allocated flats in new buildings in Sykhiv. Typical socialist housing blocks were built in Sykhiv between 1975 and 1985, and factories organized the distribution of workers among the residences. This new district in the south of L'viv, built on the remains of former villages, became a semi-autonomous neighbourhood, almost completely cut off from the city. It was a marginal district, a dormitory for workers (*spalnyi micro-raion*).

'New' Sykhiv (*novyi* Sykhiv) was imbued with state ideology in its architecture, setting, and urban culture. The village and its surrounding fields were turned into a modern satellite town in the vicinity of L'viv. In addition to big blocks of flats, the state planned all the buildings a Soviet citizen would need: hospitals, shops, kindergartens, schools, a cinema, and, opposite it, party headquarters. New Sykhiv increasingly contrasted not only with the traditionalism of Galician village life but also with the multicultural, urban identity of L'viv. The socialist order was there to eradicate the past, and its successful transformation of the territory including the former village expressed progress and modernization. The new 'spaces of everyday life' – places of leisure, learning, consumption, and domesticity – were no less important than more obviously socialist spaces as sites for ideological intervention (Crowley and Reid 2002: 5).

3.1 Visible and Invisible Communities in Sykhiv

Religion and churches were not supposed to play a role in socialist urban life, and the state undertook all means necessary to isolate the church from society. In Sykhiv, the two village churches were untouched by the new construction, but they soon found themselves located, together with a few village houses, in an isolated area on the margin of the new district. There was no possibility for building a church in new Sykhiv, so the 'visible', or official, religious life of the entire neighbourhood became centred on the only functioning church, St Mykhail's. The now Orthodox congregation there continued its Greek Catholic practices, unaltered by the so-called reunification. Although the first priest, Tarnavsky, was a reunited Greek Catholic who could still be associated with Greek Catholicism, subsequent parish priests were of Orthodox background. 'They were not ours' (*ne buly nashyi*), people used to say. This did not influence parishioners, who were happy that their church remained open and had a priest, and so they continued to attend services in the same building.

The Institute for Church History (ICH) of the Greek Catholic Church, which aims to reconstruct the life of the underground church in the Soviet Union, has conducted interviews with older residents in Sykhiv. The institute's attempt to trace opponents to the reunion with Orthodoxy among Sykhivians was unsuccessful. Interviewers were quickly discouraged by answers like that of Maria Onysko, one of the old inhabitants of the village.[105] 'Tell me please', asked the interviewer, 'those priests were already Orthodox and were preaching [in the church]; did people in Sykhiv follow them or were there people who didn't want to go to [an Orthodox] church but looked for a Catholic priest?' Onysko responded: 'You know, we were all going [to church]. There were no people like this. We didn't go for them [priests], we went for God, we went to church, but not to them. 'Our Father' is the same, isn't it? We don't have anything with them [the priests], we just went there' (ICH, Maria Onysko, 2 July 1994).

Indeed, the community was not hostile to the change, for it was largely unaware of the differences between the two churches. Villagers wanted religious services to continue, the priest to stay on in the village, and their church to remain open. New church members were few, because newcomers in Sykhiv had no connection to the church and so rarely attended it. Instead, they continued to attend churches in their nearby villages of origin. In the home villages it was less dangerous for practising believers to attend church services, and people returned nearly every week to visit their families and participate in community events, including religious celebrations. Religious practice remained the same everywhere as reunited parishes continued to observe Greek Catholic religious practices rather than Orthodox ones. And although the new priests were obliged by church rules to impose certain modifications of ritual practice, any external observer would have noticed that rituals were performed in accordance with established local traditions. People's observances of weekly rituals such as Sunday masses decreased

[105] This attitude was widespread in western Ukraine. Priests had the same opinion of the laity, namely, that they lacked both knowledge and theological understanding of the differences between Orthodox and Greek Catholic Christianity, and so they could not properly understand the significance of the reunification, unless for political reasons.

during Soviet times, and eastern Christian holidays became the most common occasions of collective religious expression.

In rare cases Sykhiv residents made use of the services of an underground Greek Catholic priest. Such practice was uncommon in urban areas, and most of these priests' activities took place among rural believers. New Sykhiv had little underground life, but occasionally Greek Catholic priests performed illegal religious services in private houses, having either been associated with the family before 1946 or found through personal networks.[106] The ritual they most commonly conducted was the blessing of the house, in order to christen people's newly obtained socialist flats in Sykhiv. The standard ritual was not lengthy, consisting of a blessing of water and a short prayer, but the private invitation provided a good occasion for the priest to celebrate a liturgy. This practice was part of the adaptability of priests and the laity in the face of religious restrictions. When a family took the risk of inviting a priest to perform a religious service, the repressive political atmosphere made the service religiously charged, so all the now inaccessible sacraments (confession, communion, blessing, and preaching) were carried out in one session. This single short service provided the basic spiritual and pastoral care that churches had offered their members in the past.

In a socialist block of flats it was difficult to perform a proper liturgy. The gathering of fifteen to twenty people in one apartment and the traditional song and response of the eastern liturgy were sure to arouse the suspicions of neighbours. Among the interview transcripts archived at the Institute for Church History is a description of a visit to Sykhiv made by an older woman, Kateryna Radkevych, who accompanied an underground priest to bless a friend's home:

> We went to Sykhiv with Father Gavryliv. We were a bit afraid, but he was more courageous. I told him, 'There will be more people there . . . please, Father, we should take care . . . Don't take anything with you, no liturgical objects, no vestments . . . give them all to someone, to me or to another person. We went there, it was a new building, my acquaintance had just moved there . . . She received [by state distribution] a flat in Sykhiv and wanted to bless the house. People, neighbours, asked why there were so many people, and we, without fear, explained that she was inaugurating the house and that

---

106 Home visits by priests were part of a more general phenomenon of 'domestication' in which not only underground but also regular priests entered people's houses more often in order to offer religious and pastoral services. This was an effective means of getting around the restrictions imposed by state authorities and a safer way of providing religious services to a familiar audience.

> we were guests. And there we had the liturgy and the priest was very happy . . . Honestly, it should have been the house inauguration and it was a liturgy [instead] . . . We sang in a low voice . . . They [the participants] didn't understand, but we sang Our Father, and even the Creed could be sung (ICH, Kateryna Radkevych, 29 September 2003).

Such events were unusual and completely separate from routine religious life in Sykhiv. Religious services related to family events were held at St Mykhail's or back home in village churches, and Sykhivians rarely asked for illegal services. The most commonly practised underground ritual during the Soviet period was baptism. People were baptized at all ages, and the ritual conveyed both an expression of faith and an anti-atheist, anti-Soviet sentiment, particularly in cases of adult baptism. The practice of collective baptism existed throughout the region in both rural and urban areas.

Although it was better for underground priests to operate in the countryside, it was safer for them to live in the city. The anonymity of the large districts of blocks sometimes offered better cover for an active priest than a village community kept under surveillance by local apparatchiks. Priests were also forced to take jobs as both cover and means of support, usually as simple workers or functionaries in industry. Such was the case with Father Vasyl Voronovsky, a Studite monk who moved to Sykhiv in 1982 when the factory that employed him gave him accommodation in one of the new blocks.[107] He moved to the flat with his brother, Iulian, also a Studite, who became an underground Greek Catholic bishop in 1986. Vasyl Voronovsky was one of those underground priests who, while living in the city, continually travelled to surrounding villages and farther, to other oblasts, performing religious services for Greek Catholics. He remembered the busy rhythm of the days when the church was emerging from underground and taking advantage of glasnost to increase its public presence:

> On Saturdays more than once [I celebrated] two or three [liturgies] . . . and on Sundays I went out to the villages, and even after returning I celebrated [mass] in Sykhiv . . . If I was not going to a village, if nobody was coming from a village after me, then [I could perform] three or four liturgies in Sykhiv . . . at different houses . . . They took me [from one house to the other] . . . If I was blessing a house, then I

[107] The Studites are a monastic order specific to the Ukrainian Greek Catholic Church. The order was founded by Metropolitan Sheptytskyi in 1904 with the aim of renewing monastic life in the church by rediscovering its eastern spirituality. The Soviets closed the order down in 1946 and it went underground, thus providing a good base for the activities of the underground church.

> immediately celebrated the liturgy also . . . For every liturgy I had no fewer than twenty people (ICH, Vasyl Voronovsky, 3 January 1999).

The Voronovskys' flat was a meeting place for the Studite community and a spiritual centre for other monks and priests in the area. After Iulian Voronovsky became a bishop, he received priests there, held regular theology courses for young monks wanting to become priests, and provided advice and assistance with organizational issues. Meanwhile, Vasyl Voronovsky continued his activities in rural areas. Both being monks, the two followed an intense liturgical regime at home, maintaining a condensed version of the monastic rules adapted to their circumstances.[108] As Vasyl Voronovsky described it: 'Every day before sunrise [we had] the morning prayer, the liturgy, and the Liturgy of the Hours . . . In the evening [we had] vespers and the midnight service . . . We left nothing aside . . . Our neighbours were nice . . . We had blessed their house and we were not afraid of them' (ICH, Vasyl Voronovski, 3 January 1999).

The presence of the two brothers and their work in the district can be seen as part of the 'invisible' religious life of Sykhiv, in contrast to the official activity of St Mykhail's Church in old Sykhiv. The pair's activities were unknown neither to the authorities nor to the area's residents, but the monks were generally restricted to acting in the private sphere, with small audiences, employing a mode of religiosity particular to the underground church. Iulian and Vasyl Voronovsky and their flat in Sykhiv served as an important centre of activity for the Studite order. At the same time, the two were part of a larger network of clergy and laity: the so-called underground church, which existed across the Soviet Union but was particularly strong in western Ukraine. Hence the two priests were part of an alternative religious structure distinct from the official structure of the Russian Orthodox Church in Ukraine. The network of Greek Catholic clergy to which they belonged, which weathered the repression of the Soviet era and grew during the glasnost period, was the starting point for the Greek Catholic Church when it emerged from under ground in 1989.

In the 1980s, St Mykhail's parish in old Sykhiv underwent its own significant changes. The Orthodox priest, Father Kuzytski, who had served there for sixteen years, had to retire, and a new priest, Father Volodymyr

[108] Father Vasyl Voronovsky was born in 1929 and became a priest in 1959 in the underground church. He was arrested three times (in 1970, 1985, and 1989) before he moved to Sykhiv. There, according to his statement, he was no longer bothered by the police, because in the mid-1980s the repression of Greek Catholics was less intense and their activity increased significantly.

Tsiopka, was sent to the parish in 1986.[109] A second priest, Father Volodymyr Kuzio, came to the parish around the same time, and the two celebrated mass together at the same church. Former parishioners were inconsistent in their descriptions of this period. Some of the villagers from old Sykhiv held the newcomers in disfavour. They complained about Tsiopka's attitude and the fact that he did not show respect to the older priest when he arrived to replace him. Stories were spread in the parish about Tsiopka's connections to the secret police. This caused some of his parishioners to stop attending his services and the parish church. Instead, they went to another Orthodox church in the centre of L'viv, the Church of the Transfiguration (Preobrazhenska tserkva).[110]

Those who became closer to Tsiopka later remembered how, before 1989, the two Orthodox priests seamlessly collaborated and shared the parish work. Oleh, an older man who was born and lived in old Sykhiv, used to attend St Mykhail's and for many years was its caretaker, also assisting the priest during religious services. His wife, Olea, had come to Sykhiv in 1946 with her family during the Ukrainian resettlement from Poland, when she was six years old. Since then she had married, worked, and attended church in Sykhiv, never leaving the district. The couple remembered the years between 1985 and 1989 as good ones for their church, in contrast to what followed during the Greek Catholic revival. 'Here everything was beautiful,' said Olea. 'One [priest] celebrated one liturgy, the other celebrated the second, there were no conflicts, nothing; everything was beautiful. Then the revolt [*zakolot*] started in the west, Catholicism went on the offensive here [in L'viv] and then [came] to our place.'

3.2 Redefinition of Spaces and Practice

This revolt, the 'Catholic assault', began in November 1989 when the first church in the centre of L'viv was taken over by Greek Catholics. People gained entrance to the Church of the Transfiguration by climbing through a window and opening the church to a crowd of Greek Catholic supporters gathered outside. This sort of takeover of a church by a spontaneous popular

[109] Volodymyr Tsiopka studied at the Orthodox seminary in St Petersburg and was ordained in 1961. He came to Sykhiv in 1986 from Sokal, a town in L'viv oblast.

[110] 'Preobrajenska' was a Greek Catholic church before 1946, situated right in the centre of L'viv. It remained part of the Greek Catholic tradition even during Soviet times, when a L'vivian eastern ritual centred on this church; on the Friday night before Easter, participants would surround the church in a chain while holding candles. The church's symbolic status for Greek Catholics became visible a few years later, in 1989, when Greek Catholics took it over in a spectacular manner. It was the first Greek Catholic church reopened in L'viv, and it set an example for the takeover of other Orthodox churches.

movement became a pattern in western Ukraine before local authorities began to regulate the allocation of church buildings through a referendum mechanism.

The wooden church in Sykhiv, the Church of the Blessed Trinity, was reopened in early 1990 when a member of the local council, Yury Hrynchyshyn, took the keys of the church, then a museum, from the L'viv Art Gallery and gave them to the old Sykhivians living next to the building. As an empty Greek Catholic church, it was the most convenient place for reinitiating Greek Catholic services. No contention surrounded the church, and the former villagers felt it was rightfully their own. The first Greek Catholic priest to minister in the newly acquired church was Father Olexander Prylip, a Studite monk from Briohovych. He belonged to the same order as the Voronovksy brothers, and Iulian Voronovsky was his superior in both the order and the underground church hierarchy.

In early 1989 the bishop asked Prylip to quit his post in Ternopil in order to come to L'viv in preparation for the Greek Catholic revival. In 1990 Father Olexander began officiating in Sykhiv, and Metropolitan Sterniuk gave him a special document acknowledging him as the sole Greek Catholic priest in the Sykhiv district.[111] He was assisted by Vasyl Voronovsky, who was already known to some Sykhivians because of his underground activity. When the two Studite monks began preaching in the small wooden church, many people moved (*perekhodyty*) to it from nearby St Mykhail's. First came the cantor, followed by the choir, and soon afterwards the entire community (ICH, Oleksander Prylip, 5 February 2000). During his first celebration of mass, Voronovsky announced to the people of Sykhiv that private home visitation would end, and from that point forward, religious services would be performed in the proper church. The Studite monks thus became direct competitors of the Orthodox priests of Sykhiv.

The unexpected appearance of two Greek Catholic priests 'out of the blue', according to St Mykhail's Orthodox priests, was felt as a threat to the Orthodox parish. The Orthodox priests, Tsiopka and Kuzio, aware of attacks on other churches in L'viv, feared for the safety of their own, so they started to preach against their new neighbours in their Sunday sermons. They portrayed Catholics as a dangerous group who wanted sacrilegiously to attack the church. The situation intensified after a large portion of the Orthodox congregation moved to Blessed Trinity. The St Mykhail's church committee suggested that the church be relinquished to the Greek Catholics, but the Orthodox priests opposed such concessions. The main priest, Tsiopka,

[111] Archbishop Volodymyr Sterniuk (1907–1997) was the acting head of the underground church between 1972 and 1991 and the first leader of the official church after 1989.

wanted to join the newly formed Ukrainian Autocephalous Orthodox Church (UAOC), not the Greek Catholic Church.[112]

Meanwhile, Greek Catholics were putting pressure on the remaining congregants of St Mykhail's. The Studite monks celebrated daily liturgies in front of the wooden church, and people came from all over the city to participate. Father Vasyl Voronovsky was a renowned exorcist, and after each liturgical service he performed healing prayers for participants and their ill relatives. Orthodox congregants perceived the growing number of people attending Greek Catholic services just a few metres away from their church as threatening. Olea, who was involved in the events on the Orthodox side, recalled that the Greek Catholics

> brought people from villages on buses. And our people and our priest locked the church and celebrated outside. They [the Greek Catholics] wanted to attack us, because there was a priest . . . Catholic . . . he was standing next to the railway. He was waiting for people to take over the church so that he could come in to celebrate . . . No, we don't know who the priest was! We know those people who came [with him], but they were our neighbours, the ones we call *our brothers in faith,* they were all rushing towards us, asking why the church was closed, why we were celebrating outside. And our [people] were afraid because, had they attacked the church, they could have desecrated it. And [our] priests were preaching that this is desecration because those who attack the church have no God.

In May 1990 the city council proposed a solution for resolving conflicts related to church buildings. State representatives would conduct local referenda on contested churches, and the results would determine property usage rights. A group of laypeople from old Sykhiv went to the head of the district council, Yury Hrynchyshyn, whose family lived in the neighbourhood and was involved in parish life. The group was led by Volodymyr Tkatchyk, a resident of Sykhiv who, though not a regular churchgoer, had been involved in the reorganization of the Greek Catholic parish. The group asked Hrynchyshyn for St Mykhail's Church back, for the use of Greek Catholics.[113] In 1990 Hrynchyshyn was head of the Lenin district council, representing the

---

[112] The Ukrainian Autocephalous Orthodox Church was founded at about this time (May 1990) and attracted Orthodox priests who wanted to belong to a Ukrainian church rather than to the Russian Orthodox Church, but who refused Catholicism.

[113] Hrynchyshyn lived in old Sykhiv, in the house of his parents-in-law, until 1974, when he was allocated a flat in another district of the city. He maintained contacts with the old place through his wife's parents, who still lived there in 2004 and attended St Mykhail's Church.

new state authority connected to the national movement for independence (Rukh).[114] He remembered how he received the delegation from old Sykhiv:

> [Tkatchyk came] and said: 'We want to make the church Greek Catholic' – that's what people said. This was the initiative of lay-people . . . The priest was Orthodox and he wanted to remain Orthodox. In 1990 nobody could say whether there would be an independent Ukraine or not . . . There was no independence then, it emerged only in 1991, in December, and [they came] to me, the head of the council, saying, 'We want St Mykhail's Church to be Greek Catholic' . . . and the process [revival] was already starting throughout L'viv.

Hrynchyshyn and the district officials proceeded according to city council regulations by organizing a referendum on the church. The committee administering the referendum was headed by Hrynchyshyn and included council deputies and representatives from the St Mykhail's church council (*dvadtsiatka*). The committee prepared 300 printed ballots on which was written, 'Which church do you want St Mykhail's to be: Greek Catholic, Orthodox, or other?' Having found an official way to organize the appropriation of the church, the committee took care of the remaining details, posting announcements in the vicinity of the church and preparing the social club of one of the nearby factories as the site of the balloting. According to Hrynchyshyn, only inhabitants of the streets surrounding St Mykhail's, mostly in old Sykhiv, were to be permitted to vote in the referendum, even though the church in question was the only church available for the entire district of 100,000 people. The decision to restrict the process to a few hundred people rather than open it to the entire district was intended to allow the committee to better control the referendum.

The Orthodox priests refused to accept the procedure, keeping the church locked during the referendum and prohibiting the posting of public announcements in the church. They also urged their parishioners to abstain from voting. In the end, the Orthodox parishioners did not vote because they were afraid – the parish community was already split, and the more vehement group was the newly formed contingent of Greek Catholics. The Greek Catholic cause was aided by the strong wave of Ukrainian national revivalism and the struggle for independence that had taken over western Ukraine. The parishioners who continued to attend St Mykhail's were accused of

---

[114] Lenin district was an administrative territory of L'viv that included Sykhiv and other parts of the city. Hrynchyshyn had once belonged to an association for the promotion of the Ukrainian language, founded in January 1989. This association was later transformed into the National Movement for Reconstruction (Narodnyi Rukh Ukrainy), which took part in the political changes of that year.

opposing Ukrainian independence and thus of having Russian sympathies. Olea and Oleh, the old couple attached to Tsiopka, who had been unaware of any underground activity in Sykhiv before 1989, remembered being surprised by the resurgence of Greek Catholics in Sykhiv – led by their own neighbours, 'underground' Greek Catholics.[115] Olea recalled:

> Neighbours were inciting [each other]: 'Orthodoxy is from Moscow!' . . . They called us *Moskali* and shouted at us[116] . . . We were going to church and they shouted at my husband – they didn't shout at me as I'm just his wife, but he is from here, they all knew him – 'To whom did you go? What are you doing?' But we didn't reply to all the terrible things they said to us, I can't say those words . . . We were *Moskali* and they were Ukrainians! People were pointing at us: 'Look at them, communists [*komuniaky*]!'

The referendum was held without incident, and despite the committee's attempt to restrict voting to the immediate neighbourhood, many people from other parts of L'viv came to vote, mobilized by Greek Catholic priests. Even in 2004 people remembered the results of the referendum and stressed the importance of the support they received from other L'vivians. There were more than 200 votes for Greek Catholic affiliation, 14 for Autocephalous, and 7 for Orthodox, so the church was to be given to the Greek Catholics. According to the state representatives and the winning party, the democratic exercise worked well, but one practical question was still unresolved: how to convince the Orthodox priests to give the church to a group of laypeople who claimed to represent the parish community. Tsiopka and Kuzio refused to recognize the results of the referendum and remained in the church. The authority of the referendum committee was limited during those times of uncertainty, and it could not force the priests to relinquish the church.

The actual handover came a few weeks later through an action that was equal parts official repossession and illegal seizure. Again, accounts of what transpired differed. Greek Catholics said they convinced the cantor to give the church keys to Yuryi Hrynchyshyn, the 'state authority' who could mediate the transfer. Orthodox parishioners recalled that the turnover was achieved by force; a group of Greek Catholics guilefully entered the church and forced the cantor to give them the keys. That Saturday Greek Catholics

---

[115] Opinions varied about how secret the activity of underground priests actually was. For example, some of the neighbours of the Studite monks living in Sykhiv found out only in 1989 that they were Greek Catholic priests and about the religious life in their flat. Other neighbours knew them and frequently asked them for private religious services.

[116] *Moskali* is a pejorative term used in western Ukraine for Russians or people connected to Russia.

occupied the church and barred the Orthodox priests and those neighbours recognized as Orthodox from further entry to the premises. As Oleh told the story:

> The second day was Sunday, it was a holy day, [so] we went to church, and at the doors there were two guards. The mass was going on . . . the Catholic one! The two guards were at the door and Mr. Tkatchyk, the one who was commanding there, [he was] a parish member who only rarely came to church. So there he was, standing next to the door showing who should be let in and who not . . . And an old woman who was standing next to the fence told me: 'Don't upset them, they can kill you!' And I said: 'Woman, I know all of them, they won't do me harm!' That was it, they didn't let the priests in, didn't give us the keys, and haven't let us in the church ever since.

That Sunday service was conducted by the Studite monks Olexander Prylip and Vasyl Voronovsky, who simply crossed the street from the old Church of the Blessed Trinity to St Mykhail's. The two priests continued to celebrate daily liturgies and to preach and perform healing prayers in these neighbouring churches in old Sykhiv. People came from all over L'viv to take part in the Greek Catholic services, which were still too infrequent for the heightened interest people had in religion. People recalled how these few months passed in a climate of religious effervescence and how the frequency of rituals performed reached remarkable numbers.[117]

At this time, 1990, a fierce battle was raging between the Autocephalous Orthodox and Greek Catholic churches over control of church buildings. Each side competed to recover parishes and property from the Russian Orthodox Church. Priests and deaneries in western Ukraine, L'viv included, oscillated between the two churches, both of which people considered Ukrainian and therefore 'ours', in contrast to the Ukrainian Exarchate, which was still connected to the Moscow Patriarchate. The revival of the Greek Catholic Church in 1989 and its links to the national movement seemed to tip the balance towards Catholicism among the western Ukrainian Orthodox. However, the emergence of the UAOC, which claimed to be the legitimate successor to Ukrainian autocephaly, attracted a significant number of Orthodox clergy. Both churches were nourished by intense nationalist feelings, and although in the first few months of 1990 Greek Catholics could distance themselves from the Orthodox by playing the nationalist card, the birth of a Ukrainian Orthodox church redressed the balance.

---

[117] Vasyl Voronovsky still recalled the baptism of sixteen children during a single Sunday mass in Sykhiv as a special event in his life.

There appears to have been no definite pattern to the choices of church affiliation made by parishes and local priests at the time. Although priests' and parishioners' opinions sometimes converged, leading to the decision not to change affiliation, often disagreements led to conflicts in which a church was taken over by parishioners or a stronger group within the village community. In such cases the priest was forced either to yield to the will of the parish or to leave the church. Hence, the best rule for a priest to follow was that once he secured a church, he must maintain good relations with the parish community and prevent other priests from interacting with his congregation. That was precisely what Voronovsky did in Sykhiv after taking over St Mykhail's from the Orthodox priests. By maintaining an intense schedule of liturgical services he was able to mobilize the local community, and the two Orthodox priests were prohibited from entering the church again. He told me:

> Every day there was a liturgy, every day preaching . . . [The Orthodox] priest couldn't celebrate . . . He still wanted to say goodbye, but they didn't let him . . . I said: 'Don't allow him [to come and] say goodbye, because he settles his accounts with them and half the people will follow him' . . . I insisted he should not be accepted because I already had some examples . . . In the Ternopil region people allowed [the Orthodox priest] back in to speak to the congregation, [and] the priest complained [to them]: 'How am I going to make a living? . . . I served you so long' . . . and then they threw out the Catholics.

3.3 Mechanisms of Church Formation

Meanwhile the Orthodox congregation, numbering only twelve people, followed the two Orthodox priests expelled from St Mykhail's into the parish house behind the church, which had been built by Father Volodymyr Tsiopka. From there the priests continued conducting religious services while trying to recover St Mykhail's with the help of the city council. Tsiopka did not take the step of joining the new UAOC, and he lost some of his remaining parishioners to that church in the centre of L'viv. St Mykhail's parish was now split into three groups that identified themselves, respectively, as Greek Catholics (Ukrainian Catholics, symbols of anti-Soviet resistance and the Ukrainian religious tradition), Autocephalous Orthodox (Ukrainians, symbols of the Ukrainian religious tradition and anti-Russian attitudes), and simply Orthodox (preserving the religious tradition and a certain attachment to a particular priest and hierarchy).

The future of the Orthodox group was uncertain, and this affected the remaining parishioners. They were able to remain in the parish house for a few months until the spring of 1991, when they were forced to vacate the building after a court order transferred the house to the now Greek Catholic parish council. Tsiopka and Kuzio relocated with their small group to an empty part in the main square in Sykhiv, an empty space in the heart of the district meant to have been populated by a Soviet complex of buildings that was never built. An improvised chapel made of wood and sheets of plastic became the space for religious services held every Saturday and Sunday morning. Meanwhile the local council granted the priests authorization to build a permanent church on the premises.

The stigma surrounding their involvement in the St Mykhail's conflict followed them to their new location, and being neither Greek Catholic nor Autocephalous Orthodox, they continued to be addressed as *Moskali*. Nevertheless, the small community did think that a national Ukrainian church should exist alongside an independent Ukraine. When discussing the options the parish had at the time, Olea expressed thoughts similar to those of many, if not most, other western Ukrainians: 'We were talking like this: Rome is not our father, Moscow is not our mother. We are already worthy of our own [church]. We were crying that we must have our own. I say even now that we must have our own church, Ukrainian'.

The general consensus favoured the idea of having a Ukrainian Orthodoxy, but not all Orthodox Ukrainians agreed that the self-made UAOC was the true Orthodoxy, particularly because it was unrecognized by the rest of the Orthodox world.[118] Priests and laypeople who had not joined the UAOC in its first stage were unsure about the outcome and refused to break with the Orthodox hierarchy, which maintained a link to the Moscow Patriarchate and the state and was still perceived as the official Orthodox church in Ukraine. The two priests could not reach an agreement regarding their church's affiliation. While the older priest, Tsiopka, intended to join the UAOC, the younger, Kuzio, rejected the idea.

In 1991 the two priests began to build a small church next to their makeshift chapel. They raised the building in two years with the help of devoted parish members and donations from factories in Sykhiv. People were receptive to the idea of building a church in the centre of the Soviet district, and they donated construction materials and labour. The laypeople who formed the core of the project became part of the church council and at the time of my fieldwork still spoke with great emotion about the church built through their efforts. When the construction was nearly complete, a

[118] The first patriarch of the postsocialist UAOC, Mstyslav Skrypnyk (1898–1993), was a renowned church figure, bishop of the UAOC's predecessor during the Second World War, and the leader of the UAOC in the American diaspora, which, unlike its Ukrainian correspondent after 1965, was a canonically recognized church.

second split took place in the community. After the emergence of the UOC-KP in mid-1992, it was for a short time the strongest church in western Ukraine, only to split again in early 1993. It was at this moment that the two Orthodox priests decided to go their separate ways. Tsiopka, following the diocese-wide trend, switched to the UOC-KP. Indeed, most of the Orthodox parishes in the oblast, including those led by Bishop Andrii Horak, left the Russian Orthodox Church and joined the UOC-KP. The Sykhiv parish community could finally proclaim its Ukrainianess; 'We are as much Ukrainian as the others [Greek Catholics]', said Olea. The younger priest, Kuzio, insisted on following the official line of the Ukrainian Orthodox Church–Moscow Patriarchate (UOC-MP), thus creating a split in the parish when he refused to administer communion to Tsiopka. Each of the two new groups tried several times to seize the church they had built together. In the end, the larger group, led by Tsiopka, managed to force Kuzio and his followers out.

Plate 3. Orthodox splintering in Sykhiv: the UOC-MP and UOC-KP chapels, 2004.

The 'Russians', as the UOC-MP group came to be called, relocated to the improvised chapel the congregation had used before, just ten metres from the new chapel. No more than ten people gathered around Kuzio, and for a long time the parish was unable to officially register itself as such. The local administration repeatedly prohibited both the registration of new 'Russian parishes' in L'viv and the construction of churches by members of the UOC-MP.[119] In 2001 Kuzio's church was at last officially registered, and the priest broke ground on a parcel of land already occupied by the UOC-KP church. He was stopped by Tsiopka, who had similar plans for that location: he dreamed of someday raising a bigger church ('for a thousand people') in the very place his one-time colleague was claiming. In 2004 both priests were unwavering in their positions, mutually preventing each other from initiating new church construction on the common site.[120] Construction materials were scattered over the plot of land intended for the two buildings, each set of supplies carefully demarcated by a sign displaying the church's name.

At the time of my fieldwork, these two Orthodox parishes were significantly smaller than the other religious communities in Sykhiv. Father Tsiopka, the UOC-KP priest, consistently attracted a crowd of older Sykhivians, but their ranks never grew beyond 500 participants, and that only during important religious celebrations. The UOC-KP chapel had no visible sign indicating its confessional affiliation. Sykhivians saw the church as 'Ukrainian Orthodox' and as 'ours' but were rarely able to differentiate whether it belonged to the UAOC or the UOC-KP.[121] At the religious services of both the UAOC and the UOC-KP, hymns were sung in Ukrainian, and the liturgical style was close to that of the Galician tradition. Tsiopka emphasized more the connection between the church and the nation in his sermons and in the activities of his parish, but the patron saint of the church, St Volodymyr, the founder of Kievan Rus, was also the patron saint of the nearby UOC-MP church.

The improvised chapel of the UOC-MP was always identified by Sykhivians as 'the church of the Russians'. The small community started with five to seven people and by 2004 had grown to fifty on a typical Sun-

[119] The reason for this prohibition was that it was unnecessary to build another Russian church in L'viv, because there was already one in the city centre. This point was underscored by the priest as well as by representatives of the local administration. The case of the Sykhiv parish reached an international audience because of the Moscow Patriarchate's lobbying and publicity, and the event was often referred to in reports discussing freedom of religion in Ukraine. In 2004, only two UOC-MP parishes were registered in L'viv, and the Sykhiv parish was one of them.

[120] Tsiopka, over seventy in 2005, had found a successor, a young priest who joined the parish that spring. Kuzio, by then secretary to the bishop of the UOC-MP in L'viv, was assisted in his parish by a young theologian who had studied in Warsaw and might eventually replace him.

[121] There is a UOAC church in the district, but it is located farther from the central square, which houses the other churches. The UOAC church was built only in 2001, with less public support than these first churches.

day. Its run-down chapel, overflowing with icons and religious objects brought by parishioners, was open only on Sunday mornings and for religious holidays. Participation in the life of this community required regular attendance at church services or close contact with one or more of the parishioners who regularly attended. The congregants, who felt under constant threat from their Orthodox neighbours, displayed a strong sense community.[122] Their discourse echoed that of the Moscow Patriarchate: the only true church was theirs, because they adhered to the canonical line of Orthodoxy, unlike the other two Ukrainian Orthodox churches. Because of their symbolic ties to the Moscow Patriarchate, the parishioners of the UOC-MP believed themselves to be part of the 'true church', which was persecuted by the 'uncanonical' (*nekanonichnyi*) churches.

Plate 4. The UOC-MP chapel on the day of the Dormition of the Mother of God, Sykhiv, 2004.

Members of the UOC-MP parish, however, were not Russian, and only a few were Russian speakers from eastern Ukraine.[123] The UOC-MP's distinction from other Orthodox churches lay in its religious practice: the liturgical language was Old Slavonic, vespers and morning prayers were part of the regular religious service,[124] confessions were heard regularly, processions

---

[122] Community spirit was lacking in the 'established' Orthodox parishes, and more active priests criticized it as their parishioners' passivity (*pasyvni*; *bayduzhi*).

[123] Proportionately, there were many more Russian-speaking churchgoers in the Greek Catholic church in Sykhiv.

[124] Such services are considered Orthodox in comparison with the Galician religious tradition, and only 'easternizing' priests perform them regularly. See chapter 2.

were performed counter-clockwise, and there was no veil kissing (*plashchenytsia*) during Easter. Some aspects of the local tradition were preserved, including the blessing of Easter food (*pasky*) and processions with icons, flags, and the cross around the church. But the liturgical practice of this parish encompassed more Orthodox characteristics than were seen in the liturgy of the nearby UOC-KP parish. Furthermore, the priest, Ukrainian by origin, commonly spoke with his parishioners in Russian, and the general preference among the congregation was for Russian over Ukrainian. The parish's perseverance in following a more 'spiritual' (and thus 'truer') path than that of its neighbours was underscored by the use of Old Slavonic as the liturgical language, while the parish's belonging to the Moscow Patriarchate was implicit in parishioners' use of Russian as a congregational language. Nevertheless, the everyday language of most parishioners outside the church was Ukrainian.

Opposite the disputed territory of the two Orthodox groups, Greek Catholics constructed one of the largest churches in L'viv. The Greek Catholic community that gathered at St Mykhail's made its first step into the central square of Sykhiv in 1990, on the advice of former underground priest Voronovsky. He thought the parish church was too small and isolated from new Sykhiv. On Easter Tuesday, 17 April 1990, a large procession left St Mykhail's in old Sykhiv, walking through new Sykhiv to the central square. There, Greek Catholic priests blessed a tall wooden cross in the memory of Ukrainian martyrs and celebrated the first public liturgy in the former socialist district.

Father Voronovsky continued to celebrate liturgies every day next to the newly erected cross. Thus his congregation first symbolically appropriated land for a new church before receiving permission from the authorities for new construction on the site. Looking back on those days at the time of my fieldwork, many Greek Catholic priests recalled the general sentiment of goodwill and gratitude they experienced at the time: the 'authorities were more open' at the beginning of the 1990s. Everyone was enthusiastic about having a church in socialist Sykhiv, and the priests began to receive substantial support for its construction.[125] In September 1991 they were able to purchase a large aircraft hangar and install it next to the cross to serve as a church.[126]

---

[125] In the early 1990s local authorities supported Greek Catholics all over western Ukraine by offering them church buildings, land for construction, and financial support.

[126] Before that they conducted services outdoors, keeping the altar and icons in an improvised shelter. The hangar chapel survived in 2004, by then transformed into an office for parish priests and church activity.

Plate 5. The hangar chapel that became the first church in new Sykhiv, with the Pentecostal church in the background, 2004.

The parish priest who followed the Studite monks, motivated by the large number of people attending the Greek Catholic church, began to make plans for erecting one of the largest church buildings in L'viv. Construction began only in 1995, however, soon after a new, young priest, Orest Fredina, came to the parish to replace his controversial predecessor.[127] The new Church of the Nativity of the Most Blessed Mother of God (Rizdva Presviatoii Bohorodytsi) became the largest postsocialist construction project in Sykhiv, and many inhabitants identified closely with it. The building project attracted a large number of people from Sykhiv and L'viv and even Greek Catholics from the diaspora.[128] Some residents dedicated their free time to working as construction labourers, technical specialists, and engineers. As in the case of the hangar chapel, considerable donations of money, construction materials,

[127] After Voronovsky left the church, an older priest, Evhen Boyko, led the parish. Because of financial problems, Boyko was unable to initiate construction of the new church. He was replaced in April 1994 by Father Orest, one of the most charismatic priests in L'viv, who still headed the parish in 2004.

[128] The original plan, designed by a Canadian-Ukrainian architect, Radoslav Zhuk, called for erecting a complex of buildings surrounding the church. The full project never came to fruition, because of the enormous amount of work and money spent on building the church.

and technical equipment came from local factories, whose directors or specialized personnel were often involved in the work. The nearby UOC-KP chapel, although built to a smaller scale and funded solely by donations and local support, also showed that Sykhivians saw the construction of their own churches as a vital necessity, a compensation for their struggle to practise their religion during Soviet times. Indifferent to the confessional affiliations of the churches, people offered their help to both construction projects.

Plate 6. The Greek Catholic Church of the Nativity in Sykhiv's central square, 2007.

The Church of the Nativity emerged as the 'church of the district' because of the efficient management of the parish priests combined with the widespread participation of Sykhiv residents. Before the 1980s, new Sykhiv was mostly homogeneously Ukrainian. Russians and Russian-speaking Ukrainians lived in a few blocks given to the army and to industry specialists, and in 1986 a large contingent of people was relocated from the Chernobyl area after the explosion of the nuclear reactor there. The majority of new Sykhiv residents, however, were villagers from western Ukraine who, in spite of social transformation projects, maintained a traditional peasant lifestyle. Rural religious practice was successfully reproduced in the city, at first in private forms but after 1990 in a way that permeated all aspects of social life. The local religious tradition found its best expression in the large Greek Catholic parish of the Church of the Nativity.

The intense religious activity of the parish was the primary focus for the majority of the Nativity church's congregants, but the parish went beyond religious ritual and involved itself in the life of the community.[129] Employees of the district administration were also members of the parish, and although official support was less visible in 2004 than it was in the early 1990s, the church's activities exceeded those of any other church in town. Greek Catholics were involved in schools, kindergartens, and hospitals. Most residents perceived the Nativity church as the main church in Sykhiv, and its priests and parishioners behaved accordingly, considering the entire district their parish. During the annual festival known as the Jordan ceremony, held on 19 January, church priests visited every flat in the district in order to bless the houses. They sought out their own parishioners but invited other Sykhivians to attend their church as well. By noting which householders refuse to accept them inside the house, the priests gathered data about local residents' religious affiliations and marked their territory against other religious groups.

Apart from this, the parish offered religious activities and community services for all age groups without making ethnic or confessional differentiations. It was the openness and efficiency of the parish's priests and laity that made it different from other eastern churches and attracted so many people.[130] One of the cantors at the Nativity church, who also served at St Mykhail's, said that many people came to the clergy looking for help with personal problems and, finding themselves warmly received regardless of background, kept returning to the church. 'There are still some Russians who go there to [the UOC-MP church]. But most [people] come to us. Look, we just had a service and an entire Russian family came to the liturgy, their girl died. They came, spoke Russian, and that was it, we don't have the right to tell them anything. Even if you speak Russian, you came to pray to God,' the cantor told me.

The Church of the Nativity gained recognition not only because it successfully combined the traditional model of a village church with western, pastoral-oriented activity. In addition, being the centre of other significant events in the district, the church took on symbolic meaning for local

---

[129] According to parish statistics from 2004, about 3,000 people were present on a regular Sunday and more than 10,000 at Easter. The church also hosted thirteen religious organizations, a choir, a parish journal, and a printing house. At any given time there were seven priests working in the parish.

[130] The Catholic concept of pastoral care, so alien to Orthodoxy, was applied extremely well in the Nativity church.

identity. In 2001, during his visit to Ukraine, Pope John Paul II met with Catholic youths in L'viv. The meeting took place in the square in front of the Nativity church, and the parish played a large role in organizing the event. People came from all over Ukraine, as well as from Poland and Belarus, but Sykhivians were there in the front row. The papal visit was a boost for the Greek Catholic parish: parish priests taught young Sykhivians how to organize, and many local residents volunteered to help with cleaning, repairs, and completing construction of the church. Each person wanting to participate and see the pope had to register on a list kept by the parish priests.[131]

Plate 7. The Nativity church during a Sunday mass. The statue of John Paul II is a reminder of his memorable visit to the parish. Sykhiv, 2003.

The pope's visit was important to Ukrainians on many levels, both religious and political, but for the Nativity church it was a paramount event. The phrase 'the church where the pope came' (*tserkva de Papa buv*) remained a marker of the church and increased Greek Catholics' authority in the district as representatives of the local religious sphere. Father Ruslan, a Greek Catholic priest in Sykhiv in 2003–2004 and one of the organizers of the event, considered that the pope's visit was the best possible advertisement for his church: 'Even those people who generally consider themselves 'against confessional differentiations' [*pozakonfesiynymy*], they come here

[131] These lists were still used by the church for fundraising purposes and various church-related activities during the time of my fieldwork.

anyway because the church is bigger; the pope was here, and after all, the advertisement works.' The pope's visit brought together religious groups that previously had ignored each other, such as the Roman and Greek Catholics of Sykhiv. The pope, aware of the implications of his visit to a place with a tradition of religious pluralism, showed consideration for both religious traditions and addressed equally Orthodox Christians and Catholics, Ukrainians, Poles, and Russians.

Only four years before the pope's visit, in 1997, Roman Catholics had moved to Sykhiv, taking over a house containing a small chapel and a flat for the Polish priest. As was the case everywhere in western Ukraine, a strong Roman Catholic presence had existed in old Sykhiv, a half-Polish village, before the 1940s. The church called St Mykhail's after 1946 had originally been Roman Catholic, and in 1990, during the fight for control of that building, there could have been a third contender, about which both parties had completely forgotten. But the Roman Catholic Church did not attempt to recover the building. Instead, the new Roman Catholic community started from scratch, attracting only the few families of mixed ethnicity living in Sykhiv, mostly Ukrainians with Polish origins.[132]

Natalia's case reveals how family relations developed around religious choices in the mixed confessional environment. In 2004 Natalia was an eighteen-year-old member of the new Roman Catholic parish. Her mother was ethnically Polish but had grown up in Ukraine, and her father was Ukrainian Orthodox from eastern Ukraine. Natalia was baptized in the Orthodox tradition, but before 1989 she went with her father to the Orthodox church and secretly accompanied her mother to the Catholic cathedral in L'viv. After the new Roman Catholic parish was established in Sykhiv, she began to attend services there regularly. She said she made this choice because she admired the priest, and the strong ethic of community pervading the parish appealed to her more than the Orthodox tradition with which she was familiar. Natalia learned Polish and became involved in the life of the community, working with children, organizing pilgrimages, and helping with pastoral activity.

Natalia's parents had little contact with the Roman Catholic church and believed she was too involved in church life. She thought their discontent came from her father, who 'doesn't know what he is' and distrusted

[132] In western Ukraine, Roman Catholics recovered only 10 per cent of their churches after the fall of the socialist regime. Most of the church buildings were given to Greek Catholics by local authorities who argued that Polish communities were either very small or non-existent. In order to avoid property disputes, the Roman Catholic Church since 1990 has chosen to build new churches rather than ask for the return of old ones. The Roman Catholic parish in Sykhiv counted about 300 parishioners in 2004.

churches. When she and her mother went to the Roman Catholic chapel in Sykhiv, he attended the Greek Catholic church. The entire family attended an Orthodox church affiliated with the Moscow Patriarchate whenever they were in the father's parents' village, because there was no other church around. During religious festivals (*sviata*) in L'viv, the entire family went to both the Catholic and Orthodox churches. Natalia's parents had not had a religious marriage, because her father did not want to upset his parents by getting married in the Catholic church (*v kosteli*) and her mother did not want to marry in an Orthodox church (*v tserkvi*).[133] Their not having had a religious marriage created problems for the family when they attended Roman Catholic services.

Although she was aware of the difference between Greek Catholics and Orthodox Christians, Natalia often used the term 'Orthodox' (*pravoslavnyi*) to describe Greek Catholics, and she said of the Orthodox Kyiv and Moscow Patriarchates that they were 'of different faith' (*insha vira*). Natalia's family illustrates the way local religious practices can be intermingled as a synthesis of the eastern and western traditions. The case shows that not only were 'Greek Catholic' and 'Orthodox' at times interchangeable confessional identities (grounded in the same religious tradition, their similarities were more conspicuous) but perhaps so too was Roman Catholicism, although it was a more clearly differentiated tradition. Possible family conflicts stemming from overlapping religious allegiances were overcome by attending multiple churches and falling back on common practices. The permeability of confessional boundaries favoured the frequenting of more than one church and the mixing of religious practices by Sykhivian Roman Catholics, though admittedly to a lesser degree than I found among Orthodox Christians and Greek Catholics.

Despite their different religious traditions, a basic common ground existed between these last two confessional groups, owing to both longer-term historical trajectories and recent circumstances. During Soviet times, some Greek Catholics in western Ukraine attended Roman Catholic churches, having identified more strongly with the Catholic component of their religion than with the eastern tradition they shared with the Orthodox Church. This choice was also political, expressing the anti-Soviet sentiments of many western Ukrainians. Moreover, some underground Greek Catholic priests were absorbed into Roman Catholic communities, which allowed them to continue functioning as priests under this disguise. These interactions

---

[133] In addressing the issue of marriage this way, the mother refused both the Orthodox and Greek Catholic churches while the father refused the Roman Catholic Church. Usually such mixed couples reach a compromise, marrying in the Greek Catholic church, but that was not the case with Natalia's parents.

strengthened the links between the two communities and influenced Greek Catholics' religious practices.

The Roman Catholic tradition had always been part of the organically occurring religious pluralism of Galicia, and the boundary that separated Roman Catholics was always ethnic rather than related to rite.[134] In the Roman Catholic church in Sykhiv, as in the UOC-MP church, there was a vernacular language (Ukrainian) and a liturgical language (Polish), and people did not wish to mix the two. Attempts made by the Polish priest in Sykhiv to introduce Ukrainian as the liturgical language were rejected by the small Roman Catholic community, which was predominantly Ukrainian, even though some members could trace their Polish roots.[135] Actual practice again contradicted the strong competition that existed in Ukraine in 2004 between the two branches of Catholicism.

The possibility of transcending confessional borders through a common religious tradition becomes more problematic with reference to the last two religious groups that were part of the local plurality while I was in Sykhiv. Pentecostals came to the district in 1992 and rented a cinema hall in the central square for their Sunday services. A year later they broke ground for their own church, just behind the Greek Catholic Church of the Nativity, close to the forest.[136] Like the Church of the Nativity, the planned building was monumental, but its enormous proportions proved too much for the capabilities of the local community, and the structure remained unfinished at the time of my fieldwork. The completed portion of the Pentecostal building included a parish church and a theological seminary for future Protestant pastors.[137]

---

[134] In western Ukraine it is a common practice in mixed families to attend services at several churches for major holidays such as Easter and Christmas.

[135] This attempt was part of a larger push for the 'Ukrainization' of the Catholic Church in Ukraine.

[136] Initially the Pentecostal community wanted the lot next to the Nativity church, but they could not obtain the approval of the local authorities, because of objections from the Greek Catholic parish. Greek Catholics explained that they wished not to have another church in such proximity. This plot of land was later occupied by a shopping mall.

[137] It is a relatively traditional Pentecostal church, with home prayer groups and little public preaching in the nearby villages. The community has between 500 and 700 members. Its ritual practice is moderate, with little charismatic influence.

Plate 8. The Pentecostal church in Sykhiv, 2004.

Not far away, in a large building close to the square, were the Jehovah's Witnesses, the most recent newcomers to Sykhiv, who arrived in 2000. Their organization replicated the standard structure of Jehovah's Witnesses worldwide, and all members from Sykhiv met in separate groups according to geographical divisions. The activity of the group involved frequent preaching throughout the district and regular visits to Sykhiv residents. Jehovah's Witnesses were thus the only religious organization in the neighbourhood that frequently met other religious groups and challenged people's religious identities by questioning their confessional belonging.[138]

[138] The centre of Jehovah's Witnesses activity in Ukraine was on the outskirts of L'viv, where it had been well established since the early 1990s. Like Pentecostals and Greek Catholics, this organization also had underground structures and was heavily persecuted by the Soviet regime. The community in Sykhiv had more than a thousand members from the district in 2004.

Plate 9. Jehovah's Witnesses leaving a gathering. The building behind them is the Kingdom Hall. Sykhiv, 2004.

Each of the religious groups I have described has had the possibility of developing its own community and creating its own space in the district. Shared buildings and land spurred the conflict between Greek Catholics and the Orthodox congregation, and later between the Orthodox of different affiliations. In the early 1990s, clashes over church buildings took place all over western Ukraine, but despite its disputes, Sykhiv remained relatively peaceful. This was the impression of many residents, priests, and pastors, regardless of the small Orthodox conflict that persisted. The two Orthodox priests remained unreconciled at the time I was in Sykhiv, and their congregations, though separated by only ten metres, stood separate.

Residents of Sykhiv quickly absorbed the district's vibrant religious activity, and new groups were able to acclimate easily. Priests often emphasized the 'religious thirst' of the district, which they believed explained its exceedingly high level of religious activity. Under-urbanization made Sykhiv a district of rural immigrants who maintained strong links to their villages around L'viv. Urban religious practice sustained traditional forms of devotion revolving around the family and important religious holidays. Most clergy, notwithstanding confession, understood the particularities of religious practice in Sykhiv and conformed to this type of religiosity.

Plate 10. Waiting to bless *pasky*, Easter food, at the Nativity church in Sykhiv, Easter Sunday, 2004.

The most notable religious events in the district revolved around the Greek Catholic Church of the Nativity, the largest religious enterprise in the area, but all the other religious groups were able to pursue their activities in Sykhiv. Since 1990, because of their relations with local authorities, Greek Catholics had influenced the religious dynamics of Sykhiv and the establishment of other religious groups. Yet even in this powerful position they did not become intolerant of other religious groups and attempt systematically to obstruct their founding and activities, as was the case in other post-socialist countries where a majority church dominated the entire religious field.

At the time of the pope's visit in 2001, the Greek Catholics' influence was felt strongly in the religious life of the quarter. One incident had to do with the conflicting presence of 'the Russian church', the UOC-MP chapel, in the vicinity of the Nativity church. This small community faced repeated refusals from state authorities to grant it official recognition. On the eve of the pope's visit, the head of the Ukrainian Greek Catholic Church (UGCC), Cardinal Husar, intervened on behalf of the UOC-MP congregation in order to obtain it a parcel of land from the local authorities.

The smaller communities got their start in Sykhiv by moving from larger communities they had already established in L'viv. When the Roman Catholic parish was founded, announcements were made at the other two Catholic churches in L'viv, encouraging Sykhivians to attend the new chapel. Nevertheless, only about half the Roman Catholics living in Sykhiv actually moved to the new church; the rest remained at the cathedral in L'viv. When a Pentecostal church opened in their neighbourhood, Sykhiv Pentecostals also moved closer to home from other churches in L'viv. These communities cultivated stronger ties between parish members than did the Orthodox and Greek Catholic communities in Sykhiv, putting greater pressure on newcomers to integrate and stay.

This incursion into Sykhiv's recent history shows how religious pluralism started in a former village church on the periphery of a Soviet district emptied of religious life. Within a few years of the postsocialist religious revival, religious activity completely reshaped the public sphere. With the 'making of churches', people did more than recycle Soviet spaces and symbols into religious ones (Lührmann 2005); they created new ones. Religious life in Sykhiv in 2004 revealed the flexibility of confessional borders and the weak commitment many people had to religious institutions, mostly with respect to the traditional churches.[139] Weak confessional affiliation had been an important factor in the emergence of a manifest religious pluralism.

Those following such undifferentiated religious practices can be referred to as 'free-floating believers', a category emphasized in several sociological studies.[140] This phenomenon is found in eastern and central Ukraine as well as western Ukraine, a region with higher levels of religious commitment. In western Ukraine, such pluralism seems to have historical roots visible in the instability of individual confessions over time and the continuous ambiguity of religious borders. Non-institutionalized religious practices were reinforced by the domestication of religion ('home belief') during Soviet times and by the characteristic late-socialist distrust of all institutions.

3.4 Emerging Patterns of Religious Practice

The survey I conducted in Sykhiv in 2004 showed that intense, non-institutional religiosity was characteristic of the district. Of the 312 respondents, 97 per cent had been baptized, and 96 per cent considered themselves

---

[139] I consider the traditional churches to be the Orthodox, Greek Catholic, and Roman Catholic Churches.

[140] Boyko and Rousselet (2004: 39–50) labelled the category of believers without clear institutional affiliation 'individual believers'. Casanova (1998: 95) wrote about the 'unchurched', and Borowik (2002: 503), about the 'Orthodox with undefined affiliation'.

to be believers. People frequently performed individual devotional activities (47–68 per cent of respondents reported doing so), and most church-related religious activity took place in the family around religious holidays. Families were major sources of religious education and support (65 per cent said this was the case), whereas churches were less successful in their attempts to provide religious education for adults and young people. The only successful church-based education was the children's Sunday schools provided by the Greek Catholic, Pentecostal, and Roman Catholic communities.

Most respondents (85 per cent) declared that churches influenced their religious lives in a significant manner. More than half of those interviewed (55 per cent) attended church at least once a week – usually the Sunday mass – and 45 per cent attended with family. Almost all respondents (97 per cent) had attended church at least once in their lives. However, the meaning of 'church' for Sykhivians was more 'a place of prayer' (80 per cent) than 'a hierarchy' (11 per cent) or 'a national institution' (21 per cent). This confirms the idea of a non-institutionalized group of practising believers who see the church building as a locus of spirituality rather than as representative of a specific religious denomination. It also makes it easier for churchgoers to remain attached to one physical place of prayer even if the institution to which it belongs changes.

Respondents preferred to stick to one church (80 per cent) that most closely fitted their beliefs (60 per cent). Factors such as proximity, comfort, and social networks had less influence on respondents' choice of church (fewer than 30 per cent reported that these factors were influential).[141] The sense of 'a church that fits one's beliefs', however, was based not on confessional differences but on the shared tradition of religious practice of Orthodox Christians and Greek Catholics. When asked to differentiate the two churches, people tended instead to address their unifying characteristics. 'Each church teaches the good. There is no difference [between them],' said one respondent. 'We do not make the difference; Orthodox and Greek Catholic are our churches,' said another.

Congregations' collective expectations of church and priest imposed certain practices that were maintained in spite of confessional changes. The accommodation that took place with each attempted innovation in religious practice was usually achieved through a negotiation between the priest and the community. When the new generation of priests came to the Church of the Nativity in 1995, for example, the parishioners asked them to continue devotions from the Latin tradition.[142] In the Roman Catholic parish, the

[141] These factors are more important in villages in determining people's choices of church.

[142] The priests refused, insisting on adhering to the main line promoted by the church after 1990 – namely, Byzantinization. There are still parishioners who, either by visiting other

Polish priest had to give up some classic Catholic rituals in order to make space for traditional rituals requested by his parishioners.[143] He found it difficult to introduce new rituals that were not part of the local tradition, and he had to celebrate rituals and religious holidays that were important for his community but were rarely observed in the Latin rite. Thus, even in the case of traditional churches, Sykhiv residents shaped their newly built religious communities according to local cultural practices deriving from a distinct religious tradition. Catherine Wanner (2004) recognized the same process in Protestant communities in Ukraine.

By tracing the history of religious plurality, one can see how, despite a church's having switched its 'official' affiliation several times in the recent past, the religious practice of its community continued relatively unchanged. Rituals remained the same, or if they changed, they did so through gradual alterations, allowing time for their acceptance by the community. Usually the same priest continued to lead the parish, making the change even less dramatic. It is not surprising, then, that the great majority (86 per cent) of survey respondents in Sykhiv stated that they had not changed their confession or church since 1990. Even though there had been only one Orthodox church in Sykhiv before 1989, whereas now there were at least six different religious groups, the number of real converts was extremely small. This result confirms the idea that instead of perceiving ruptures, Sykhivians had weathered the splitting and making of churches without conceiving of these cosmetic changes as affecting the actual content of their religious belief and practice.[144]

Many respondents wanted to see the creation of a national church, stating that they wished churches would unite to become one (*obiednuetsia*). But this choice was not oriented towards any particular confession such as Orthodox or Greek Catholic. A large majority (70 per cent) believed that confessional identity was not necessarily related to national identity, affirming that being Ukrainian did not depend on being Orthodox or Greek Catholic.[145] Because confessional identities were weak, people tended to opt for

---

churches or in private, continue their own style of worship and in parallel attend the Byzantine services in Sykhiv. I discuss such a case in chapter 7.

143 Parishioners asked for services that also existed in the Latin tradition but were more important in the Orthodox Church, such as the blessing of water. The Roman Catholic priest renounced Marian prayers and rogation days, which were practised in the Polish Roman Catholic Church.

144 During the interviews, not a single respondent from either the Orthodox or the Catholic community referred to his switch from one church to the other as a conversion. Wanner (2003: 276) found just the opposite in the case of new Protestant movements.

145 What mattered, according to the survey, was language – 'speaking Ukrainian' (75 per cent) – and patriotic feelings, or 'feeling Ukrainian' (77 per cent).

identities that were capable of incorporating religious differences. Being Christian or Ukrainian was more important than being Catholic or Orthodox.[146]

Sykhiv residents indicated different levels of acceptance of the religious groups present in the district.[147] Greek Catholic seemed to be the most accepted category (55 per cent of respondents expressed a positive attitude towards Greek Catholics).[148] The large number of Greek Catholic residents and the presence of the Nativity church, a symbol for the entire district, might together have accounted for such a favourable reception. Half the respondents expressed neutral attitudes towards other traditional churches, such as the UAOC, the UOC-KP, and the Roman Catholic Church. Pentecostals and members of the UOC-MP were viewed with some suspicion (negative attitudes towards them were expressed by 28 per cent and 21 per cent of respondents, respectively). The survey included a broad, ambiguous category, 'sects', which were referred to as such (*secty*) in common language. This category, usually identified with Jehovah's Witnesses, was strongly rejected by almost half the respondents (49 per cent), who considered sects 'bad for Ukraine' (*pohanyi*) or not to be 'true' (*ne spravedlyvyi*) churches.

These results are better understood when one considers the distance of each religious group from the local religious tradition and the cultural understanding of 'church' and its role. The boundaries of this collective representation of what religion is about are manifested clearly when it comes to Jehovah's Witnesses. The story of Hanna, the woman introduced earlier who had been forced to change churches three times – each of them belonging to the same eastern Christian tradition – and who had finally settled in the UOC-KP, illustrates where the imagined religious community stops, leaving Jehovah's Witnesses outside:

> I came here [to the Greek Catholic church] with them and I didn't see any difference: that the prayer was different, that the preaching was different, that they read a different Gospel . . . and it seems to me that that is how the Orthodox faith was from the beginning . . .

---

[146] Ukrainian (16 per cent) and Christian (27 per cent) were the most important identities selected from a total of 32 choices given in the questionnaire, including religious, ethnic, moral, gender, and age markers. In comparison, 4.5 per cent of respondents chose Greek Catholic, even though 60 per cent of the sample population consisted of self-identified Greek Catholics.

[147] The following results were obtained from a scale of social distance introduced in the questionnaire.

[148] This result was directly influenced by the proportion of Greek Catholics in the survey sample (60 per cent). Their over-representation reflected the heavy presence of Greek Catholics in Sykhiv and in L'viv oblast (56 per cent of the population).

> So there was one, and then [the other] . . . It was not our fault [but was the fault of] those patriarchs, they thought of their own and divided . . . and since then they separated . . . But the faith should be one, this is how I think. One God, we cannot divide [*dilyty*] him. Look, you walk and meet Jehovah's Witnesses on the road . . . There was also an acquaintance of mine [who was a Jehovah's Witness] and I said to her, 'Christ is risen!' And she laughed at me . . . You know how much it hurt me, and I thought, 'Woman, you even went [to church] up to now . . . and to me it doesn't make a difference which church you go to, to the *kosciol*, or to the Autocephalous, or the Orthodox, or to the Catholic, but you go to pray to God . . . and all [of them] say, 'Christ is risen!' And you don't [say it]!' And I think about her: How is it possible that she lost her way completely?

3.5 Conclusion

When I started my work in Sykhiv in 2003, I was attracted by the exemplary case it offered as a post-Soviet site of religious boom. Sykhiv was interesting because of its multitude of churches situated in such proximity. As one of the last urban transformations in L'viv, heavily industrialized in the 1960s, the district and its central square were supposed to bring socialist ideology into people's everyday lives. Instead, from 1991 onwards, religion came increasingly to assert its presence and prominence there. In late 2003 Sykhiv's central area accommodated Greek Catholics, Orthodox Christians affiliated with both the Moscow and Kyiv Patriarchates, Jehovah's Witnesses, and Pentecostals. Dispersed in nearby neighbourhoods were other, unfinished churches and chapels: one Roman Catholic, another Autocephalous Orthodox, and a few more Greek Catholic.

This plurality of churches had to have started somewhere, and my effort to discover its initial moment sent me to the former village, old Sykhiv, and the two village churches, the Roman Catholic Blessed Mary (St Mykhail's) and the Greek Catholic Blessed Trinity. The history of old Sykhiv was a history told by a small group of Ukrainians who had survived its multiple tragedies. My account has followed their view of events, a view that was part of a larger narrative of Ukrainian martyrdom that I address in the following chapter.

The dual-confessional character of the village ended with the rise of the Soviet regime, which allowed only a single church officially to exist. Public forms of religious practice remained confined to St Mykhail's, then Orthodox. However, an alternative religious life, hidden from state authorities, grew up within the Soviet district. Greek Catholic priests, in order to survive repression, de-institutionalized and adapted their religious practices.

Significantly altering their mode of religiosity, they managed to preserve and transmit the religious tradition in Sykhiv. The moment it became possible, in 1989, these underground priests surfaced and re-entered the public sphere, first by occupying traditional religious spaces and then by moving into the empty central square of the socialist district.

The first new, postsocialist religious communities in Sykhiv appeared through the successive splitting of the Orthodox parish, a process that was repeated all over western Ukraine. In L'viv in 1989–1990, public pressure mounted for people to turn away from Orthodoxy, following an intense national mobilization. Lay activists and underground priests preached a return to the Greek Catholic Church, which had traditionally defended national ideals in western Ukraine. At the same time they denounced Orthodoxy for being Russian and thus anti-Ukrainian. The formation of the Ukrainian Autocephalous Orthodox Church further complicated the religious revival. Defections of priests and entire parishes from Russian Orthodox churches led to the takeover of church buildings by Greek Catholics and later by Ukrainian Orthodox congregations – often the same community, which had merely changed its name. Yet the making of churches was more than the simple replacement of Orthodoxy with Catholicism. It was a process of successive splitting, reunification, and fluctuation at various levels of religious life.

Together with the social dynamic, which involved significant institutional changes, forms of religiosity were also transformed during this time. Changes resulted from the re-entry of religion into the public sphere and the deliberate modifications made to church ritual by clergy wishing to differentiate their churches from newcomers on the scene.

The case of Sykhiv shows how Ukrainian religious pluralism came into being in a specific setting, shaped by the relationship between the majority church and state authorities, and how this pluralism functioned at a particular moment. In spite of a complete reorganization of institutional religion, the everyday experience of confessional diversity was connected to less institutionalized forms of religious practice based on the local religious tradition. Thus, people related to a common basis of practice and belief that, instead of consolidating confessional boundaries, permeated them. The relation between the general transformation of religious structures and the transition from a mode of religiosity specific to the underground church to a mode of religiosity employed by institutionalized religion is the subject of the following chapter.

Chapter 4
Making Orthodoxy in the Ukrainian Greek Catholic Church

In this chapter I engage with the institutionalization of the post-1989 Ukrainian Greek Catholic Church (UGCC), looking particularly at the roles of eastern and western trends in the religious tradition of the church. I bring together the historical and theological concepts introduced in previous chapters in order to analyse a recent case of excommunication of a Greek Catholic priest. I focus on a particular community of practice, the traditionalist movement in the UGCC, which retains a nostalgia for the church's underground years. Marginalized by the church, this group has looked for alternative spaces in which religious practice might preserve the mode of religiosity specific to the underground period. Their story illustrates the attempt by a religious institution emerging in the postsocialist religious sphere to consolidate its structure by redefining the orthodoxy of the local religious tradition.

The theological particularities of eastern Christianity have given a certain trajectory to the evolution of this religious tradition. The eastern Christian model of decentralized authority based on revelation rather than on authoritative interpretation permitted the development of various local traditions, each an authentic expression of the same belief. The blurred distinction between practical and doctrinal religion in eastern Christianity allowed for relatively easy exchanges between popular practices and beliefs and church doctrine. Popular interpretations of dogma were unproblematic as long as they stayed within the salvation idiom of Christianity, while church doctrine incorporated novel sources of inspiration from practice in order to renew itself. The natural evolution of the religious tradition, then, was based on the ways in which popular exegesis and practice shaped theological knowledge. Turning from Lossky's (1985) 'Tradition', writ large, to 'tradition', writ small, or 'religion as practised', I described in the previous chapter how the body of practices and beliefs that forms the local religious tradition developed through the interaction of two great traditions, eastern and western Christianity. What resulted from the process of local elaboration was a distinctive tradition, a creative synthesis of multiple influences and historical strata.

Among Ukrainian churches, the Greek Catholic Church stands apart as a perfect illustration of the local tradition and its embedded ambiguity. An analysis of the Greek Catholic Church reveals the particularities of the local religious tradition. The Uniate, or eastern Catholic, churches are part of eastern Christianity, together with the eastern Orthodox churches (more commonly known as autocephalous national churches) and the separate eastern churches.[149] Among the eastern churches, the Uniates (Greek Catholics) have a somewhat unclear status because of their liminality, being of eastern origin and practice but following the western model of authority and doctrine. Several writers have evoked the east-west 'orientation problem' of the UGCC as a continuous dilemma that has pervaded the church's history (Hann 2003b; Boyko and Rousselet 2004; Yurash 2005a). By maintaining a slight distance from the Roman Catholic Church in order to preserve their distinctiveness, and by retaining their unique identity vis-à-vis Orthodoxy, Greek Catholics have always stressed the differences between the two great traditions while equally highlighting their unifying characteristics. Throughout the history of the UGCC, one or the other of these influences has predominated, but since at least the late nineteenth century, the times of Andrei Sheptytskyi, a line of thought has conceived of the Uniate Church as a bridge between east and west, 'a bridge to unity'.[150]

Greek Catholics prove their connection to the Western world through their recognition of the authority of the Catholic hierarchy and ultimately the pope, a condition that is reflected concretely in the reproduction of the church's hierarchical authority. The pope is at the head of the church, followed by the actual head of the UGCC, the major archbishop, who in 2004 was Lubomyr Husar. After his release from a Soviet labour camp and his move to Rome in the 1960s, Cardinal Josyf Slipyi, the exiled leader of the UGCC between 1944 and 1984, argued that the UGCC should become a patriarchate. He and his successors continued, unsuccessfully, to look for recognition from Rome.

With the beginning of its revival in the 1980s, the UGCC had to rethink its structure, starting from the temporary hierarchy that had developed

---

[149] These are autocephalous churches (Oriental Orthodox) that accept only some of the Ecumenical Councils but remain in full communion with the other eastern Christian churches (Nestorians, Monophisite, Coptic, Ethiopian, and Armenian).

[150] Andrei Sheptytskyi, the most celebrated figure of the twentieth-century UGCC, was the head of the church between 1901 and 1944. He regarded his own church as a model for the attainment of this church unity, although later in life he came to see that a different approach, an ecumenical movement, had a greater chance of success (Husar 1989).

in the underground period in Ukraine but also taking into account the diaspora church, which had grown large and influential.[151] Although Volodymyr Sterniuk, the acting head of the UGCC since 1972, continued to lead the church throughout its revival period, the official leader of the UGCC after Slipyi's death was the archbishop of Philadelphia, a diaspora Ukrainian named Ivan Lubachivsky. In 1991 the pope recognized ten bishops consecrated in the underground, and following a synod of the UGCC held in Rome that February, Cardinal Lubachivsky returned to Ukraine in March 1991 to take over his position as major archbishop of L'viv, head of the UGCC in Ukraine and abroad. The acknowledgement by the pope of an established church hierarchy resolved some of the recognition problems both outside and inside Ukraine, even if the Ukrainian bishops were not completely satisfied. The Code of Canons of Oriental Churches, a product of the Second Vatican Council, was also accepted at that time as church law for the UGCC, creating a legal framework for institutional functioning.[152]

Because of various implications of the Code of Canons, the re-establishment of the Greek Catholic hierarchy was not straightforward. High-level discussions between the Vatican and Moscow, undertaken without the input of the UGCC, provoked frustration and dissension among Greek Catholic leaders. The political moves of the Vatican, which tried to avoid upsetting the Moscow Patriarchate in order to sustain the ecumenical dialogue, were apparently not in the best interests of the UGCC, which felt neglected and constrained in its newly acquired freedom.[153] Nevertheless, the church continued to grow in western Ukraine, owing to the favourable attitudes of local authorities and leaders of the nationalist movement (Rukh) towards its underground leaders, as well as the full support of diaspora Greek Catholics. The 'making of churches' in the early 1990s that I described in chapter 3, taking place beyond the level of church politics, led to the creation of new churches through the grassroots reorganization of parishes and local communities, with almost no top-down control by religious authorities. Individual and collective choices about which church to attend, which Orthodox congregation to join, and whether or not to become Greek

---

[151] The two Ukrainian Greek Catholic metropolitanates in the United States and Canada and various other eparchies spread around the world, starting in nearby Poland.

[152] In conjunction with the Code of Canons of Oriental Churches, which is used by all Uniate churches, the UGCC has a 'particular law' that includes canons established by the church itself. The Synod of Bishops of the UGCC passed a series of such laws in 2000, which complement the Code of Canons (Babiak 2004).

[153] A detailed description of Vatican policies towards the revival of Greek Catholicism in Ukraine and Greek Catholic reactions to the political moves of both Moscow and the Vatican is offered by Plokhy (1995).

Catholic depended on very different reasons from case to case.[154] This grass-roots dynamics ensured the formation of an extremely heterogeneous UGCC, which made great efforts to find an identity shared by all its members. In addressing the question of church institutionalization in this chapter, I refer mostly to the search for a common identity expressed in the redefinition of tradition rather than to the structural processes that re-created the church as a religious institution. The two processes, however, were strongly interconnected.

I said in chapter 1 that eastern Christianity illustrates the equilibrium state between the two modes of religiosity. It is a religious tradition that, although doctrinal in essence, manages to draw on imagistic practices to renew its message and keep people engaged. Imagistic and doctrinal rituals act within the religious tradition in both directions: to preserve a continuity of practice and belief and to accommodate change and adjust the religious message accordingly. Yet in certain moments one can distinguish a trend within the tradition that seems to favour one mode of religiosity over the other. A proliferation of imagistic practices seems to have characterized the underground church, whereas a strong tendency towards the doctrinal mode accompanied the postsocialist institutionalization of churches. Since the early 1990s, conflicts over what constituted the distinctiveness of the local religious tradition emerged frequently among the Ukrainian churches, particularly in western Ukraine. One of the high points of this struggle was reached in the case of the 'traditionalists', a small group of Greek Catholics nostalgic for the underground years. Their case is particularly interesting because it illustrates the shift from the imagistic towards the doctrinal in the UGCC and the role of the underground church in shaping the present tradition.

4.1 A Splinter Group Emerges

In February 2003, Vlodko Hitsiak, a student at the Ukrainian Catholic University (UCU), published an article in *Patriyarkhat*, the official journal of the UGCC, writing about the traditionalist movement within the church. The lengthy article described a group of Greek Catholics who called themselves traditionalists (*trayitionalisty*) and named the parishes and priests belonging to the group from every eparchy in western Ukraine. Hitsiak presented the traditionalists as a well-organized movement led by a charismatic leader that had successfully established a structure parallel to that of the official church.

---

[154] There was indeed no visible pattern, though some general tendencies at the level of decanates (*blahocenia*) could be determined (Yurash 2005a). A decanate is an administrative jurisdiction of the church comprising six to ten parishes delimited by a certain territory.

Moreover, he made several connections between Ukrainian traditionalists and the Lefebvrist movement in the Roman Catholic Church.[155] He concluded the article with accusations that the lax attitude of the hierarchy of the UGCC in the L'viv Archeparchy had allowed this traditionalist group to develop.

Hitsiak articulated several factors to account for the emergence of the traditionalist movement, but in his opinion the primary cause was the existence of two influences, 'pro west and pro east' (*prozakhidnyi i proskhidyi*), in church tradition. Another factor, in his view, was the general attitude of practising underground Greek Catholics, who believed that suffering was a unique marker of faith under the old regime and that an appreciation of this suffering was indispensable to the proper understanding of the local tradition. The movement was further fuelled by the negative 'influence from abroad' that Hitsiak detected in the repeated missions of western Lefebvrist priests to Ukraine since 1990. Among the people and places of importance mentioned in the article, one particular priest, Vasyl Kovpak, was held to be the undisputed leader of the traditionalist movement.[156]

The article in *Patriyarkhat* was the first to bring traditionalists into the public eye, portraying them as an organized group associated with a foreign movement and implying that they posed a threat to the church. It was not by chance that the article was written by a student at UCU. From its inception the university, officially inaugurated in 2002 as the successor to the L'viv Theological Academy, was a major player in the reconstruction of the UGCC in western Ukraine and the strongest progressive voice within the church.[157]

At that time Vasyl Kovpak was the parish priest of Peter and Paul Church in Riasne, one of the newer suburbs of L'viv, a Soviet 'dormitory' built in the 1980s. People in Riasne remembered the period preceding the 'changes' as a quiet time for religious practice, irrespective of confessional identity. During Soviet times one underground Greek Catholic priest, Father

---

[155] The Lefebvrist movement got its name from Marcel Lefebvre, a French bishop who refused to accept some of the decisions of Vatican II and the revision of the Catholic mass. This anti-modernist movement belongs to the larger trend of traditional or traditionalist Catholicism within the Catholic Church. The group is represented worldwide by the Society of St Pius X (founded in 1970), led today by Bishop Bernard Fellay, who, having been consecrated without papal approval, is considered uncanonical by the Vatican.

[156] Apparently the movement spread in the early 1990s when a priest who was a member of the Society of St Pius X came to Ukraine. The priest made contact with a group of Greek Catholics that was in favour of religious practices derived from the Latin rite, as this had been an important component of their underground practices.

[157] The L'viv Theological Academy, which was closed in 1946, reopened in the fall of 1994. The UCU was founded on the basis of the academy.

Muravskyi, a returnee from Siberia, conducted liturgies in the homes of residents who knew him. Other underground priests sometimes came to Riasne for religious services, but such visits were rare. People attended either the Roman Catholic cathedral in the city centre or the Orthodox church nearby, which was administered by an Orthodox priest, Father Babych.

Kovpak became a priest in 1990, when the UGCC was first emerging into public life, registering hundreds of new parishes and in need of new priests. He had studied theology during the underground period in the seminary belonging to the Basilian monks, and he headed the third Basilian order, an uncompromising, radical group of Greek Catholics who accepted no relation to Orthodoxy, 'reunited' priests, or the Soviet state.[158] Kovpak left the Basilian order soon after being ordained a priest, having observed that the community was altering the tradition it had fought so hard to preserve during the underground period, now adapting to the general tendency of church renewal. In his parish in Riasne Kovpak practised what he considered the 'true' (*pravdyvyi*) rite while developing contacts with Ukrainian and foreign priests who shared his ideas. In the early 1990s he started preparing young Ukrainians for the entrance exam to the newly opened official seminary of the UGCC, the Holy Spirit seminary in Rudno, L'viv. In the beginning Kovpak's students successfully gained entry to the seminary, but by 1998–1999 they were no longer being accepted, because they were regarded as *kovpakyvtsyi* – Kovpak's students.

While running the Riasne parish, Kovpak had surrounded himself with a small group of priests and supporters who cherished the religious experience of the underground. The parish became Kovpak's base of activity as his parishioners became full supporters of the traditionalist movement. Greek Catholics in Riasne who did not agree with the priest's hard-line change of course switched to other parishes in the city. Three priests who served as assistants in the parish were sent away because they would not follow the traditionalist line. At first glance, Kovpak's base of support seemed to be composed of elderly people who remembered 'the way things were done before' and refused any recent changes introduced by the church. In reality, the traditionalist community was much broader, and its discourse was fo-

[158] The order of St Basil the Great was the first centralized monastic order in the Kyivan church. The present version of the order was created by Metropolitan Veniamin Rutskyi (1614–1637) by joining five autonomous monasteries with the centre at the Holy Trinity monastery in Vilno in 1617.

cused on the idea of maintaining 'the old traditions of the Greek Catholic Church and staying away from Orthodoxy'.[159]

Although some of Kovpak's supporters were indeed older people who remembered the period before 1946, he found most of his supporters among Greek Catholics who had participated in the underground church. These were entire families spanning several generations and people who had kept in close contact with one another through their common involvement in illegal religious services, domestic devotions, and clandestine, informal networks. For former participants in such surreptitious activities, memories of those times evoked a strong sense of nostalgia every time they were recounted.[160]

Daria, a woman of middle age living in Shchirets, a nearby village, had met Vasyl Kovpak in the underground church in L'viv. After 1990 she asked him to prepare her son for theological studies. Although her son did not, in the end, become one of the *kovpakyvtsyi,* and she had not met the priest in recent years, Daria approved of Kovpak's move to reclaim the spirit the UGCC once had under socialism. She portrayed the image of the 'true church', which, she and others said, was experienced and could be understood only by those who had actively participated in the underground: 'The church is strong when it is persecuted. It was in those times that the church was strong, when we went to liturgies in houses, covering windows . . . The true church was that one.'

Like Daria, other people in L'viv agreed with and supported Kovpak to a certain extent in the spirit of solidarity generated by their common feeling of having been part of the underground community. Religious life in a traditionalist parish to some extent followed the model of the underground church. Devotion was more intense, with each parish priest promoting his parish as a 'place of pilgrimage' for neighbouring areas, thus drawing larger crowds on Sundays than his local community could provide. On Sundays and holidays, religious services took place three times a day in Riasne, and the Sunday liturgy lasted for two and a half to three hours. The main religious celebrations took place outside the church in the middle of the neighbourhood, and on every occasion traditionalists organized long processions through the locality. The community was strongly united by its common opponent, re-enacting the model of 'defender of the faith' common to the times of repression. This model, which presupposed clear-cut attitudes

---

[159] From an interview with Volodia Havalko, head of the Riasne parish council, in Maria Sholomytska, 'Hreko-katolytski neporozuminnia [Greek Catholic misunderstandings]' *Postup* 37, no. 1346, 16 February 2004: 3.

[160] Similar feelings for the underground church can be witnessed in the Romanian Greek Catholic Church, which went through a similar experience from 1948 to 1989 (Mahieu 2003).

and a firm moral stance, mobilized the community and reproduced the former determination of the underground believers.

Plate 11. Greek Catholic traditionalists led by Father Vasyl Kovpak gathering for a Jordan ceremony mass in Riasne, 2004.

In recent years the traditionalist group had also attracted new converts and Greek Catholics disappointed by the daily routine of church practice. Among them, one family of former Communists, now Catholic converts, who owned a large factory in L'viv offered full support to the group. The owners opened a floor of the factory building as a chapel and conference hall for the traditionalist community. This family, under Kovpak's guidance, integrated religious practice into the daily routine of the factory, conducting a religious service every morning for the 800 employees, in addition to spiritual readings carried out during common meals.

Every eparchy in western Ukraine had traditionalist parishes similar to that in Riasne. Kovpak's activism and his claim to represent traditionalism in the UGCC attracted many priests, nuns, and candidates for priesthood who had been forced towards the periphery of the church since 1989 because of their wish to 'keep the tradition'. Some of these people were already problematical for the church hierarchy. In the Ivano-Frankivsk and Ternopil-Zboriv Eparchies, local bishops quickly responded when a parish priest displayed his inclination towards traditionalist practices, immediately suspending him from the parish.[161] The parishes in Riasne (Riasne-1 and Riasne-2) became the core of the traditionalist movement, and other priests joined Kovpak without being removed from their own parishes. Additionally, a small group of nuns who were forced to leave the Basilian order in 1995 because of their traditionalist ideas joined Kovpak's movement and subsequently opened a traditionalist convent.

Plate 12. Traditionalist nuns, formerly members of the Basilian order, during the Jordan celebration in Riasne, 2004.

In 1999 Vasyl Kovpak and two other Ukrainian priests asked Lefebvrist bishop Bernard Fellay to become their spiritual leader. With this initiative Kovpak hoped to receive approval and support for organizing the incipient structures of the traditionalist movement. Candidates for the priesthood who had been refused by the Greek Catholic seminary were to become part of a private seminary led by Kovpak. In September 2000 he and six other priests and the nuns formed the Society of St Josaphat, headed by him. Upon the Lefebvrist bishop's visit to Ukraine in November 2000, this almost-splinter group from the UGCC was ready to receive the Episcopal blessing and thus to re-enter world Catholicism through a back door opened by another splin-

[161] Such was the case of Father Lubomyr Haievsky, from Bohorodchan, Ivano-Frankivsk, who was suspended from his parish in September 1999 and excommunicated in 2002 by Bishop Sofron Mudryi for continuing his priestly activity in the village.

ter group, the traditionalist Catholics of Marcel Lefebvre. At a retreat organized for followers of the traditionalist movement, the bishop inaugurated the Immaculate Heart of Mary Seminary, gathering eight students and the congregation of Basilian Sisters of the Divine Mercy, a community of ten nuns.

Some accusations against Ukrainian traditionalists held that their priests maintained contact with Lefebvrists only for material reasons. Indeed, the connection with the Lefebvrite society brought significant advantages and assistance to the community, which would not have survived and developed to such an extent had it been left to its own devices. Three Lefebvrite priests from the Society of St Pius X in Poland regularly visited to instruct seminarians. Since 2001 the Society of St Josaphat had published a bimonthly journal, *Bells of Fatima* (*Dzvin z Fatimy*), and, among other items, a collection of traditionalist Christmas carols, a book about the apparition at Fatima, and Kovpak's 2003 book, *Persecuted Tradition* (*Peresliduvana tradytsia)*.

The book appeared in response to an investigation into the traditionalist movement launched by Cardinal Husar, head of the UGCC, in September 2003.[162] In it Kovpak reflected on how the church had developed since 1989, finding a continuous thread of 'traditionalist ideas and practices'. He offered a detailed explanation of the formation of the traditionalist movement, an account of his attempts to discuss his ideas with the hierarchy of the UGCC, and a critical evaluation of the contemporary situation of the church. He enumerated the individual instances in which priests, monks, and nuns had been forced to leave the church since 1989 because of their wish 'to keep the tradition', claiming himself to be one representative of this widespread trend. The book included an autobiography that explained how, by experiencing the underground, Kovpak arrived at the idea of becoming a 'defender of the Greek Catholic tradition' because of his disappointment with the official church and 'the immorality of church representatives'. The book ended with eleven open letters written by theology students at Kovpak's seminary and addressed to Cardinal Husar. The students explained how they were discriminated against and barred from entering the Greek Catholic seminary as followers of Father Kovpak. They asked for the right to pursue their theological studies and thus realize their vocations.

---

[162] In March 2003, a month after the publication of Vlodko Hitsiak's article, Cardinal Husar formed a commission to investigate the traditionalist movement in the L'viv Archeparchy and traditionalist practices among Greek Catholic believers. The clerical commission was to interview Kovpak and his followers and then decide to what extent their activity diverged from the official line of the church. See 'Dekrety' [Decrees], *Bells of Fatima,* May–June 2003: 11.

Following the investigation, the results of which were not made public, Cardinal Husar announced at a press conference on 10 February 2004 the church's decision to recall Vasyl Kovpak as administrator of the parish and to suspend his status as a Greek Catholic priest. The official statement said that Kovpak 'of his own free will has ceased to belong to the UGCC and the Catholic Church in general' because of his recognition of the Lefebvrist Bishop Fellay.[163] Husar stressed that 'the road to return to UGCC is always open to Kovpak and his followers on the condition that they denounce their affiliation with the foreign [*chuzhynets*] bishop'.[164]

The announcement of the suspension was published in religious and secular media and was posted at several churches in the city. The Church of the Nativity in Sykhiv, for example, posted the announcement at its entrance, and parish members discussed the subject intensely in the following days. The Nativity parish was connected to the case because its main priest, Orest Fredina, had an administrative function in the L'viv Archeparchy as chancellor (*syncellus*) for clergy, and in this capacity he dealt directly with the excommunicated priest. Outside L'viv, the Greek Catholic church in the village of Shchirets was silent: no announcement was posted and there was no mention of the case in the church. The village priest expressed interest in Kovpak's suspension only in private, after the service.

On Sunday, 15 February, a few days after the announcement was made, two priests were sent from St George Cathedral, the chancellery of the UGCC, to replace Kovpak in his function as parish priest. Upon hearing of this, Kovpak's parishioners gathered in front of the church and threatened the two priests, turning them away and telling them never to return. A week later the priests returned with Orest Fredina from Sykhiv, who was extremely popular among Greek Catholics in L'viv. Father Orest attempted to reason with Kovpak's parishioners, hoping to convince them to accept the two new priests. The two sides remained intransigent and the parishioners became irritated, declaring that 'the parish already has its own priest!'

The case became notorious in L'viv, attracting media coverage and the attention of Greek Catholic believers, for whom it became a matter of debate. At the time of this conflict in Riasne, I was accompanying a group of pilgrims to Lishnia, a recent apparition site frequented by Greek Catholics from all over western Ukraine (see chapter 7). Most of my travelling com-

---

[163] 'Tribunal Excommunicates Lefebvrite Priest from Greek Catholic Church', RISU News, 14 June 2004, www.risu.org.ua.

[164] *Chuzhynets* is a pejorative word for a foreigner. In this context its usage was ironic, because two months before the press release Husar had appeared in newspapers holding his Ukrainian passport and being quoted as saying, 'I am not a mason or a foreigner' (*Ya ne mason i ne chuzhynets*). *Vysokyy Zamok* 206, 30 October–2 November 2003.

panions, who came from parishes in L'viv, were regular visitors to 'alternative' devotional sites; they were 'churched' people in the sense of being knowledgeable believers rather than passive churchgoers. Some actually belonged to the group of Greek Catholics that had been involved in underground activities during the socialist years, participating in 'illegal' religious services and visiting such sites of popular devotion.

After the liturgy at Lishnia, celebrated by two priests who also were perpetuators of underground practices,[165] animated discussions began among the pilgrims regarding Kovpak's case. The main issue of debate was whether or not the priest was 'on the right track'. Pilgrims showed sympathy for the his plight and identified with his struggle for 'our tradition', but they were also concerned about the possible split with church authority that was implicit in Kovpak's position. The pilgrims discussed whether or not the pope's authority had been defied, given the known relation between the schismatic priest and the Lefebvrist bishop. They were less concerned with Kovpak's alleged insubordination to the Greek Catholic hierarchy.

The conflict over Kovpak went on until the first of June 2004, when the church tribunal of the UGCC, after an additional investigation that had been started two months earlier, excommunicated him. The decision was announced in a decree signed by Cardinal Husar. Kovpak was prohibited from performing religious services in the UGCC, and all Greek Catholic priests were forbidden to associate with him in any religious activity. Aside from the condemnation of Kovpak's connection to Bishop Fellay, the priest was accused of 'popularizing the movement among other priests and establishing illegal institutions on the territory of the major archbishop of the UGCC'.[166] From the perspective of the church, this act was the culmination of a case that had begun with minor differences over rituals such as kneeling during communion and had boiled over into open defiance of church authority.

The mission of the underground church was to preserve the tradition of the Greek Catholic Church, and traditionalists considered that 'being traditionalist means knowing and protecting the traditional knowledge of the church' (Kovpak 2003: 134). Their mission continued that of the underground, and they saw themselves as its successors. They opposed anything that did not belong to the Catholic tradition and that could pervert the only 'true church'. The response of the UGCC hierarchy to the traditionalist

---

[165] The two, Father Mykhailo Koval, a Basilian monk, and Father Yury, a Redemptorist monk, belonged to the category 'travelling priests', who undertook intense missionary activity in popular places of devotion (see chapter 7).

[166] 'Tribunal Excommunicates Lefebvrite Priest from Greek Catholic Church', RISU news, 14 June 2004, www.risu.org.ua.

movement made use of the same idea of 'true tradition', which it regarded as completely different from the Catholic tradition. The claim of the new leaders repositioned the entire debate over tradition by reinterpreting the entirety of church history from an Orthodox point of view, thus creating a new orthodoxy. In the words of a church leader representative of this new direction:

> The UGCC began with the baptism of Volodymyr the Great. We [churches] are all one Kyivan Church, which simply split under different jurisdictions – Moscow, Rome, Constantinople . . . We want to return to our ancient traditions. This is why the Greek Catholic rite has to unite us with the Orthodox . . . Now we continue to look for a name – Greek Orthodox, Orthodox-Catholic, Kyivan Catholic . . . When we fulfil Christ's instruction 'to be one', then there will be no sense in the existence of a separate group of 'Greek Catholics'. We want to be one Kyivan Orthodox-Catholic Church.[167]

4.2 Continuities and Ruptures in a Church Tradition

In the conflict over authority that emerged in the Kovpak case, the 'true' Greek Catholic tradition became an object of contestation and competition between different religious actors. The church tradition that traditionalists so fiercely protected had changed significantly since 1989. During the underground period the Greek Catholic rite was modified to a large extent. The 'practical adaptability' that most clergy and laity chose in order to preserve the Greek Catholic rite meant that significant transformations were made in both life-cycle and liturgical rituals (Shlikhta 2004a: 192). Forced to adapt to the disappearance of their church, Greek Catholics had to choose whether to switch to Orthodoxy together with their parish priest, to begin frequenting a Roman Catholic church, few of which remained open, or to refuse both options and go on with private, individual religious practices, infrequently interspersed with clandestine religious services.

In reality the choice was not so clear-cut, and people could and often did move between these options, praying at home and attending Sunday mass in a Catholic church but also attending underground liturgies when the occasion presented itself. Sometimes rituals were performed multiple times, just to be sure the 'right thing' was being done for the occasion. For example, a family might have an Orthodox priest perform a funeral and later, at night, have an underground Greek Catholic priest bless soil from the grave

---

[167] Mykhailo Dymyd, 'Vony vzhe poza Tserkvoiu' [They are already against the church], in 'UGCC Became Orthodox Church', *Hazeta Argument,* 14 January 2004: 4–5. Also, personal communication with Father Dymyd, chancellor of the L'viv Archeparchy at that time.

site (Shlikhta 2004a). The laity developed a preoccupation with performing rituals as they had once been performed, following 'the tradition'. The tradition they sought to preserve was a synthesis of eastern and western influences, which made the mission easier. Western Ukrainians could adjust to either Roman Catholic or Orthodox churches by following one or the other set of characteristics already present in their own practice.[168] Underground Greek Catholic priests sometimes attended the two Roman Catholic churches still open in L'viv and heard confession in both Polish and Ukrainian. 'When a Ukrainian came to confession I spoke to him in Ukrainian; when a Pole [came], I used Polish. And I encouraged people to find Catholic priests and listen to their liturgy,' recalled Father Vasyl Voronovsky (ICH, 3 January 1994).

Greek Catholics in L'viv, knowing that their priests could be found at one of the Roman Catholic churches, would go there in order to confess to 'their own' priest, afterwards partaking of the Latin mass. This situation created problems for the Roman Catholic Church, whose position was already insecure. Sometimes Roman Catholic priests were afraid to accept 'illegal' Greek Catholic priests into their churches. But Roman Catholic priests such as Father Rafal Kiernicki, from the cathedral, who later suffered under the Soviet authorities' repression, were also popular among Greek Catholics.

The majority of Greek Catholics, however, ended up in the Orthodox Church, although this switch had little effect on the rite itself. Most priests serving new Orthodox parishes were 'reunited' Greek Catholic priests, who had signed the agreement (*pidpysaty pravoslavia*) to join the Orthodox Church.[169] They and their parish communities retained the rite as it had been, making use of the same Greek Catholic prayer books (though they were forbidden in 1949) and maintaining the specifics of the local religious tradition: the kissing of the veil on the Friday before Easter (*plashchenytsia*), the blessing of Easter food (*pasky*) on Saturday afternoon, commemorating the dead on Easter Monday, singing carols (*koliadky, shchedrivky*) at Christmas, and performing a popular religious play (*Vertep*) dedicated to Christmas. May and June remained special months, with devotions dedicated to the

---

[168] The accommodation was not straightforward because of language differences and other rite barriers. However, most of these difficulties could be overcome with the help of a sensitive priest.

[169] The term under which priests were 'reunited' means 'undersigned' (*pidpysani*) and comes from the act of signing a declaration stating that they accepted the Orthodox faith. The text of the declaration was usually made more neutral, in order for the priests not to break with Catholic canons by signing it. The declaration had to be confirmed by the signature of a bishop (the canonical legalization) in front of a representative of the Soviet Committee for Religious Affairs (Shlikhta 2004a).

Mother of God (*maivky*) and the Sacred Heart of Jesus (*haivky*). Other acts and objects were preserved in liturgy, processions, and devotions, including the Latin prayers of the rosary (*vervytsia*) and the Way of the Cross (*hresna doroha*). Galician popular religiosity was actually better preserved in the reunited church than in the underground church.

Later attempts by the Orthodox hierarchy to the 'Orthodoxize' the Ukrainian exarchate came to nothing. Western Ukrainian Orthodox priests, now trained in Russia, tended to adapt their religious practices to the local tradition. State authorities in charge of religious issues regularly reported that 'reunited parishes continue to observe the Uniate rituals rather than the Orthodox', and from the 1960s onwards they reported that church rituals in Orthodox churches were performed in accordance with an 'established local tradition' (quoted in Shlikhta 2004a: 349–350). In spite of the fact that it had absorbed some influences from Orthodoxy, the local religious tradition maintained its particular character (Jepsen 2005: 76). Even by the late 1950s, with the return of exiled Greek Catholic bishops and priests, many reunited priests resumed their contacts with the clandestine church. According to various testimonies, hundreds of priests returned to the underground church, and while they formally maintained their Orthodox affiliation, they reactivated their connection to the UGCC.

Although the literature depicts the underground period as 'the time of the laity' because people to some extent controlled religious practice and adapted it to their needs, priests continued to play important roles. The sacrament of confession became a highly important event because it offered the laity the possibility of legitimating their religious actions. Confession confirmed to the priest the worshipper's status as a practising Christian, which was particularly important in such risky, illegal services, and it symbolized the worshipper's belonging to a larger community of faith represented by the priest. During confession a believer could obtain a blessing to attend Catholic mass, an injunction against attending Orthodox liturgies, or the approval to perform certain rituals at home with a suggested private devotional routine. Priests provided believers with the means to carry out rituals such as the blessing of holy water in the priests' absence. Individual confessions, even if sporadic, were spaces of negotiation of the orthodoxy of ritual practice and provided a mechanism for the adjustment of church tradition to particular situations.[170]

Historians researching the catacomb church tend to disagree on the effects of this practical adaptability on official church doctrine. William

---

[170] Particularly during Lent, when the number of people requesting confession was larger than usual, priests would accept public confessions, a clear break from official church doctrine (Shlikhta 2004a).

Fletcher (1981) maintained that theological conservatism and practical adaptability were distinct features of the underground experience, and changes brought on by the pressures of Soviet times did not undermine official church dogma. Natalia Shlikhta's argument (2004a), which is corroborated by my research, was that practical adaptability brought significant changes to rites, thus challenging and forcing a rethinking of theological concepts. Bearing in mind the peculiarities of eastern Christendom, it is evident that the church tradition absorbed transformations that affected the teachings of the church. Underground priests walked a fine line between preserving the Greek Catholic tradition, through which people could differentiate Greek Catholicism from Orthodoxy, and implementing small-scale changes that would revivify religious practice.

Furthermore, the UGCC, in its provisional underground form, could not communicate a uniform message regarding its religious tradition. Differences between Latinizing and easternizing tendencies within the church were perpetuated during this period, each being promoted by a different monastic order. In a simplified view, Basilians championed the Latinization drive, which in this case meant preservation of the pre-1946 tradition, in contrast to Studites, representatives of the eastern orientation.[171]

During Soviet times 'the persistence of the church [was] mainly due to the spirit of monasticism' (Wynot 2002: 63).[172] Underground monastic orders organized themselves to solidify their communities and provide religious services for larger audiences. Although in the 1950s monks and nuns had been sent either into exile or back to their families, in the 1960s they began to gather and reorganize in small groups. Up to six people might live together in a house or flat that functioned as a sort of domestic monastery where residents' schedules and duties mirrored those of a normal monastery. Monks would find employment in low-profile jobs that would give them the time to pursue their spiritual paths (Keleher 1993: 71). On the whole, monasticism was better able to adapt to the difficult conditions of the time and retain aspects of Greek Catholic tradition. Other elements belonging to the common tradition were retained in reunited 'Orthodox' churches.

Among the Greek Catholic orders active in the underground, there were also lay associations centred on various devotions and third-order

---

[171] Metropolitan Andrei Sheptytskyi founded the Studite order to renew eastern monasticism in the church. The first renewed monastery of the Studite order was established in 1904 in Sknyliv, near L'viv.

[172] Jennifer Wynot (2002) discussed secret monasticism in the Soviet Union before the Second World War. The features she described were also present in the Greek Catholic underground: 'urban monastics', 'monasteries in the world', 'wandering monks', and 'personified monasticism'.

monastic communities. The lay forms of religious associations survived the repression in better shape than the religious institutions themselves and constituted a basis for religious practice under the Soviet regime. Tertiary orders – Franciscan, Basilian, and Redemptorist – consisted of consecrated laypersons who continued their secular lives with work and families, remaining 'in the world' while simultaneously pursuing spiritual lives similar to those of monks. Third-order Basilians were the most determined defenders of the rite. Inspired by the tertiary orders of the Roman Catholic Church, this community adapted perfectly to underground life: its members, all laity, maintained a secular existence but made vows and adopted a monastic regime that gave them monk-like obligations. Under the guidance of underground Basilian priests, the Basilians adopted a survival strategy that allowed no compromise. They unequivocally opposed the idea of Greek Catholics attending Orthodox churches and refused to open their doors to recently reunited priests. They regarded the changing of one's confessional identity, even if only as a façade, as betrayal, and they incriminated all accommodations of Orthodoxy.

When the underground was first emerging to the light of day in the glasnost years, the Greek Catholic Church emphasized its difference from the Orthodox Church in order to create a necessary distance. This campaign went beyond the labelling of Orthodox Christians as 'Russians' and the use of nationalist discourses; it actively promoted Latin-rite devotions in local practice. In the 1980s, for example, the phenomenon of religious apparitions became a means of civic and religious mobilization in Ukraine (see chapter 7). Large pilgrimages to sites such as Hrushiv, where an apparition of the Mother of God was made public in 1987, were occasions for church leaders and religious activists to inculcate practices and ideas about the Greek Catholic tradition and to reinforce the orthodoxy of the rite. In Hrushiv, visionaries communicated divine messages encouraging the committed practice of Latin devotions: to Christ the King, for the souls in Purgatory, to the Sacred Heart of Jesus, and in the daily practice of the rosary. These visionaries asked people to pray for the pope and the church hierarchy: 'Follow the leaders of the church boldly and you will win your own country, gaining love among the nations of the world' (Terelya and Brown 1991: 277). Such sites of popular devotion were also spaces where people simultaneously confronted devotional practices from the underground and found common religious expressions with which to represent the emerging Greek Catholic community.

The underground experience represented a liminal period for the UGCC, and the ambiguities resulting from it had to be cleared up quickly after the church's revival. More than aspects of doctrine or rite, the most visible aspects to be settled were those surrounding the status of priests and bishops consecrated in the underground, who were to be confirmed or refuted. Ordination ceremonies for bishops, priests, and deacons had often been shortened, left incomplete, or performed without witnesses because of constraints on the operations of the underground. The inclusion in the institutionalized church of clergy ordained in the underground was not a smooth process, and it generated many surprises and conflicts.[173]

Whereas in the 1980s there were fewer than 500 active underground priests, with additional members of monastic orders, at the end of 1989 more than 600 Greek Catholic parishes had applied for official registration. Some 300 churches were already functioning, and 200 Orthodox priests were prepared to become Greek Catholic. By mid-January 1990 the numbers had risen: Greek Catholics had 600 churches, 350 'converted' priests, and 700 parishes that had applied for registration. There were ten bishops and an acknowledged head of the church, Volodymyr Sterniuk. The church was starting to look like an institution again, with religious structures developing all over western Ukraine. Its supporters were extremely heterogeneous, which added to the growing list of problems besetting the institutionalization.

The older priests, who had been ordained before 1946 and remained Greek Catholic during the underground times, played a pivotal role in the first years of church revival. They had remarkable biographies of suffering and resistance and constituted moral examples for Greek Catholics in their devotion to the rite and the church. Together with the example of those who had died and become martyrs for the church, these people inspired the first generation of rediscovered Greek Catholics. They were objects of much admiration, but their legacy was soon transformed into an 'official memory' that created the martyr aura of the present-day Greek Catholic Church. The old priests preserved the pre-war Greek Catholic tradition of Metropolitan Sheptytskyi, which was held to be the authentic tradition from the times of 'the true church' (*pravdyva tserkva*), as Father Vasyl Kovpak maintained. Kovpak himself was inspired by such priests and legitimated the traditionalist movement by reference to their model of faith.

Members of the catacomb church had also consecrated younger priests during the underground years. These priests studied in Roman Catholic seminaries in Riga or Kaunas during the Soviet era and later returned to

[173] One such case was that of Father Vasyl (Iosaphat) Kavatsiv, the parish priest of the Annunciation Church in Stryi, a 'self-declared' bishop who claimed he had been ordained as a bishop in the underground but was unable to provide either proof or witnesses. Though unrecognized by either Rome or the UGCC, he received great popular support because of his celebrated underground past.

western Ukraine to become priests.[174] Their orientation was Latin, which was an advantage in the early 1990s but would become a problem later, when the UGCC changed course towards Orthodoxy. More priests emerged from the underground seminaries in Ukraine, and several priests were clandestinely educated and ordained by the underground bishops. Their theological knowledge and style of worship depended on the monastic order in which they were educated. Studites were more inclined towards the eastern Byzantine influence, whereas Basilians embraced the Latin tradition. Redemptorists had incorporated the changes brought by Vatican II, while Basilians maintained the pre–Vatican II rite.

In spite of the preservation of religious structures during the Soviet period and the illegal ordination of priests, there were too few underground priests to suffice for the rapidly developing Greek Catholic Church in the early 1990s. New priests from various backgrounds were hastily ordained, some of whom had a genuine interest and some of whom joined the church for status and material benefits. Among the new recruits were many who, motivated by enthusiasm for the religious revival, were eager to try a new option. Their studies were brief – two to six months before their ordination – because the church needed priests quickly in order to register parishes and regain church property throughout western Ukraine. This was a widespread phenomenon not only in the Greek Catholic Church but also in the Orthodox churches (Mitrokhin 2001). Between 1988 and 1998 the number of religious communities in Ukraine more than tripled, requiring qualified personnel who did not exist at the time.[175]

It would have been extremely difficult to prepare priests in such a short time, considering that an institutionalized theological education system was not in place. Before 1989 there was one official Orthodox seminary in Odessa, but most priests from western Ukraine studied in St Petersburg or Moscow. The Greek Catholic Church had to build its pedagogical system from scratch. The first two institutions appeared in 1990: the Basilian Theological Institute in Krekhiv and the Holy Spirit Seminary in Rudno, L'viv. These two institutions were supported by the diaspora church and run by 'returnees', Greek Catholic priests from abroad. Looking back to that time, today's professors at the Ukrainian Catholic University think the selection

[174] The only legal Roman Catholic seminaries in the Soviet Union were in the Baltic countries.

[175] There were 6,179 religious organizations registered in 1988, and 19,780 in 1998 (Mitrokhin 2001: 181).

procedure was too permissive and the educational program too brief and improvised to have yielded high-quality results.[176]

Plate 13. Models of priesthood: Father Anton, a celebrated Basilian monk from the underground church. L'viv, 2004.

In addition to the underground priests, a nearly equal number, 400 priests, left the Orthodox Church to become Greek Catholic. These were not the reunited priests from 1946. They came from western Ukraine, had trained in theological seminaries in St Petersburg and Moscow, and had their own parishes before 1989. Many other priests of this generation did not even consider becoming Greek Catholic but switched to the Autocephalous Orthodox Church or, later, to one of the other Orthodox churches. Reasons for changing confession varied from priest to priest, with each one's decision contingent upon whether he could convince his parishioners to support the

[176] This is why the university proposed a series of evening courses that would provide further training for this generation of priests (Taras Tymo, UCU, personal communication). The issue is of serious concern because, according to UCU estimates, around 70 per cent of these priests are far from being ideal parish priests as far as the university is concerned.

change, even if it was against the general trend (as in two cases I discuss in the following chapter), or whether he was forced by his parishioners to leave the church (as was the case of the two priests in Sykhiv described in chapter 3). Sometimes priests became competitors in the same village, like the Greek Catholic and Orthodox priests in Shchirets, who had studied in the same seminary, practised a similar rite, but now belonged to different churches (see chapter 5). For some, the switch was a strategic move, opening better career opportunities and gaining the support of the Roman Catholic Church. Others returned because of family tradition. Regardless of the reasons for their 'conversion', these priests had their unique understandings of the rite and the church and were regarded with suspicion by the 'true' Greek Catholic priests, who were survivors of the repression or returnees from abroad. In fact the 'converted' priests best represented the local religious tradition as it developed throughout the Soviet period.

Plate 14. Models of priesthood: Father Ruslan, a young, post-1990 Greek Catholic priest going for house blessings in Sykhiv, 2004.

Overall the model promoted for the emerging church was that of the underground martyrs, but those advocating it were diaspora priests. Few diaspora priests returned to Ukraine in the early years of the revival (about forty by 1993), but they occupied all the leading positions in the UGCC, from the head of the church to the founders of its new educational system. These people were better educated in the spirit of the post–Vatican II Catholic Church, had been closer to the Vatican, and, being better connected to the Ukrainian church abroad, could provide more for the emerging church. Representatives of the underground church were slowly marginalized, together with the trend they represented in the UGCC. Priests ordained after 1994–1995, who had completed a full program of theological studies, were better prepared but also eastern oriented, given the direction of the UGCC established by the new elites.

In spite of the hierarchy's attempts to impose guidelines for the recreated church, the UGCC remains today a heterogeneous institution whose mass of believers follows a local religious tradition shared with Ukrainian Orthodox churches. This constitutes an advantage as understood by the Greek Catholic elites. When the UGCC re-established itself in western Ukraine, its regional influence was extremely important for the development of local structures. Those who supported the foundation of the new church were pro-Catholic and nationalist, rejecting any connection to Orthodoxy and thus to the eastern roots of the UGCC.[177] This orientation changed radically with the takeover by the diaspora elites, who redirected the church towards the goal of becoming a national church through its belonging to the Orthodox imaginary (see also Yurash 2005a). The journey from local to national meant switching emphasis from Catholicism to Orthodoxy, understood in this context as the eastern Christian tradition of Kievan Rus. This was visible not only in the moving of the patriarchal seat from L'viv to Kyiv, in the establishment of new exarchates in eastern Ukraine and Central Asia, and in the discourse of church officials regarding the recognition of the UGCC's status as a patriarchate. It was also apparent in the 'purification of the rite' (Mahieu 2003: 206) and the redefinition of church tradition starting in the mid-1990s.

This unexpected rethinking of Greek Catholicism caught many people off guard, and the first casualties of the purification of the rite were those underground heroes who, once fixed in the representation of the martyr church, became marginalized by mainstream discourse and practice. The representatives of the underground, either real survivors or self-created

[177] It was even proposed that the diaspora church take the name 'Ukrainian Catholic Church'.

protagonists, found themselves and the tradition they stood for in direct opposition to the church.

Most of the problems came from the fact that Greek Catholic churches draw implicitly on two models of authority: the Roman Catholic hierarchical model and the Orthodox model of diffuse authority. This paradoxical position is reflected in the Roman Catholic canonical code for eastern churches, which establishes the frames for the functioning of the Uniate churches but encourages them to preserve and follow the 'particular heritage of the eastern churches' (Congregation for the Eastern Churches 1996). The latter represents a completely different model from that of the Catholic tradition. The entire idea is questioned today by church hierarchs who seek to reinterpret 'Uniatism' and their relationship with the Catholic Church. By questioning the status of their own church, Ukrainian hierarchs aim to challenge the actual separation between east and west.[178]

Even though the church was able to quickly re-establish a clear hierarchy with the pope as symbolic head, for the laity institutionalization generated many conflicts, which started to appear just after the religious boom of 1989–1990. Apart from conflicts related to the church hierarchy and illegal bishops, questions surrounding monastic orders fuelled further clashes. Having been well adapted to the underground, some monks and nuns found it difficult to emerge from it after 1990. Many individuals could not or did not want to change their pattern of life. Either too old or still devoted to a mode of religiosity that had secured their personal survival and religious tradition, these people looked for possibilities to carry on.

Some, like Vasyl Voronovsky and other missionary priests supporting popular devotions, continued their active lives dedicated to the lay communities they had served while in the underground. One young Studite brother, a colleague of Voronovsky's, commented on Voronovsky's particular rhythm of life, which perpetuated his religious routine from the underground but contrasted with the rhythm of the monastery: 'One never knows when he is in the monastery, he comes and then he just disappears, a car comes and picks him up and he is gone for two or three days.' Nevertheless, in comparison with other monks or nuns who preferred to remain clandestine, living in the 'underground' even in 2004, Voronovsky was somehow reintegrated into the life of the church. The priests, nuns, and laity who gathered

[178] This is what Cardinal Husar did in Rome in 2006 when he asked whether, for unity between Catholics and Orthodox Christians, there was a need for more than the common Eucharistic celebration. Sitting at the margins of two great religious traditions, the Greek Catholic Church might be in a position to question the centre. The peripheral position of the church could thus become its strength.

around Vasyl Kovpak and formed the traditionalist movement were just one facet of the inability or refusal to adjust.

Differences between members of the monastic orders and clergy were not only related to the preservation of a style of religious life but were also ideological. Throughout the underground period, monastic communities had maintained their identities, and upon the legalization of the church, the differences between the values and practices of these orders and the church became even more pronounced. Each monastic order illustrates a major tendency in the UGCC today. Basilians, as champions of the Latinization drive – which in this case means the preservation of the pre-1946 tradition – contrast with Studites at the other end of the spectrum, as representatives of the eastern orientation.

Basilians are the oldest monastic order in Greek Catholicism and have retained an independent streak over the course of their existence. The present form of the order came about as a result of the Jesuit reformation in the nineteenth century. Under strong Jesuit influence, Basilians became the Latinizing factor in Uniate churches. Most of the ritual practices that are today considered to represent Latin influences on the Greek Catholic rite were introduced by Basilians in the nineteenth century. The Way of the Cross (*Kalwaria, hresna doroha*), prayers to the Virgin Mary in May (*Maiuvky*), the Adoration of the Blessed Sacrament, the Sacred Heart of Jesus, the Apostleship of Prayer in June, and the devotion of the first Friday of every month became popular at all levels of the church. The consecration of the Sacred Heart of Jesus was a mass phenomenon that produced impressive numbers of personal and collective devotions. Most of these devotions were preserved during the underground period and are practised even nowadays. Basilians introduced a trend of having lay associations centred on various cults and devotions affiliated with particular monastic orders. They were the preservers of most non-liturgical devotions of Latin inspiration.

In the aftermath of the Greek Catholic revival, the Roman Catholic Church had undergone one of its most important transformations, owing to the Second Vatican Council. This added problems to the revival of monastic orders. The Vatican II reforms reached the UGCC during its underground period and were inconsistently applied. In the early 1990s these inconsistencies were among the first causes of conflict. In 1995 a group of Basilian nuns led by the head of the female Basilian order, Liuba Ilnytska (1992–1994), was forced to leave the order because of strong disagreements over ritual practice. Some of the nuns adhered to the pre-war Basilian rite, whereas others had adopted the post–Vatican II influences under the guidance of Redemptorist fathers. The conflict between the two Basilian groups proposing different views of the Greek Catholic rite could not be contained within the Basilian community, so the traditionalist nuns had to leave the order. They formed a separate convent independent of the established order. Later, at the time the Greek Catholic Church was attempting to bring its doctrine in line with Catholic doctrine, these nuns were excommunicated and their convent was closed. The nuns then restructured their community around Vasyl Kovpak and the new traditionalist movement connected to the Lefebvrists.

The traditionalist splinter groups described here contrast strongly with another monastic group that provides the subject matter of chapter 6. That monastic community, in Kolodiivka, was also a splinter group originally part of the Basilian order. The reasons for its separation were related to its interpretation of church tradition, part of a search of a spiritual model closer to the roots of eastern Christianity. Its path was different from those of both the traditionalists and the Basilian tradition. The common cause uniting traditionalist groups was the need to preserve a mode of religiosity specific to underground practices.

By putting the memory of the underground church in the service of their ideas regarding the 'true' church, traditionalists began to compete with the church hierarchy over the memories of martyred bishops and priests. Thus they became actors in one of the most important processes taking place in the UGCC – the 'recovery of memory'. The intense activity of discovering and describing the underground church preoccupied both church elites and members of the monastic orders, and both groups used the symbolic importance of the underground in equal manner. Traditionalists appeared in this process as those who would preserve the character of the underground, in opposition to the others, who would preserve only its memory. Each group claimed to be the legitimate heir to the catacomb church. The official institutional memory of the church has been revised since the 1990s through the standardization of the collective memory of the underground experience and the creation of 'exemplary biographies' (Naumescu 2004). In this way some events and heroes were retained and promoted in the official narrative of the past while others were marginalized and some disappeared altogether. The creation of the 'martyrs of the church', which culminated in the canonization of twenty-seven underground figures by Pope John Paul II in 2001, was a strenuous process of memory recovery and selection.

4.3 The Uses and Abuses of Memory

The synod of the UGCC that was held from 14 to 21 October 1996 established a commission for beatifications and canonizations. The commission was supposed to use the work of the Institute for Church History (ICH), which had been initiated in 1992 to create profiles of underground bishops and priests who might be named Catholic martyrs of faith. The institute, founded by Father Borys Gudziak, a representative of the diaspora church, started by gathering materials about clandestine religious activities during the Soviet period, with a particular focus on Greek Catholic clerical involvement. By mapping out all the underground religious networks and practices, this oral history project illuminated a distinctive image, that of the catacomb church, whose main actors became the martyrs of the UGCC. The institute managed to incorporate a great variety of individual memories and produce a standardized memorialization of the underground that would later be elevated by the church to become its official history. The ICH and most of the other institutes of the Ukrainian Catholic University acted to standardize various dimensions of church life, thus providing for and endorsing the official ideology of the UGCC.[179]

In the institutionalization of the church, the symbolic level of reorganization occupied an important role. The symbolic restructuring of the UGCC after 1990 required the creation of '*lieux de memoire'*, or places of memory (Nora 1989). Church elites and local communities initiated an intense process in which human remains – Katherine Verdery's (1999) 'dead bodies' – were transported over great geographical distances and reburied in places of symbolic significance for the church in its mission to reclaim various sites. Similar processes were taking place in other postsocialist spaces (Gal 1989; Verdery 1999). Among Greek Catholics, enthusiasm was aroused by the reburial in L'viv of the remains of Cardinal Slipyi, who had been a figurehead of the resistance and head of the UGCC in exile. Slipyi had died in 1984 in Rome, and his remains were transported to L'viv and buried in St George's Cathedral in 1992 in a symbolic reconsecration of the most important Greek Catholic church, less than a year after it was recovered from the Orthodox Church. More than a million people came to view Slipyi's grave in the week following his reburial.[180]

Although the relocation of 'the Patriarch' was the most visible case of reburial, his journey was one in a long series of transports. The remains of Father Oleksii Zarytskyi (1912–1963), who died in a labour camp in Karaganda, Kazakhstan, were also brought back and reburied in his former parish

---

[179] Apart from its influence on generations of students, laity, and clergy, which together formed the new generation of church elites, UCU incorporated a series of institutes specialized in the most important aspects of the religious sphere: the Institute for Church History, the Institute of Canon Law, the Catechetical-Pedagogical Institute, the Institute of Marriage and Family, the Institute of Theological Terminology and Translation, and the Institute for Liturgical Studies for the standardization of rite.

[180] The reburial of Cardinal Slipyi in L'viv preceded a similar reburial in Romania, that of Inocentiu Micu Klein, the Romanian Greek Catholic bishop, whose remains were transported from Rome to Blaj in 1997 (Naumescu 2004; Verdery 1999: 55–93).

in the village of Riasna-Ruska, close to Riasne-1. The case of Zarytskyi is interesting because it shows that the transport of bodies was more than mere political manoeuvring (Verdery 1999). Similar to the procedure in other cases, the remains were located by Zarytskyi's former parishioners, who also took the trouble to bring them back, in a closing of a symbolic circle of collective memory. Zarytskyi had been taken away from his community by the Soviets but was repatriated by the community of its own initiative.[181] In chapter 7 I further discuss symbolic reappropriations of distant spaces, this time through the mobilization of religious symbols for the eastward expansion of the UGCC.[182]

Another case, important because of its apparent failure, is the journey of the probable remains of Hryhoryi Lakota (1883–1950), the auxiliary bishop of Przemyśl, Poland, who died in Siberia, near Vorkuta. The bishop's body was brought to the Church of the Nativity in Sykhiv in 2001 for the occasion of the pope's visit to Ukraine and the celebration he was to lead in Sykhiv. It was escorted by the parish priest, Father Orest Fredina, and Jaroslav Shyiko, a parishioner whose wife was a relative of the late bishop's. The two had recovered the body from Abez, near Vorkuta, and, convinced of their successful find, expected the pope to acknowledge the martyr's presence in their church. However, they could provide no evidence that the remains were Lakota's. The recognition of Lakota's relics was in hiatus in 2004 because, according to Father Roman Terehovsky, who was in charge of the recovery of martyrs' relics for the UGCC, the remains were still held by the Nativity church and had not been handed over to the church authority (Derdziak 2002). As long as the commission could not determine the authenticity of the remains brought from Siberia, the Nativity parish could not publicize them and thus benefit from their presence. The remains of the bishop were to lie in the chapel of the Nativity church until ownership became clear.

The remains of Bishop Josaphat Kotsylovskyi (1876–1947), a Basilian monk, the main bishop of Przemyśl, and a colleague of Hryhoryi Lakota's, who died in a camp near Kyiv, were also kept away from public devotion. In 2004 they were located in the Annunciation Church in Stryi, on the property of Father Kavatsiv, the self-proclaimed but officially unrecognized bishop of

---

[181] Filmed interview with Kateryna Tytych, Riasne-Ruska, 24 January 2004.

[182] This is illustrated by the symbolically reversed journey of Father Zarytskyi from L'viv to Karaganda through the creation of a *lieux de memoire*. A monument to the new 'saint' was erected in the village of Dolinka, Karaganda, in Kazakhstan, where Zarytskyi died in the prison hospital on 30 October 1963. A chapel dedicated to him was opened in 2001 at the Church of the Protection of the Mother of God in Karaganda (RISU News, 02 March 2006).

the Greek Catholic Church. Kavatsiv's ownership of one of the new 'saints' of the church increased his spiritual authority and legitimacy.

Contemporary devotion to the new Greek Catholic 'saints' is a continuation of the underground devotion once dedicated to these celebrated figures of the martyr church. In the preceding examples, those relocating the bodies were able to circumvent church authority and the standardization of the martyrs' cult. The most popular unofficial saints during the socialist period were Metropolitan Sheptytskyi and Bishop Mykola Charnetskyi (1884–1959). Charnetskyi, a Redemptorist monk, returned to western Ukraine after spending eleven years in prison and remained active in the church for another three years, until his death. During those last years he ordained several underground priests and allowed reunited priests to return from Orthodoxy to Greek Catholicism, a move that surreptitiously brought hundreds of ostensibly Orthodox priests back to the Greek Catholic Church.[183]

In the early 1960s Charnetskyi's remains were brought from Kulparkivskii to Lychakivskyi Cemetery in L'viv. In both places his grave was a site of intense devotional activity. People believed that the earth from his grave had miraculous powers, and they visited the tomb for relief from health problems.[184] The popular cult surrounding the saint, as he was known, disturbed authorities, who tried unsuccessfully to stop the pilgrimages. On the occasion of the papal visit to Ukraine in June 2001, Bishop Charnetskyi was one of twenty-seven Greek Catholics beatified by the pope. In order to be able to contain and standardize the popular cult of the new 'martyr of faith', the church hierarchy decided to move his remains to St Josaphat's Church in L'viv on 4 July 2002. Since then, the relics of the 'Blessed Mykola Charnetskyi' have sometimes been displayed for the veneration of pilgrims, and the church itself has become a site of devotion.[185]

The locations of a saint's grave and that saint's site of devotion rarely match as they do in the case of Charnetskyi. Even with the making of the sanctuary and the formal devotion to Charnetskyi, alternative cults dedicated to him survive, escaping church authority. The image of the bishop has travelled throughout western Ukraine to various sites of popular religiosity, such as the apparition site in Lishnia. There, Charnetskyi appeared to vision-

[183] According to Father Vasyl Voronovsky, Charnetskyi oversaw the return of 180 to 300 priests who had agreed to become Orthodox priests in 1946 and repented later (ICH, 3 January 1999).

[184] Father Ihor Tsar, *Chiudesni podarunky vid Mytropolyta Andreia* [Miraculous gift from Metropolitan Andrew], L'viv, 1998, quoted in Hurkina 2002.

[185] RISU News, 'Remains of Blessed Charnetskyi Transferred to Church', 5 July 2002, and 'Relics of Greek Catholic Martyr Venerated in L'viv', 4 April 2006.

aries and pilgrims together with the Mother of God, and these apparitions opened the possibility for the reappropriation of the saint by ordinary people. The church could not control devotion to the saint because it could not prevent the use of the symbol by its direct contestant, the traditionalist movement. The relation between the underground and the postsocialist community was straightforward in this case: Charnetskyi's former house in L'viv, an emblematic nucleus of the underground church, hosted the small community of traditionalist Basilian sisters that had separated from the Basilian order and reappeared as the convent of the traditionalist group led by Father Kovpak.

4.4 Conclusion

The institutionalization processes I have presented go beyond the simple restoration of religious structures to the Greek Catholic community as described in chapters 2 and 3. One of the most important endeavours of the re-established church was to begin the recovery of its underground memory – the standardization of collective memory that created new 'saints' as martyrs of the church. This accompanied the reconstruction of the church hierarchy alongside 'purification' of the Greek Catholic rite and the redefinition of church tradition. Following the spectacular revival of the church, it began to distance itself from its underground past while recovering memories of the underground. Various groups within the church competed to valorize this memory in a particular manner. The underground heroes became revered symbols, and their tragic stories became constituent of the social memory of the Greek Catholic Church. At the same time, survivors' understanding of the rite was revoked and underground practices were abandoned.

Recollections of religious events from the underground church, emotionally charged and extremely detailed, remind one of the differentiation between episodic and semantic memory in Whitehouse's model of the modes of religiosity. In this sense the model may explain how a type of ritual transmission favours a particular social structure, a specific community of practice. With the traditional parish community destroyed by Soviet policies, a new kind of relationship developed between clergy and believers, out of which emerged new forms of collective practice. Restrictions placed on religious activities triggered a proliferation of imagistic practices, which increased believers' motivation and fortified the community of practice. Considering Catholic communities in other parts of the world (Stirrat 1992), one can suggest that when facing suppression and church disintegration, religious communities turn towards imagistic religiosity, cultivating a closer relationship to the divine.

The Ukrainian experience of the underground favoured individualized, highly sensitive rituals making use of Catholic imagery and powerful symbolic rhetoric. These rituals, often improvised and tailored to specific needs, were practised occasionally by small, cohesive communities of family and trusted companions. When the institutional church resurfaced, it strove to replace this form of practice with a routinized, standardized rite, controlled by a centralized religious authority that promoted orthodox doctrine and tradition. Whereas the imagistic mode of religiosity was better suited as a successful engine of religious transmission under the Soviet regime, the situation has changed completely since the 1990s, when the UGCC reinforced the doctrinal mode.

Yet people had no difficulty mixing the two modes, either in the underground or afterwards. They tended to participate in all kinds of rituals, some more imagistic and others more doctrinal, both private and church related. Keeping the two modes separate by promoting a unified practice and doctrine was a concern of the religious elites that had emerged since the 1990s. More than a conflict between modernists and traditionalists, the case of Kovpak's traditionalists was about trying to keep the modes of religiosity separate. In such cases, conflicts result from the subjection of one of the two modes to the other through political manoeuvring. Thus, power and authority are variables neglected by the modes theory, which fails to read the historical and political context of the case.

The dilemma of East and West remains an essential challenge to the church. 'Easternizers' and 'Westernizers', 'Latinizers' and 'Orientalizers', 'modernists' and 'traditionalists' are all labels that have changed over time, being applied at different moments to different groups within the Greek Catholic Church. Depending on historical context, such markers were used in different associations, and their political meaning changed frequently. The actual dynamic behind these trends corresponds to distinct modes of authority available in Greek Catholicism and the question of who defines the orthodoxy of the religious tradition.

Religious authority in the UGCC is disputed at the centre as well as at the margins of the church. The Greek Catholic hierarchy and monastic orders are competing actors, and the case of the traditionalists is part of this structural dynamic. The Lefebvrist movement offered Kovpak the legitimating doctrine and the basis for founding a structure parallel to the one from which he had splintered off. The rebellious priest's effort to de-localize the conflict by connecting it to a transnational Catholic movement was successful and repositioned the struggle in a wider context. Through this move Kovpak made use of the model of authority specific to the Latin tradition, changing his status by switching from the authority of one (Greek) Catholic bishop (Husar) to a different (Lefebvrist) Catholic bishop (Fellay). He thus challenged the established Greek Catholic hierarchy, making use of the larger Catholic framework to which the Lefebvrists also belonged. The choice made by Kovpak's splinter group to use the 'western connection' contrasts with the choice of the Basilian splinter group that I analyse in chapter 6. This group established an independent monastery by making use of the eastern monastic tradition, which favours the establishment of autonomous monasteries independent of monastic orders but still within the church structure.

The underground experience was essential in the realization of Kovpak's project to form a traditionalist movement. Church hierarchs understated Kovpak's influence in their public addresses, but their extreme reaction to him – excommunication – showed the church's determination to undermine his popularity and get away with the re-actualized past. The community supporting Kovpak was bound by its common need to preserve and re-enact a mode of religiosity specific to the underground. Traditionalists' main task was to preserve the 'feeling' of the underground church, and Kovpak's supporters were linked by an emotional relationship stemming from their common experience of the underground.

For traditionalists, the high moral and spiritual standards set by the underground priests, from among whom appeared the new martyrs, constituted the criteria for a 'true church' similar to that in which Greek Catholics had fought and suffered for their faith. Traditionalists remained committed to preserving the model of Christian life that differentiated Greek Catholics from others, Orthodox or Catholic. More than a conflict between modernists and traditionalists, the case of Kovpak's traditionalists is about modes of religiosity coming into conflict. Traditionalists' move from away from nostalgic re-enactment of the underground experience and towards organized political activity attracted the attention of the church authorities, who imposed sanctions on their initiative. For Kovpak's supporters, traditionalism was a revival of the underground experience they missed and a reaction to changes that sent them from the centre of Greek Catholic revival to the periphery of the Greek Catholic Church.

Chapter 5
Religious Routine and the Continuity of a Religious Tradition

To complement the picture I have painted of religious life in an urban setting, Sykhiv, in this chapter I offer an overview of patterns of ordinary religious practice in rural western Ukraine, especially as I observed them in the village of Shchirets. I look at the characteristics that make the local religious tradition an original synthesis of eastern and western Christianity. The local religious tradition was the tie that initially bound together the churches belonging to the eastern Christian tradition in the 1990s. Since then several factors beyond the religious sphere have shaped the making of churches, and the churches themselves, through institutionalization, have created distinct orthodoxies that have led them to drift apart. Yet in spite of institutional pressures, people have managed to preserve the unifying aspects of local practice.

Routine religious practices in Shchirets illustrate the contrast between these and the unconventional, imagistic practices presented in the following two chapters. The particularities of rural religious life and the forms of ritual transmission displayed in Shchirets favour a doctrinal mode of religiosity, in contrast to the imagistic mode described later for the Kolodiivka monastery and for apparition sites.

Of my two major themes in this book, mechanisms of reproduction and mechanisms of change in religious tradition, I concentrate in this chapter on the former – on patterns of religious expression preserved in local practice. I look at ritual transmission, types of rituals, frequency of repetition, frequency of individual participation, spaces of practice, language, and the actors involved. My intent is to grasp differences between rural and urban practices in ritual form and content and their variations over time.

During the socialist period, rural space remained the main site of religious practice. Rural people maintained a certain continuity of religious practice expressed as part of traditional rituals and so-called traditional culture, which continued to be encouraged and ideologized by the socialist state (Kligman 1988). The 'reunited' parishes in western Ukraine were the main preservers of the local religious tradition in that region. There, most churches remained open, and reunited priests could continue performing their usual rite undisturbed. With religious institutions repressed under the Soviet regime, religion could best survive through popular religiosity. Even in villages where churches were closed and public religious practices suppressed, religion was preserved through different mnemonic devices – bodily practices and places of memory (Naumescu 2004). Rural and urban practices, I found, did display strong similarities, because rural religiosity extended into the city suburbs. I expected confessional segregation to be a greater source of conflict in the village than the city, because of the closer social contact in the rural community. However, just enough church buildings were available in Shchirets not to provoke an insoluble conflict.[186]

What Shchirets adds to the picture of western Ukrainian religious life is the continuity of religious practice during socialism, secured by the maintenance of the two churches that remained open in the village, the Roman Catholic and the Orthodox, but also by the lack of local underground activity. Because of its proximity to the city, Shchirets enjoyed considerable religious mobility, and residents regularly attended churches in the city in addition to participating in village religious life. Only a few villagers maintained a consistent interest in alternative devotional sites. I spent enough time with these people to be able to follow their religious devotion beyond the village and to elaborate on the idea of a rhythm of religious life and alternation between two modes of religiosity, the imagistic and the doctrinal.

5.1 Religious Practice in Village Life

The village of Shchirets lies south of L'viv, in a nearby *raion*. It officially numbered 5,500 inhabitants and 1,200 households in the 2001 census, but in reality far fewer people live there, because many have left the village to work in Spain, Italy, Poland, and Russia. The majority of the inhabitants are Ukrainians, with just a few mixed Polish-Ukrainian families. The village was once a typical small Galician town with an ethnically mixed population, but the multiculturalism once representative of historical Galicia (Himka 1998) was obliterated during the two world wars. It reappeared in a weaker form only after the 1990s with the emergence of different churches, under the name 'multiconfessionalism'.

---

186 Had there been one church building instead of three, the religious situation would have looked different, as was the case in the nearby village of Serditsia, where the two congregations, Orthodox and Greek Catholic, fought over one church.

At the turn of the twentieth century the town's population was composed of Catholics (Poles and Ukrainians) and Jews in almost equal numbers, and each group had its own place of worship, cemetery, and school.[187] The synagogue and Jewish school in the town centre were destroyed during World War II, and the only trace is the old Jewish cemetery, two kilometres from the centre, now completely run down and overtaken by a thick forest.[188] The majority of Ukrainians lived in Ostryv and Lany, two adjacent villages to the north and south of the town.

Plate 15. The abandoned Jewish cemetery in Shchirets, 2004.

The tragic end of such towns, in which multi-ethnic coexistence was actually possible (Himka 2005), came when the fighting and ethnic cleansing of two world wars left few survivors.[189] Poles who survived the war were displaced

[187] The earliest known Jewish community dates to the seventeenth century. At the turn of the twentieth century there were 1,607 Jews and 1,205 Catholics living in Shchirets (Pustomytivschyna 2003). Other figures are 835 Jews out of a population of 1,754 in 1880; 1,324 Jews of a population of 1,730 in 1900; and 1,264 Jews out of a population of 1,614 in 1910. There were 2,000 Jews in 1912, but by January 1939 the number had dwindled to 890. There are no Jews left in Shchirets today.

[188] The approximate size of the cemetery is three hectares, and there are hundreds of tombstones, a few of them dating back to 1836. The last known Hasidic burial was in 1941.

[189] The First World War caused a massive decrease in population, which continued between 1918 and 1945, when the area came under the successive occupations of Polish (1918), Russian (from 1939), German (from 1941), and again Russian (1944) administrations.

to socialist Poland after 1945 in a massive exchange of population.[190] In return, Ukrainians from south-eastern Poland were resettled into now deserted villages (*pereselentsi*) of Soviet western Ukraine. In just a few years the multi-ethnic and multi-religious composition of the village disappeared, destroying what might have emerged after the war as a 'community of memory' (Irwin-Zarecka 1994). Today there is no collective process of 'memory recovery' in Shchirets apart from that of remembering the Ukrainian past. This is actively pursued by a few nationalist Ukrainians who commemorate Ukrainian partisans in the village.

Plate 16. The 'church on the hill', dating from 1557 and disputed by Orthodox Christians and Greek Catholics in the early 1990s. Shchirets, 2004.

At the beginning of the Soviet period Shchirets had three churches. One, erected in 1557 on a small hill overlooking the village, was Shchirets's oldest stone building. In the eighteenth century, when Shchirets was controlled by Polish nobility, a Roman Catholic *kosciol*, St Stanislaw's, had been built in the town. A third church went up between Shchirets and the nearby village of Ostryv in the 1860s. Both this church, referred to as the

[190] The Ukrainian and Polish populations were killed by each other's militias, and the entire Jewish population was deported to the concentration camp in Belzec in 1942.

'church in the centre' (*tserkva v tsentryi*), and the one on the hill were Greek Catholic parish churches until 1946.

Under the Soviet regime, each of the three churches in Shchirets had its own fate. The church on the hill, called the Church of the Nativity of the Blessed Mother of God, accepted Orthodox reunion and continued operating through a regular succession of priests throughout the Soviet era. The church in the centre, the Church of the Blessed Trinity, functioned for a time but was closed in the late 1950s. During the re-registration of parishes and priests, part of a broader campaign against religion, churches were barred from functioning as parish churches and eventually were closed.[191] St Stanislaw's, on the other hand, was among the few Roman Catholic churches in the region that remained open during the Soviet period and into the 1990s.

The parishioners of the Nativity church were residents of Pisky, Lany, and Zahorodkyi, villages that had no churches of their own and for which the Nativity church was their parish. After 1946, most people from these villages continued to attend the church on the hill, which was considered 'their' church and where they were familiar with the priest. When the Blessed Trinity church closed its doors, villagers from Ostryv and Shchirets who had attended it moved to the Nativity church. Some villagers refused to follow the conventional shift to Orthodoxy. The reasons for their decisions, as well as their choice of practice, differed from case to case. It was rare for someone to stick to one option; instead, people combined them, visiting different churches in the village and in L'viv.

A few Greek Catholic families from Ostryv decided not to attend the Orthodox Nativity church because, as they put it, 'We are Catholics, we go to the Catholic church'. As the Roman Catholic church in the village remained open, this family and others from Shchirets went to services there. They remembered how attending the church meant risk of harassment, persecution, and even arrest by local authorities. A family member named Oxana told me: 'People could go to *kosciol* [in Shchirets], but they were always being watched: who comes to church, why . . . they were persecuted. And many people who wanted to come to church couldn't take the risk to attend.'

In spite of their different religious traditions, the two Catholic churches in western Ukraine share a basic common ground, owing to both historical and recent circumstances. In Shchirets, Greek Catholics who chose to attend the Roman Catholic church during Soviet times considered their Catholic identity more important than the eastern tradition they held in

---

[191] It was unusual to have two Orthodox churches open in the same village, and when this did occur, one of the first measures taken by local authorities was to close down one church, if not both.

common with Orthodox Christians. Their choice was also political, determined by anti-Soviet attitudes. Such connections strengthened the links between the two communities and brought Greek Catholics' religious practices even closer to the Latin tradition.

There appear to have been no cases of Greek Catholics dissembling about their identity in Shchirets or of worshippers and priests conducting 'illegal' services there. The families I interviewed, as well as others who had remained Greek Catholic and thus had contacts in the underground church, mentioned no underground activity.[192] Their option was to attend church in L'viv. The anonymity of the city provided enough space to choose between either one of the former Greek Catholic, now nominally Orthodox, churches in the city or services at the Roman Catholic cathedral or St Anton's Church.[193] One might tour the churches of the city or perhaps choose one church for confession and another for a particular devotion or blessing obtainable only there. Some families from Shchirets went to L'viv for weddings or to have their children baptized by an underground priest, who was often an old acquaintance or recommended by someone trusted. These visits were rare and were saved for special occasions: baptism, marriage, and confession, all of which stood as exceptional moments in the religious lives of these villagers. The nostalgia felt for the underground church, so important to splinter groups such as the traditionalists described in chapter 4, was nourished by such feelings towards the past.

The only remarkable public initiative from the Soviet period that later remained in the collective memory of the village was the preservation of the church in the centre, Blessed Trinity. The building had been closed for years when its roof collapsed in 1980. The director of the village school and some of the local intelligentsia thought about ways to save it and, inspired by a solution found in other places, began to transform the church into a museum of atheism (*muzei ateisma*).[194] With this move they could obtain local party approval and start repairing the building legally. The interior of the church was preserved as such, but by adding anti-religious slogans and ideological texts, villagers created the appearance of an educational space for young people. The edifice was thus preserved, to be reopened in 1990 as a Greek Catholic church. Indeed, the first signs of religious revival in the village

[192] There is no mention of any activity by underground Greek Catholic priests in Shchirets in the oral history archive of the Institute for Church History.

[193] As I mentioned in chapter 3, the Orthodox Church of the Transfiguration (Preobrazhenska) was the main symbol of continuing underground activity, and people from the countryside usually chose to visit it while in L'viv.

[194] This was a frequent practice in the early Soviet years, when church buildings were transformed into museums or anti-religious centres (Conquest 2002: 209), but it was uncommon in the 1980s.

were connected to the reopening of Blessed Trinity in 1990. The first priest to celebrate mass in it was a retired Orthodox priest, Father Stepan Hrynchkiv, a formerly reunited priest who returned to Greek Catholicism and now followed the villagers' wish to reopen the church as it had once been.

The official priest of the village, Ivan Mykytyn, who served in the church on the hill, remained Orthodox until 1991, when he sided with the Ukrainian Autocephalous Orthodox Church, which appeared to be the strongest candidate against Greek Catholicism and Russian Orthodoxy. Neither change in their priests' allegiances had much effect on the residents of Shchirets, who, having both churches open, relocated to the more convenient of the two, the church in the centre. The village elites, including local apparatchiks and the heads of the cooperative and the factories in Shchirets, all began to attend the Greek Catholic Blessed Trinity church soon after its reopening. Their relocation followed a wave of political changes that were resoundingly confirmed with the independence of Ukraine in 1991. Upon seeing former socialist leaders rediscover themselves as devout believers, however, the first of many villagers decided to return to the Church of the Nativity on the hill. Their reaction was a statement against the mixing of politics and religion, the dangerous combination of which was disapproved of by people in both Shchirets and Sykhiv.

Over the years, other people returned to the church on the hill, but this had more to do with the charismatic young priest who came to the village in 1992. Father Andriy Aftanas, from the UAOC, came to replace Father Ivan. He entered a church that was caught in a dispute putatively about confessional identity but really having to do with property rights. Greek Catholics from nearby villages who had once attended the church on the hill wanted to obtain it for their own use. In theory, people from Shchirets could not claim a second church in the same village, and the inter-confessional committee that was at the time working in the oblast was in charge of supervising this agreement. Nevertheless, Greek Catholics provoked an argument over the actual ownership of the church, claiming that the parcel of land on which it stood was part of another village, Pisky. The community in Pisky was therefore entitled to the church, and being majority Greek Catholic, they tried to convince the priest to change affiliation. The conflict culminated in the sequestration of the Orthodox priest in his house. Being new to the village, he had little support from his own parishioners. Only a small group, composed of people from the nearby villages who considered Ukrainian Orthodoxy to be just as patriotic as Greek Catholicism, were satisfied with the new priest and supported him. The conflict continued until 1995, when the local administration of the Pustomyty *raion,* to which Shchirets belonged, put an end to the issue by deciding to give one church building to each religious community in Shchirets and authorizing the construction of a church for the Greek Catholic community in Pisky – an initiative that arose from the oblast administration in L'viv. Thus Shchirets became truly multiconfessional, with coexisting Orthodox, Greek Catholic, and Roman Catholic communities.

While the dispute between Orthodox Christians and Greek Catholics, fuelled by local interests, continued in a nationalistic tone, Roman Catholics from the village stayed aside. The Church of St Stanislaw was never closed during Soviet times, although it had no permanent parish priest until the 1990s. Instead, priests from L'viv came regularly to hold religious services, and since the church in Shchirets was the only other Catholic church open in the region (where the majority of larger villages had once housed large Polish communities), all the Catholics from nearby villages gathered there. People came to Shchirets from Semenivka, Debianka, and Serdytsia for the Sunday liturgy. There were Poles and Ukrainians, Roman and Greek Catholic villagers who could speak Polish or who, even if they spoke Ukrainian, had learnt the mass and hymns in Polish by heart. From 1990 onwards, in all other villages churches were reopened or, when there was no church, chapels built (as in Serdytsia), and so these families no longer came to Shchirets. Instead, the parish priest from Shchirets visited the other villages. The young priest (*ksionts*, the Polish word for priest, used in western Ukraine for Roman Catholic priests), Father Tadeusz, was in charge of five villages in the region: Shchirets, Navaria, Semenivka, Debianka, and Serdytsia. His parishes were part of Zolochiv deanery, which included thirteen more parishes and was one of the eleven deaneries belonging to the archdiocese of L'viv. Father Tadeusz was a diocesan priest depending directly on his bishop in L'viv. For practical reasons he lived in Semenivka, five kilometres from Shchirets, but he made regularly scheduled weekly visits to each of his parishes.[195]

Most of his parishioners in 2004, around 200 people in Shchirets, were mixed Ukrainians and Poles (*pomishani liudy*), members of the second generation of mixed families, with one Polish grandparent. In one family, for example, the grandmother attended the *kosciol;* the father, the Orthodox church on the hill; and the mother and child, the Greek Catholic church in the centre – a situation not unusual. It was still common in mixed families for a daughter to take on the confession of the mother, and a son, that of the father. Such diversity was generally accepted and could best be observed during religious holidays (*sviata*) that were celebrated at different times because of discrepancies between religious calendars. These holidays were

[195] Tadeusz came to Shchirets in 2001 and first lived in a rented house, later moving to Semenivka when one of his parishioners donated her house to the church.

often celebrated twice by the same family, with the entire family attending each church where the particular holiday or special ceremony was held.

The regulars of the Roman Catholic parish were old people who attended services throughout the week. They were mostly Ukrainians who frequented the church because it provided the only weekday religious services, and it also allowed them to carry out various personal devotions. Although the liturgical language of the parish community was Polish, immediately after the church service people began speaking Ukrainian. Many of them, especially the young, spoke no Polish at all. In Shchirets, as in the new Catholic parishes like the one in Sykhiv, youngsters who did not know Polish were starting to learn the language, first through liturgical practice and then more consistently through courses organized by the parish.

For the newer members of the parish, rediscovered Poles, the language was more than the liturgical idiom; it was a strong identification with the west and their entry to western Europe.[196] Even if most parishioners' native language was Ukrainian, these people refused to attend masses in Ukrainian when they were introduced by the priest. The Roman Catholic Church in Ukraine tried to introduce Ukrainian as the liturgical language as part of its project of nationalizing the church, but people refused to follow. In both Sykhiv and Shchirets, the Roman Catholic priests stopped conducting services in Ukrainian after an initial attempt to introduce them, when parishioners refused to come. The 'Ukrainization' of the Roman Catholic Church was not viewed with favour by Greek Catholic priests, to whom it looked like direct competition for parishioners.

In spite of the significant Ukrainian presence, the association between the Catholic and Polish identities was strongly emphasized in the village (and the region). Throughout the history of Galicia, ethnic identity had been lodged as a means of maintaining a distance between Roman and Greek Catholicism, a distinction that fails today, with so few Poles left. The enduring association between Polish identity and Roman Catholicism was troubling for the Roman Catholic village priest, Father Tadeusz, as well. He said:

> In our church, in the *kosciol,* it is not written: 'Polish Roman Catholic Church', just 'Roman Catholic Church' . . . and this means that anybody can come here: Russians also, anybody who thinks it fits his spiritual needs. It is true that in the church we pray in Polish, but we do so because people asked us to have the liturgy in Polish . . . In other places, where people do not know Polish, the entire liturgy is in Ukrainian . . . following our [liturgical] tradition but in Ukrainian.

[196] In western Ukraine, Polish is a western European language that one can easily learn, and it has enjoyed high status for historical as well as practical reasons related to post-1990 work migration.

Himself an exception among Roman Catholic priests in western Ukraine, who usually were missionaries from Poland, Father Tadeusz came from a mixed family from the region. He had lived in Soviet Ukraine and went to study theology in Lublin, Poland, only after 1990, returning to Ukraine as a Catholic priest. For those who kept Poland as a model, Tadeusz was 'too Ukrainian, not a real Pole, but a Ukrainian one', as one of his parishioners put it. His origin as well as the fact that his predecessor had been a 'real Pole' from Poland counted against him in the eyes of his parishioners.[197]

The liturgical service at St Stanislaw's was based on the standard Latin mass celebrated in the Catholic Church, with Polish influence visible mostly in the choice of songs. The calls and responses and songs were sung by youths belonging to a catechetical group run by the priest. The rest of the parishioners had little input into the performance. The youngsters used an electronic organ as accompaniment, an improvement the community in Shchirets found objectionable. The local form of Catholicism took expression in the pre-liturgical prayer of the rosary, and during the week, while alone with the priest, the old women sang their own songs and recited the prayers as they knew them. There was little excitement in parish life, but people found spiritual inspiration in pilgrimages inside and outside Ukraine. Young people in particular were attracted by these exciting excursions and by trips to large Catholic youth meetings. These sorts of events maintained youth motivation and involvement in the parish at levels higher than those found elsewhere in the village.[198]

Unlike the distinguishing of Roman Catholics in Shchirets from everyone else, making distinctions between Orthodox and Greek Catholic churches on ethnic, linguistic, or liturgical bases is problematic. After the property conflict over the church on the hill was resolved, the Greek Catholic–Orthodox dispute evaporated, and only a few cases of individual 'shifting' occurred in the following years. The church in the centre, Blessed Trinity, remained the Greek Catholic parish for Shchirets and Ostryv. The church on the hill, the Church of the Nativity, remained the Autocephalous

---

[197] Because he was not from Poland, Tadeusz did not have the same contacts and support as other Polish missionaries in Ukraine, who received substantial support from their home dioceses. The previous priest had been Polish and from Poland, and people appreciated him very much. Father Tadeusz was young and new in the parish, so in conversations with parishioners he was always compared with the former priest, usually to his disadvantage.

[198] In Poland, parish youths go to *kalvaria Patslavska*, a big Catholic youth meeting held every year in August, 25 kilometres from Przemyśl. The group organized from the cathedral in L'viv walked from L'viv to the pilgrimage place, 25–30 kilometres per day with backpacks and sleeping bags. In Ukraine there is a similar youth meeting at Ivano-Frankivsk, Halych, and at other, smaller pilgrimage sites.

Orthodox Church and provided services for three villages, Shchirets, Lany, and Pisky.

The Greek Catholic and Orthodox priests in the village in 2004 had little contact with each other, but they shared much in common from the past. Neither of them was from Shchirets, both having arrived in the area only after 1990 in order to succeed retiring priests. At the time of these priests' arrival, both parishes already displayed unique confessional identities that had been preserved despite outside pressure. Andriy Aftanas was made a priest in 1990 by the Orthodox Church, which at that time still belonged to the Moscow Patriarchate. His first parish was in Lutsk, Volynia. Father Andriy came to L'viv in 1992, where he met Dimitriy Yarema, one of the initiators of the autocephaly movement, and switched to the UOAC.[199] He arrived in Shchirets in 1992 to replace the old Orthodox priest, who had already opted for autocephaly. Although Father Andriy's parish in Shchirets was part of the Pustomyty deanery, each of its priests had a large degree of independence from the church structure. The organization of the UOAC in a relatively loose and unhierarchical structure, respecting the origins of the church as a grassroots movement that later developed into a community of faith, was one of the practical reasons for its earlier success.

The other priest, Bohdan Kohut, had followed the same course up until 1990, when he joined the Ukrainian Greek Catholic Church instead of the UAOC. He came to Shchirets in 1996 to replace Father Stepan, the retired priest who had opened the church in 1990. Thus there were two western Ukrainian priests in the village who had graduated at different times from the same theological seminary in Leningrad (St Petersburg), had become Orthodox priests within the Ukrainian Orthodox Church under Moscow jurisdiction, and later reconsidered their options following 'the changes'.

Father Stepan, on the other hand, was a former reunited Greek Catholic priest who had served as Orthodox priest during Soviet times and returned to Greek Catholicism with the revival of that church. He seized the opportunity to return to the parish in 1990, and thanks to his high status among the villagers, he became their first Greek Catholic parish priest. He was considered a 'true priest' (*spravedvyi sviashchennyk*), raised in the Galician religious tradition. Yet he was also old-fashioned, holding to strict rules regarding fasting, confession, and behaviour, which made parishioners appreciate his character but caused some to move back to the Orthodox

---

[199] Volodymyr Yarema was an Orthodox priest who became bishop and later metropolitan of the UOAC when the autocephaly movement began to enjoy strong popular support. He was also parish priest in Shchirets between 1950 and 1953.

church.[200] When he died in 1996 and was replaced by Father Bohdan, the new priest moved into an established parish that still gathered the largest number of villagers. He benefited from the switch to Greek Catholicism by gaining access to the institutional networks provided by the Roman Catholic Church and completed his religious education with Catholic theological studies in Lublin. His two sons studied theology in Lublin and L'viv, preparing to take over the parish from their father.

In western Ukraine, priesthood is a family business, and parishes often remain in the family, passed down from generation to generation. Extended family networks and family pasts still open doors at seminary and can help priests to find good parishes after graduation. Particularly in the early 1990s, people say, the best reference for entering the seminary was to come from a family of Greek Catholic priests whose members were active in the underground. In 2004 the competition was heavier, because the number of available parishes was decreasing, particularly in western Ukraine, and few young married priests would agree to start a 'mission' in central or eastern Ukraine or farther into Siberia or Central Asia. Therefore, preparations for taking over a parish were made well in advance, not least by cultivating helpful contacts.[201]

Father Bohdan's position was also strategic from the point of view of the institutional structure: he was dean of the Shchirets deanery. In a deanery like his, priests and their families keep in close contact, visiting each other, substituting for one another when needed, and sometimes developing kin relations. They tend to form an interrelated, cohesive social group that pursues and defends its common interests vis-à-vis church authority. Group solidarity at this level was maintained during socialist times and became an important factor in the revival when decisions regarding which church worshippers should follow were made at the level of the deanery as a whole and were respected by the priests of the deanery.

Beyond their confessional affiliations, village priests maintain high social status, and their expertise in more than just spiritual problems is respected. The village priest is a religious expert with authority over spiritual problems (*dukhovna khvoroba*), but in postsocialist times of material and symbolic reconstruction, villagers greatly appreciate his managerial capabilities. The presence of an active priest is a mobilizing factor for the village community. The local parish as well as the church hierarchy value having a strong leader to oversee construction, renovation, and fundraising for the

[200] Villagers also said that he was too harsh and reproachful, and several people left because they could not get along with him.

[201] Father Andriy, too, was preparing his successor, Myron, a student in the Orthodox theological academy whom he supported.

village church. Pastoral care, particularly of children both at church and in school, and constant solicitude towards villagers' requests are highly esteemed. People seek out the priest when a child is ill, after unsuccessful visits to doctors or witches, when a husband is drinking too much, or before leaving to work abroad. If a priest pays attention to his parishioners, they remain in his church, whereas his neglect or carelessness towards them estranges them. These sorts of dynamics were well illustrated in the case of Shchirets, where, of the two priests, Orthodox and Greek Catholic, the former slowly won out over the latter, with more people from Shchirets asking for his services or joining his parish. Both priests were well-off in comparison with the average economic situation of the villagers, but their wealth provoked little anti-religious sentiment.[202] Instead, people criticized the Greek Catholic priest for of his involvement in politics, his support for the local mayor, his relations with the former socialist village elites, and the politically charged content of his preaching. They respected the Orthodox priest for being a good speaker, an intellectual, and a good manager at the same time. Yet few people remained attached to only one priest while completely ignoring the other.

The household survey I conducted revealed that almost all villagers were part of at least one religious community in the village or circulated between more than one, maintaining an adequate level of religious practice. Levels of participation in religious life of the village varied, but there was a general awareness of the 'religious routine' – that is, religious practices that were embedded in the community, producing a distinctive rhythm. Most villagers attended to the religious routine, regardless of the religious affiliation they declared.

Two small groups that had recently appeared in the village evaded the routine: Pentecostals and Jehovah's Witnesses. Even though both religious movements had almost a century-long presence in Ukraine, they were usually present in cities rather than villages. Designated *Baptisty,* a general term for the religious 'other', they were perceived as outsiders by the villagers and consequently were left aside during village rituals. Their presence challenged the local religious tradition and the certainty of the religious routine by questioning certain rituals, such as those surrounding burials in the case of Jehovah's Witnesses, and opposing common practice.

Pentecostals were too few to organize themselves in Shchirets and therefore attended Sunday services regularly in L'viv. Apart from a few older women, one family stood out as true Pentecostals among the villagers. The husband and wife had both been baptised and raised Orthodox and had

---

[202] This is unlike the situation in neighbouring Poland, where there is a strong anti-clerical movement (Buzalka 2007).

married in an Orthodox church in L'viv. However, while working in the city they came across Pentecostals who were work colleagues and converted in 1982. During the socialist period they had baptised their first two sons Orthodox, but their daughter, born after 1990, was not baptised that way. Their children were active in the Pentecostal church in L'viv. The older son also organized a home prayer group in a nearby town, a regional centre. The group consisted of eight to ten young people, among whom was a Greek Catholic who favoured their style of charismatic prayer. To accommodate her in the group they concentrated on things they had in common and avoided the differences, such as the Greek Catholic devotion to icons. This family's religious life was not connected to religious institutions in the village, and they were excluded from collective rituals and from 'extraordinary' practices, events that happened infrequently.

The other non-traditional group in Shchirets was the Jehovah's Witnesses, whom the priests particularly opposed. They were a small group gathered around one family that organized and hosted their activities. Members of this group were active in the village and maintained affable relationships with their neighbours. Several villagers read the Jehovah's Witnesses' literature, and some had lengthy discussions with the missionaries, in spite of these people's being the main targets of the priests' 'anti-sectarian' discourses. Villagers found Jehovah's Witnesses to be good in that 'they don't go against God, but pray to him and preach his word to others,' a frequent statement among both Greek Catholic and Orthodox residents. Prayer and the expression of one's religiosity were highly valued and together constituted a good reason for accepting another religious group. As several villagers put it: 'Sects also pray; they do not do any harm!'

5.2 The Routine of Religious Practice: Ordinary and Extraordinary Rituals

The religious routine of Shchirets is based on the performance of ordinary rituals. These are regular, expected rituals that take place in predetermined spaces and at preset times. These standard rituals form the core of mainstream practice and lend a particular rhythm to community life. Ordinary rituals frame the modalities through which religiosity may be expressed. The rough counterpart of these ordinary rituals is extraordinary rituals, which are religious events that develop according to a different set of social dynamics. Most of this section deals with the former kind of ritual, but at the end I discuss two rituals belonging to the latter category. Both categories tend towards the doctrinal mode of religiosity that forms the core of mainstream, standardized ritual practice.

Public religious celebrations do not take place every day in Shchirets; only individual religious practice occurs on a daily basis. Individual devotion is by default separated from church structures and standardized practice, as it was during the Soviet period. Nevertheless, individual devotion has its own forms of repetition, often based on religious structures parallel to those of the church. Daily prayer is a frequent practice among villagers, with ever more old and young people praying regularly. This practice has been preserved through religious education in the family. It consists of morning and evening prayers, two short prayers that can be individually chosen from among the usual prayers or read from a prayer book. Some people do not use a verbal form of prayer, standardized or otherwise, but still perform prayer by undertaking a ritual act such as drinking holy water every morning before breakfast. Another common act used primarily by older people is making the sign of the cross before or after meals.

The boom of religious activity following the collapse of the Soviet regime was accompanied by an impressive production of and trade in religious objects. Under the old regime the trade and, at times, possession of icons, Bibles, prayer books, and figurines were forbidden, but they flourished after 1990. Houses in the village are often full of such objects, in addition to posters, plastic water-filled figurines, miraculous medals, blessed flowers, holy water, and *proskury*.[203] One rarely sees old icons, however. The type of devotion represented by each religious object has become extremely specialized. There are prayers and small icons (*obrazochky*) for everything one might experience: health, travel, family, children, household, money, and much more. This huge variety of devotions has no confessional orientation, although some can trace individual origins back to a Latin devotion, a Greek Catholic martyr, or an ecumenical saint such as St Nicholas. Such devotional objects are extremely popular, often being recommended by the devout and the clergy, and there are many occasions to purchase them. Some devotions require attention for a longer time in order to fulfil their purpose, whereas others are used only when one is in immediate need. But all such objects demand an individual form of devotion at home, church, or some other religious site.[204]

---

[203] *Proskury* are pieces of bread that have been blessed during the pre-liturgical ritual of preparation (*proscomedia*). They are used like holy water for purposes such as alleviating health problems. The cure requires one to take *proskury* together with holy water in the morning and evening.

[204] A look into the lives of such religious objects and the use of specialized devotions to fit particular requests underscores the idea that forms of religiosity are becoming more individualized.

Churches, schools, and religious groups provide a good deal of religious literature, which in the hands of villagers loses its intended confessional identity. Villagers read the Orthodox periodical that Father Andriy, its editor, sells in the Nativity church. They also read the well-known *Watchtower*, the Jehovah's Witnesses' magazine, which they receive for free without having to accept or commit to the Jehovah's Witnesses. Printed text appears to be an efficient means of religious transmission while not necessarily enforcing a particular doctrine or confession, but rather spirituality and Christian devotion. Specific devotions that have arisen at apparition sites arrive in Shchirets by way of pilgrims who disseminate devotional fliers throughout the village, enlarging the community of special devotion beyond the actual site of the apparition.

Prayer chains constitute one of the most institutionalized forms of devotion not controlled by the church. This widespread Roman Catholic practice has recently entered the Greek Catholic community, becoming a successful form of devotion. Prayer chains are de-territorialized, transnational networks that create virtual communities by maintaining a particular form of social cohesion through religious routine. The prayer network functioning in Shchirets was brought there by a villager whose son studied in the Basilian seminary in Briohovych. The students there had learned about the idea of perpetual devotion promoted by the Universal Living Rosary Association of St Philomena, a Catholic organization in the United States, and looked for members in L'viv to start their own chain.[205]

The lay enterprise in the United States puts a heavy emphasis on missionary activity in poor countries, from which most members come. The organization is simple, based on prayer groups of fifteen people centred on a rosary. Each member has to perform daily a decade of the rosary, which is a standard traditional Catholic set of prayers performed on a chain of prayer beads, theoretically combining prayer and meditation but usually resulting in automatic repetition. The member of the prayer chain has to perform eleven standard prayers at a certain hour, sharing the large chain of rosary with others praying at different hours of the day. Symbolic membership is achieved by performing the ritual while wearing a brown scapular and a miraculous medal. The group regularly receives rosaries and a quarterly newsletter from the headquarters of the movement. Instead of being asked for a small donation, which most Ukrainians cannot afford, participants are asked to pray even more for the success of the enterprise.

---

[205] Other lay associations focused on specific devotions, such as the Marian Reunion (Mariiska *druzhyna*), have a long history in the Greek Catholic Church. They are usually in active connection with the parish priest.

At the time of my fieldwork, the prayer chain initiated in Shchirets counted around 200 members in the L'viv area, had established its centre in the city, and had started conducting missionary activity in Russia. Members came mostly from Roman and Greek Catholic churches, but by entering the chain they formed their own community outside of official church structures or confessional borders. A member had the feeling of belonging to a community, which in fact never met face to face. The prayer chain functioned as a particular form of religiosity based on standard prayer and fixed hours of devotion, motivated by affiliation with a community of practice under the name of St Philomena.

Other regular rituals are usually related to the church, even if they are not necessarily part of the liturgical rite. Among the three churches in the village, only the Roman Catholic one is regularly open during the week. According to the Latin tradition, the priest is obliged to celebrate mass daily, but because Shchirets's priest has to attend to five parishes, he comes to Shchirets only three times a week. When he comes to the village, Father Tadeusz celebrates only the liturgy, leaving the community to say its own prayers before the mass starts. The group of women who form the congregation for weekday liturgies recite the rosary and, during Lent, the Way of the Cross. Because the priest does not live in the village, he has to keep the church locked, making it impossible for the congregation to gather in his absence. He arrives half an hour before the liturgy to open the church, let in the rosary group, and listen to confessions. It is these practices that together make up the ordinary religious life of the Catholic parish. The Sunday liturgy attracts more people, with around 100–150 who attend mass. Their numbers vary by season, as is the case for all churches in the village (and those in Sykhiv), because church attendance is affected by seasonal agricultural work.

Orthodox and Greek Catholic priests are not required to celebrate the liturgy every day, according to the eastern tradition, although the Greek Catholic Church advises its priests to celebrate daily. Rarely does a village priest do so, and priests are often asked by their bishops at least to alternate the liturgy with other classical eastern rituals: vespers, matins, or the acathistus. At the Greek Catholic church in Shchirets, Blessed Trinity, Father Bohdan, like most other parish priests, does not follow this rule. He comes to church on Sunday at 10 a.m., after people gather from 9.30 to recite the rosary and wait for confession. He starts the liturgy only after all those who want to confess have done so, and the others continue the rosary until all confessions have been completed. The sermon comes at the end, so the entire liturgical ritual continues uninterrupted, with the priest reciting his 'calls' and the church choir singing responses, followed by songs sung by a few of the attendants.

Only the core parishioners at Blessed Trinity come early enough to occupy the space close to the iconostasis, from where they may more actively participate in the service. Most people are separated from the priest, standing in side spaces attached to the main body of the church.[206] They know the liturgy by heart but tend to listen passively to the service most of the time. Attendance at a regular Sunday mass is between 300 and 400 people, with some late arrivals who remain until the end of mass. The liturgy may be followed by another, shorter service, depending on the occasion, either for the entire church (a prayer for the dead during the celebration of the martyr saints of Ukraine) or for a private group (baptism).

Plate 17. Father Andriy, the Orthodox priest in Shchirets, during the Jordan celebration, 2004.

There are times when an unexpected ritual, such as a funeral, is needed, and when this occurs Father Bohdan sends one of the other Greek Catholic priests from his deanery to replace him, rather than conducting the ritual himself. Because the Orthodox priest, Father Andriy, is more accessible, he is frequently asked to perform such rituals by Greek Catholic parishioners as

[206] The central part of the church was too small, so the priest built two additional corridors next to the outside walls (left and right) where people could stand and listen to the liturgy. These are usually full, so those who come late remain completely outside the church.

well. At his own church Father Andriy conducts the Sunday mass and an additional liturgy on Saturday mornings, dedicated to the memory of the dead (*panahyda*). The Saturday service is well attended by villagers from Shchirets and beyond, because the church is near the new village cemetery and people from around the area visit both. Usually the priest starts with the matins and continues with the liturgy. A small choir responds and sings during the service, while most in the congregation remain passive listeners. The priest gives the homily during the ceremony, concentrating on moral issues and applied biblical teaching rather than on political problems, unlike his Greek Catholic colleague.

The Orthodox and Greek Catholic priests perform liturgical services in similar manners, following the local tradition, and their parishes observe the same religious calendar. There are no significant differences between the two congregations in terms of rite, language, devotional practices, or organization of church space. Had there been differences between priest and community, then collective expectations about what one ought to find in the village church would have imposed on the priest the community's habits. Both churches preserve a 'Galician' style of church ornamentation, which is actually an accumulation of different layers of Latin and Slavic influences that were never erased in various 'purifications'. The two priests as well as most other local clergy, notwithstanding confession, acknowledge the similarities between the Orthodox and Greek Catholic Churches and their differences from the Roman Catholic Church. As Father Andriy put it:

> There is nothing in common with the Catholic church, because in their church everything is different. Here [in the Greek Catholic and Orthodox churches] the rite unites us, the language unites us, everything unites us [*obiednuie*] . . . Roman Catholics are practically Poles! Here in our village, there are actually no Ukrainian Roman Catholics . . . If you are Ukrainian, you must be Greek Catholic. You can be Orthodox, but it is better if you're not!

Because most Orthodox churches tend to exert little or no control over their members, who are perceived as belonging to the church simply by being born into the respective nation and formally baptized, there is no membership registration or other requirement related to individual belonging. Villagers attend church of their own free will; the village is too large and heterogeneous to act as a united community in sanctioning those who do not participate. The Sunday congregation, which best represents the whole of the UAOC parish community, is a variable group of villagers among whom only a few people play a continuously active role: the cantor, the choir members, and the caretaker. They also form the parish council , an administrative instrument that helps the priest to run the parish. Referring to Sunday attendance, priests and worshippers use expressions such as 'the church was full' (*povna tserkva*) or 'few people came' (*ridko liudei*). It takes some effort for people to remember exactly whether a particular person was there on a specific Sunday or not.[207]

The Sunday mass anchors the rhythm of rural religious life, and every Sunday in Shchirets three liturgies are held concomitantly: Roman Catholic, Greek Catholic, and Orthodox. The first is shorter and less well attended than the other two. When asked, most villagers claim that they belong to only one church, yet all agree that it makes no difference whether one attends the Orthodox or the Greek Catholic church. Levels of participation in church vary, but there is a general awareness of the religious routine, the religious practices embedded in the life of the community.

Rural religiosity, like urban religiosity as practised in the Soviet-built districts of L'viv, sustains traditional forms of devotion revolving around the family and the important religious holidays of the year: Easter, Christmas, Ascension, Pentecost, and Dormition. These holidays are observed by both Orthodox Christians and Greek Catholics; in the Roman Catholic parish they take place on different dates. The rituals connected to these celebrations are common in eastern churches and belong to the local tradition: the kissing of the veil on the Friday before Easter, the blessing of Easter food, and commemoration of the dead on Easter Monday. Both churches also sing carols at Christmas and perform a popular Christmas religious play.

There are also common devotions which, even if their origins can be traced back to a Latin or Orthodox devotion, have lost their confessional orientation and become part of the local religious tradition. The first Friday mass (*pershe piatnitsa*), for example, is a Latin-rite devotion that entered Galicia and the Greek Catholic Church by way of the Basilian order in the nineteenth century. It is connected to a popular Roman Catholic devotion, that of the Sacred Heart of Jesus, which survived the socialist period and continues today. In 1998 the Greek Catholic priest, Father Bohdan, began to perform repentance prayers related to the first Friday celebration. Since the reintroduction of this monthly ritual, it has acquired a special status in the religious calendar of Shchirets.

The Jordan celebration on 18 January is another common eastern festival that takes place at a different time from that of the similar Catholic observance. This ritual has an important function in the community, for it is the moment when priests walk from home to home throughout the village, blessing every house over the course of several days. The Roman Catholic priest visits only his own parishioners, but the other two priests walk down

[207] The priest evaluates his Sunday congregation by the sum gathered from mass offerings.

the streets of Shchirets, ringing a bell, and enter houses where they are invited or awaited. Once inside they sprinkle the house with holy water already blessed in the church and recite a short prayer for the house, with responses given by the cantor. The priests are usually invited to sit and join a meal prepared by the family, and before leaving they receive money for the church. Many residents expect both Father Andriy and Father Bohdan to visit them for the Jordan blessing, but the priests know precisely where they are unwelcome and avoid entering the homes of Pentecostals or Jehovah's Witnesses. The celebration has a practical aspect for the hosts, who are given holy water and keep it throughout the year.[208]

Plate 18. Villagers waiting for the blessing of water during the Jordan ceremony in Shchirets, 2004.

Two additional community-oriented events are held in Shchirets: first communion (*pershe prychastia*) and the name day of the church (*praznyk tserkve* or *sviata*). The celebration of the saint for whom the church is named takes place once a year in each of the three churches. It offers an opportunity for people to visit churches they do not usually attend, because the celebration is more than a parish feast. Priests from elsewhere in the deanery gather for the event, and some outside priests are also invited. The two Catholic priests

[208] Holy water is thought to prevent or cure all kinds of problems, and a household's stock is refreshed on every such occasion.

invite each other, but the Orthodox priest does not attend the ceremony. Each event starts with a liturgical service, which is followed by speeches by the invited priests. Water and religious objects are blessed at the end of the ceremony. A bazaar offering icons, prayer books, rosaries, and many non-religious items is situated next to the church during the entire celebration and is an important source of religious objects and literature for the villagers.

On this day children are let out from school. Both the Orthodox and Greek Catholic priests play important roles in the village school, so they are able to convince the directors to close the school during the festival. Many children do not come to church but instead wander around the village or stay outside at the fair. Attendance is high, around 500 people. 'The church was packed,' people would say. Twelve to fifteen priests celebrate the liturgy together. The local priest usually plays a passive role, letting the others perform, but he acts as the host at the end, offering food to lay participants outside the church and inviting the other priests to his house for a more intimate get-together.

First communion is also a Latin-influenced ritual that entered the local religious tradition and remained. It is practised by all three churches in the village, with the Greek Catholic and Orthodox churches subtly competing for children every year. The ritual is not formally practised in eastern Christianity, where children receive their first communion when they are baptized. In the Roman Catholic Church, first communion is extremely important. The ritual acknowledges a child's entry into the parish community and his or her coming of age. In Shchirets, first communion takes place once a year in each of the three churches and represents the closing celebration of the catechism cycle undertaken by youths. The occasion draws together all the children's relatives, who prepare their children and the post-ritual gathering outside the church. While a religious holiday (*sviata*) is both a community and an institutional celebration, first communion is primarily a community celebration, and the church invests in organizing the event and bringing the families together. The ritual is an occasion for conspicuous consumption, an opportunity to show off family wealth with extravagant clothing for children and significant donations to the church.

Table 5.1 shows the frequency of life-cycle rituals in each parish in Shchirets during the year.

Table 5.1
Numbers of Life-Cycle Rituals Performed in Shchirets, 2003 and 2004

	Orthodox		Greek Catholic		Roman Catholic	
Ritual	2003	2004	2003	2004	2003	2004
Baptism	57	48	27	20	3 in 4 years	
First communion	56	45	60	55	15	—
Marriages	36	39	30	20	1 in 3 years	
Funerals	49	59	35	23	—	20

Sources: Parish registers.

The events differentiated at the beginning of this section as 'extraordinary' take place only occasionally and serve to break and accent the quotidian rhythm of religious life in Shchirets. These extraordinary practices, focused on a particular devotion that is not among the common rituals, engage villagers in a more intense form of religious practice for a shorter period of time.[209] The first such event to take place in Shchirets after the legalization of the Greek Catholic Church was initiated by the local Greek Catholic parish but later was taken over by the village community. In 1993 the former Greek Catholic priest, Father Stepan, brought a travelling figurine (*figurka*) of the Virgin Mary to Shchirets. The image was supposed to pass around the village, being sheltered for one night in every Christian home that would take it in. While transporting the icon from house to house, villagers recited the rosary and sang Marian songs. Villagers remember how the figurine went to most of the houses in the village, both Orthodox and Catholic. The symbolic journey carefully avoided the homes of the Pentecostals and Jehovah's Witnesses, who would not take part in the devotion.

The other extraordinary ritual that has taken place in Shchirets since 1990 was promoted by the current Greek Catholic priest, Father Bohdan, soon after he arrived in the village in 1996. He took care to organize a village procession of the Icon of the Mother of God from Zarvanytsia.[210] The icon and its place of origin are strong markers of Greek Catholic identity, and the journey was supposed to reinforce people's sense of belonging to Greek Catholicism. A procession carried the icon from village to village. It arrived in Shchirets from Humenets, to the south, and was taken afterwards

[209] The best attended event of such a nature was the public display of a copy of the much-venerated shroud of Turin in St George Cathedral in L'viv, which most of the village flocked to see.

[210] Zarvanytsia was an important pre-Soviet pilgrimage site in western Ukraine, and after 1990 it was institutionalized and transformed into 'the national pilgrimage place for Ukrainian Greek Catholics'. The icon, the Chair of Wisdom (Prestyl Premudrostii), has at least one 'official' replica, which is the 'travelling icon' described in chapter 7.

to Pustomyty, the regional capital in the north. When the icon arrived in Shchirets, it was hosted in the Greek Catholic church, and an overnight vigil was organized for it.

Over the following days the icon toured the streets of the village, together with the Greek Catholic priest and a group of core parish members. At every crossroad the group stopped and prayed with the people of the neighbourhood who had gathered to receive the icon and the priest. During the night the icon was returned to the Greek Catholic church and the vigil continued, engaging residents who were willing to spend an hour with their neighbours praying near the icon. The Roman Catholic priest and his parishioners came out and prayed with the group when the icon passed the *kosciol*. Only the Orthodox priest, Father Andriy, refused to take part in the event, disturbed by the intimidating gathering of forces that the Greek Catholic priest had managed to stir up.

Father Andriy's reaction was reproved by the villagers, who participated irrespective of their confessional affiliation. They considered the procession an act of prayer that united all villagers, rather than a means of imposing Greek Catholicism on the village. One of the organizers, Lioba, a Greek Catholic from the local parish, remembered that many participants believed the attitude of the Orthodox priest was wrong: 'They [the Orthodox] didn't accept [the icon], saying that it's Polish! But what is the difference? Many villagers were upset that the priest stayed away from this important event.'

5.3 Conclusion

In the village of Shchirets, the routine practice of standard forms of religiosity often leaves little space for individual expressions of religiosity. I have looked here at rituals that form the doctrinal side of the local tradition. Enacted regularly, they maintain a continuity of practice. These are rituals that form the core of the church tradition: the liturgical services and certain devotions that entered the rite long ago and now pervade liturgical practice. The exegesis of each Orthodox ritual is included in the ritual itself in an explicit form, being part of the actual recitation during the performance (Stewart 1991; Dumas 2000). Because of repetition and the formalized character of the performance, people are not attentive to the exegesis but perform the ritual without conscious understanding of its meaning – much as in Harvey Whitehouse's description of the doctrinal mode of religiosity (1995: 197). During mass in Shchirets, no one thinks about *why* the priest comes out with the 'gifts' from behind the iconostasis and presents them to the people. There is an implicit awareness of the symbolic importance of the moment, which suffices for the congregation to respond by kneeling and reciting a specific sentence. There is little excitement and no creative input in the formulaic celebration from either the priest or the audience. Rarely, the priest takes care to explain in his sermon the etiology of various practices, and in doing so he underscores the dogmas behind the acts.

Another set of rituals is based on individual practice, separate from the church. Complementary forms of religious expression, usually organized by lay groups, are an important part of the Galician tradition, and during the socialist repression such forms made up the bulk of religious practice out of sheer necessity. Now these practices respond to individual needs and create alternative communities of practice, such as the prayer chain group. In this case, routine is sustained by a connection with an imagined community of prayer, and by performing the prayer one reaffirms the symbolic link.

'Extraordinary' rituals inhabit a zone somewhere between institutionalized practices and personal devotion. The figurine of the Mother of God entering each village house for one night is a return to the world of domestic religious observance specific to the underground period. The particular character of extraordinary rituals comes from the fact that they break the routine of the village and mobilize the community for a short time. The neutrality of these practices has an integrative effect for the community, in spite of attempts by each priest to claim the ritual exclusively for his own confession.

The short history of the village's three churches shows a remarkable similarity to the case of Sykhiv, where, in spite of recent confessional differentiation, there is a shared practice and understanding of 'religion'. In the context of the religious divisions of the early 1990s, each local congregation in Shchirets was obliged to define its position and its jurisdictional orientation, by either confirming its traditional identity or switching to a new one. A general process of self-identification among churchgoers meant that people had to make choices. However, while religious elites with different political visions were competing with one another, individuals maintained a sense of belonging to a common tradition of practice, which allowed them to frequent different churches.

Nowadays villagers, like people in the city, favour the unification of eastern churches, which in practice is a *fait accompli*. When prompted to discuss confessional differences, they bring up the commonality of Ukrainian eastern churches as 'our' churches, which follow 'our tradition' (*nashyi obriad*). Many say they wish the churches would unite to become one (*obiednuetsia*). By 'one church' they understand not a single Orthodox or Greek Catholic Church but a 'Ukrainian church'. It is in this sense that 'nation' still has a religious connotation. Yet few people believe in the existence a real Ukrainian church (*cysta ukrainska tserkva*) that is more righteous (*bilsh spravedlyvyi*) than the other churches. When they do, they refer to a righteous Ukrainian church as an Orthodox church that might materialize from the contemporary Orthodox imaginary.

One of my purposes in describing routine practice in Shchirets has been to highlight the need people appear to have to look for spiritual reinforcement outside of everyday village practice. Most villagers have at some point or even regularly visited religious sites of 'strong devotion' (*sylna molytva*), and such moments constitute special events in their lives, producing well-preserved memories of which they speak in detail and with passion. Well-known pilgrimage sites like those described in the following chapters represent unorthodox alternatives to mainstream religious practice. There, where exorcisms take place or apparitions of the Mother of God reveal themselves, belivers meet another type of religious experience that is far from their daily routine. It is in such imagistic practices, which facilitate an almost unmediated communication with the divine, that believers find a different expression of their religiosity.

Chapter 6
A Monastic Splinter Group and Its Imagistic Practice of Exorcism

The postsocialist institutionalization of the Ukrainian Greek Catholic Church took place within a ferment of religious unrest that saw the splintering of many religious communities. The conflicts that sparked the emergence of splinter groups can rarely be reduced to a single cause, even in terms of the interaction between the divergent modes of religiosity, the doctrinal and the imagistic. The ideal interaction of the modes, by which imagistic religiosity emerges within a doctrinal tradition in order to revitalize it, is rarely found in reality. Rather, the common situation in any tradition is that of a mixture of types of rituals corresponding to the imagistic and doctrinal modes. People do not stick to one or the other but tend to participate in all kinds of rituals. Apparently, even according to the modes theory, a religious tradition will be more successful when it promotes both imagistic and doctrinal modes. But this seldom happens, and so the two modes remain in dynamic tension. As Pascal Boyer remarked (in Whitehouse 2002: 11–12), keeping the two modes separate is actually a political move to be determined by religious specialists. In cases where the modes coexist within a single religious tradition or community of practice, most conflicts result from the subjection of one of the two modes to the other. Thus, one can argue, authority is a variable neglected by the modes theory, which does not read the role of power relations into the social context.

In this chapter I explore the case of a monastic community that separated from the pre-existing structures of a monastic order because of a reinterpretation of doctrine. This splinter group has the characteristics of a spontaneous *communitas,* and by following its short evolution, certain parallels can be found with Victor Turner's analysis of the evolution of the Catholic Franciscan order from a spontaneous to an ideological communitas (Turner 1996: 47). In the making of churches in western Ukraine there is a general tendency towards the structuring and institutionalization of religious communities. Splinter groups that form in the splitting of parish communities tend soon to adhere to an available structure, such as one of the competing Orthodox Churches or the Greek Catholic Church, and are quickly reintegrated into the mainstream tradition. Alternatively, a splinter group might align itself with an alternative religious tradition, as in the case of the traditionalists described in chapter 4. Sometimes, however, a community flourishes autonomously on the basis of an imagistic ritual. The case presented here is of just this sort. The phenomenon is likely to be short-lived, however, as the community begins to disintegrate because of a clash between two groups promoting different modes of religiosity.

6.1 Making Kolodiivka: The Emergence of a Splinter Group

The monastic community at Kolodiivka, Ukraine, began as a spontaneous, innovative movement made up of a small number of people who shared an ideal and tried to give it shape. It came into being as a splinter group of a monastic order well established in Ukraine, the order of St Basil the Great, commonly known as Basilians. The order's roots lie in the Orthodox ideal of monasticism, but it is regulated and functions according to western monastic principles.[211] Basilians follow the centralized model of Catholic monasticism by reproducing one rule, one structure, and the same ideals in all their monasteries. This principle of uniformity is unlike the Orthodox principle of decentralization, which makes each monastic community distinctive. The first effect of monastic variation is the higher degree of mobility obtained in Orthodoxy, in which monks are given the possibility of experiencing various communities without being limited by the rules of a single order.

In the early days of religious revival in Ukraine, monastic orders were the first to re-create religious institutions. Emerging from the underground, Basilian, Studite, and Redemptorist priests laid the groundwork for the reconstruction of the UGCC while consolidating their monastic structures. The Basilians benefited from the strong support they received from the large diaspora Basilian community, which allowed them to open monasteries and a theological seminary by the beginning of 1990. The possibility of freely practising religion, and the emergence of numerous religious institutions after a long period of religious persecution, triggered a boom in monastic activity. In the early 1990s a surge of young people joined religious orders, particularly the Basilian and Studite orders. They were mostly attracted by the example of underground survivors, who were living paragons of both

[211] If one can speak of a Greek Catholic monastic tradition, then Basilians and Studites are its main representatives (there are also smaller communities emanating from the two). I do not deal with the evolution of the Greek Catholic monastic tradition here, although it is an interesting subject that could be interpreted in line with other works dealing with the development of monasticism, such as those of Victor Turner (1996) and Talal Asad (1993).

Christian and Ukrainian commitment. Many young people were eager to try this path, which had been blocked for more than forty years, leaving western Ukraine with a dearth of theological formations save for the few clandestine initiatives. Novitiate houses had to be built quickly to accommodate the large number of Ukrainians ready to pursue a religious path, and Basilians were the fastest at doing so. Most of these houses, like the one in Krehiv in L'viv oblast, are now, after fifteen years, nearly empty.

One example of such young people is Brother Efhen, a monk I met in 2004 in the Kolodiivka monastery. His 'conversion' took place in 1990 in Sykhiv, in St Mykhail's Church, newly recovered by the Greek Catholics, where the two previously underground Studite monks, Voronovsky and Prylip, were daily celebrating religious services. Efhen came from a devout family of Greek Catholic priests that had given him a religious education and encouraged him towards spiritual activities. He remembered that the atmosphere at home was extremely religious, in contrast to school, where he was persecuted for coming from a religious family:

> At home it was like in the monastery. We were talking about God, everything about what God is, and more. God was with us and gave us lots of joy and love. In our house there was a great love [for God]. And when you went out of the house it was like in a prison. You went out and it was very dark and terrible on the street. This is how that life was, and this is how it remained up to the times of perestroika.

In the late 1960s, while still in school, Efhen had some inclination towards joining a monastery, but since that was impossible he studied sports medicine instead. From the moment of the first clear signs of Greek Catholic revival in 1988 he looked for a monk with whom to talk about his vocation. He learned from his neighbours about Vasyl Voronovsky, who by now was gathering large crowds in Sykhiv; the sudden visibility of a clandestine priest was a hot topic in those days. Efhen was still a student when he first met the Studite monk, and his memory of that event was clear. He arrived at the church to find Voronovsky performing an exorcism, surrounded by a throng of people, among whom were some who were possessed. He saw the priest sprinkle holy water on an ill boy caught in a crisis and then recite healing prayers over the head of the boy, who immediately felt better and calmed down. After the end of the healing prayers Efhen went to confess to Voronovsky and asked to be accepted into the monastery. The priest believed he had a vocation (*poklykannia*) for monastic life but asked him to finish his studies and only afterwards to join the Studites. So Efhen entered a Studite monastery upon graduating in 1994, and after two years as a novitiate he took the monastic cloth. After two and a half years spent in a hermitage in the mountains, Efhen visited Kolodiivka, a monastery founded by Hryhoryi Planchak, a former Basilian monk, and decided to remain there.

The founding of the Kolodiivka monastery had its roots in the splintering of the Basilian order that took place in the early 1990s. A central figure in the story was Hryhoryi Planchak, a Ukrainian monk from Croatia who came to Ukraine at that time and joined the Basilian monastery in Krekhiv as a teacher in its theological seminary. The tradition of the Greek Catholic Church was already being redefined in the wake of the rediscovery of its eastern roots, and church leaders were downplaying the centuries-old Latin influence. Planchak was at the forefront of the easternizing move among Basilians, desiring to return to the spirituality of the eastern church fathers that had inspired the Orthodox tradition.[212] Yet he also sought a different style of monastic life, corresponding more to that of the western contemplative orders: withdrawn from the world, concentrated on prayer and mystical experience. He reinterpreted 'contemplation' in the spirit of Orthodox monasticism as a solitary exploration of inner spirituality.

He was not alone in this pursuit, and a few young monks, his students from Krekhiv, became his disciples in exploring the ideals of eastern monasticism. One of those who followed Planchak, Father Mykhail, described to me what was to become the foundation myth of the new monastic community: 'One of the fathers, Basilian at that time, wanted to go deeper into spirituality and return to the sources our early fathers proposed. He wanted to live more absorbed in prayer and an inner [spiritual] life [*vnustryshnyi*]. And when he couldn't do this in the Basilian [order], he received a blessing to leave it and form a new community.'

Basilians were oriented towards an active life of missionary activity, education, pastoral care, publishing, and church politics. Planchak's aspirations were too dissimilar to be accommodated within the order. Not wanting to separate from the Basilian order, his group initially planned to transform a Basilian monastery in Lavrir into a contemplative monastery. But they were soon forced to leave the order, for it had been argued that Basilian monastic rule provided no space for the contemplative path the group was set on following. Planchak's departure was motivated in large part by his interest in exorcism, a practice he wanted to revive in the church but which was unpopular among Basilians.

Ten monks left with Planchak, and together they moved into an apartment in Ivano-Frankivsk, where Planchak began to teach in a local theological seminary. They organized themselves into a monastic commu-

---

[212] The early church fathers were theologians and Christian writers of the era preceding the first Nicene Council (325). In the Orthodox tradition the age of the church fathers is thought to have continued beyond this and to have included later influential writers.

nity, observing a spiritual and communal program. Soon after their relocation, a few nuns and female novices also joined the community, opening their own community in another apartment in the city. Instead of joining another monastic order such as the Studites, a Greek Catholic order with an orientation similar to that of the splinter group's (owing to the eastern orientation provided by Metropolitan Sheptytskyi at the order's founding), the breakaway group decided to create its own monastery. Planchak registered the new community as an independent monastery under the jurisdiction of the local bishop in 1995.

The group's wish to start a new monastery coincided with a parallel search pursued by a monastic community in Rome that was looking for young monks to populate its monastery. While in exile in Rome, Josyf Slipyi, the head of the UGCC, had gathered the monks who had escaped from Soviet Ukraine and offered them the possibility of continuing monastic life in Rome. In 1965 Slipyi opened an eastern-rite monastery for the group, under the rule of Theodore Studite, a descendent of the original Studite order founded by Andrei Sheptytskyi.[213] In spite of its name, the Studion had no real connection to the Studites in Ukraine, who at that time were trying to survive in the underground church. The Studion survived Slipyi's death, and the religious revival in Ukraine found Lubomyr Husar the archimandrite of a small monastery in Grottaferrata, near Rome.[214]

After the re-establishment of the UGCC and Husar's return to Ukraine, he tried to revive the now elderly and dwindling monastic community with new monks. In 1993 the Studion was moved from Rome to Ukraine. Husar found a convenient site in Kolodiivka, a village near Ternopil, an oblast capital, where the local authorities donated a former school near the village church. The monastic community, by then composed of only three or four elderly monks, could not undertake the reconstruction of the monastery. Husar proposed that Planchack and his group go to Kolodiivka and there establish a monastery that would be a continuation of the Studion. The two seemed to share a vision of reviving Greek Catholic monasticism through the rediscovery of eastern monastic spirituality. Planchak's community moved to Kolodiivka in 1997, remaining an independent monastery under the patronage of now Cardinal Husar, head of the UGCC.

---

[213] Theodor Studite was an influential church father whose rules of monasticism and instructions for leading an ascetic life are still followed in Orthodoxy. He revived a monastery outside Constantinople called Studion, and this name is used today for Orthodox monasteries that observe his canons.

[214] Grottaferrata is a famous commune in Rome where monasteries follow an eastern (Greek) monastic tradition dating back to the eleventh century.

The way the new community in Kolodiivka came about was unusual for Greek Catholic monasticism, and its orientation tested the limits of the easternizing trend within the church. While the community was able to preserve the course that had driven it to separate from the Basilians, to the same degree it would remain on its own, experiencing a new form of monasticism. Brother Arseny, a member of the initial group, reflected during one of our conversations on this unusual situation: 'And it came out like this, that the Studites didn't recognize this community, because it didn't use the common typikon, the Studite typikon.[215] Which is a bit outdated . . . They are not Basilians either . . . so [the Kolodiivka community] remained on its own, neither here nor there. But time showed that one can live like that.' Planchak's group forged its new monastery in the spirit of the ideal community of which it dreamt, oriented towards contemplation and spiritual self-accomplishment. The hardships of establishing a new, independent monastery were slowly overcome through the group's persistence and avidity.

The monastery in Kolodiivka is inaccessible by local train or minibus, but four regular buses a day pass the village, linking Ternopil, fifty kilometres away, with smaller towns in the south. In Kolodiivka the monks took over the village church and moved into the former school, which had been abandoned after a new one was built. The takeover of the school irked the villagers, who had hoped to see it converted into a small food-processing factory. In the beginning villagers opposed the establishment of the monastery and complained to the local authorities and later to the Greek Catholic bishop in Ternopil. The monks blamed the villagers' hostility on evil forces residing in the village, which they considered exorcising. During socialist times there had been no continuity of religious practice in Koldiivka, for the village had no parish priest, and both of its churches, Greek and Roman Catholic, had been closed.[216] As an outcome, the majority of villagers were atheists (*bezbodznyi*), which to the monks also explained the presence of evil forces there.

The monastery Planchak's group wanted to create was founded on a vision of a secluded place where monks, as hermits, would concentrate on personal spiritual growth, just as the early church fathers had done. Their path to God was to be experienced not in individual seclusion but in a com-

[215] A typikon is a liturgical book that regulates the ceremonial order and religious services in eastern churches. It is presented in the form of a calendar of religious celebrations. A typikon is also a rule of conduct or method, such as a rule regulating paintings or the arrangement of icons. The typikon plays an important role in eastern Christianity, where inscribed tradition is one of the pillars of church doctrine.

[216] The village instead had a wealthy cooperative that closed only in 1998, when most of its land was sold to a gas company in Kyiv. The remaining land was distributed to villagers, who owned small plots that they cultivated mostly for family use.

munity imagined as a 'communitas of withdrawal' (Turner 1996: 154). The group was inspired by the Orthodox image of monasteries as islands of spirituality (*oseredok dukhovnosti*) separated from the mundane world. However, Orthodox monasteries are also places to be visited by pilgrims, who take part of the holiness radiating from the monastery back into the world. Pilgrims visit Orthodox monasteries throughout the year, and their visits give a rhythm to life in the monastic community (Sarris 2000). Therefore, even if one were to try to build a completely remote monastery, people would attempt to reach it – and the more difficult the route, the more rewarding the spiritual journey. The monks in Kolodiivka were aware of this but did not consider how much their presence would be felt outside the monastery. They were prepared to live the lives of hermits rather have to deal with worldly matters.

The principles of monastic life inspired by the Studion were even stricter and more demanding in Kolodiivka than in the Studite order. To the basic Studite division of the day into three periods (eight hours of sleep, eight of work, and eight of prayer) were added further obligations. The monastery's program was centred on personal devotion, and an ordinary day started at 4.00 a.m. with matins, the morning prayer service, followed by the liturgy at 7.00. At 5 p.m. there was an evening prayer (vespers). There were two meals a day, one at 9.00 a.m. and the other at 6.00 p.m., but two days a week were governed by a harsher program (*pustynia*) including fasting and solitary prayer – a form of being in the 'desert' inside the community.[217] One night a week was dedicated to continuous prayer, and the monks took hour-long shifts during the night. All religious services within the monastery were conducted in Old Slavonic, whereas those for pilgrims and villagers were held in Ukrainian. Even when the monastery was forced to open its doors to its many solicitors, an emphasis on personal development (*pratsia nad suboiu*) remained its main goal and differentiated it from other monasteries.

When the monastery was established in 1995 it had 10 monks in addition to their leader, Father Hryhoryi Planchak. In 2004 it counted 45 members: 7 priests, 2 deacons, and 36 monks. Between 1995 and 2004 the size of the community fluctuated, with no more than 15 to 20 monks in residence at a time. Keen on pursuing the idea of hermitage, the monks opened two 'deserts' in the mountains (Verhovyna and Posich in Ivano-Frankivsk) – small places where monks and nuns could go for short periods to live a

[217] *Pustyn* (desert) is a spiritual metaphor representing the asceticism and secluded life of prayer of a hermit and his spiritual and physical retreat from the world. *Pustynia* refers to the hermitage; the monks in Kolodiivka use the term with the sense of creating a hermit-like existence within the monastery.

solitary life.[218] The experience of seclusion is highly esteemed in the community and extremely challenging for those undertaking it. The monks also established a retreat for the community in Terebolja (Ternopil oblast) and a convent for nuns in Byrki, twenty kilometres from Kolodiivka.

The monastery in Kolodiivka became the centre, or 'mother monastery' (*matirnyi monastyr*), and Planchak became the father superior (*ihumen*) for all the other communities. The structure was apparently of Greek Orthodox influence, a part of Mount Athos monasticism, although the community continuously redefined its rules as it evolved.[219] Because of such structural ambiguities, the status of a few of the monks was unclear to both the monks and the monastery itself. Apart from the monks living in the 'desert', away from the monastery, there were some who pursued theological studies and resided in L'viv. Their only contact with the monastery came during infrequent visits to Kolodiivka. This was the case for Brother Arseny, who graduated from the Ukrainian Catholic University in 2004. He was a sort of wandering monk, a common figure in the Orthodox world, close to the mystical tradition of the church. He had tried various Greek Catholic monasteries and was familiar with Orthodox monasticism. He had a strict view of monasticism and criticized Greek Catholics for their hodgepodge structure, created from imports of orders and monastic rules from the west, and their inattention to the true sources of the eastern Christian tradition. The beginnings of the Kolodiivka monastery were promising in this regard, he thought, given the contemplative Orthodox life that people pursued there.

Other monks also joined the monastery, convinced that this was a place to experience a new form of monasticism. They were either unhappy with their previous communities or dreamed of a spiritual model that seemed to have been realized in Kolodiivka. The flexibility of the boundaries of eastern churches and the fluctuation of priests and parishes characteristic of the postsocialist revival also affected monastic life. The heightened mobility of monks and nuns trying different orders and moving between monasteries was representative of the times and the institutionalization taking place within the church.[220] In Kolodiivka the ambiguity of one's affiliation was favoured by the monastery's loose rules and the long absences of the abbot, Planchak. Monastic rule was strict in regard to religious obligations but less

---

[218] The superior has to approve the hermitage period, which usually lasts from two weeks to a month. Only one monk lives permanently on the premises, and he returns to Kolodiivka once a month.

[219] Maintaining female and male branches in addition to several smaller communities is common in Catholicism but does not respect the institutional bases for Orthodox monasteries.

[220] Such mobility is uncommon in Catholic monasticism, where each order has a particular formation for its members and clear rules that make such flexibility unachievable.

rigorous in organizational matters, and the bounds were continually pushed by daily practice. The rules for novitiates, neither strictly Catholic nor Orthodox, initially established clear steps for becoming a monk. The period of probation, a status in-between secular and monastic life in which the person experiences monastic life without being tied to the monastery, became a permanent state for some monks. Few of those in the monastery had taken minor vows, and only two had taken permanent vows.[221] There was neither an actual office for novices nor someone in charge of the young monks' education.

Yet Planchak's public lectures and spiritual teachings attracted increasing numbers of theology students from Krehiv, Ivano-Frankivsk, and Ternopil. The community was growing with young people; the few priests were all around forty years old, and most of the monks under thirty. Planchak reached an agreement with other monasteries so that their monks and nuns who wanted to experience monastic life in Kolodiivka, Byrki, or one of the hermitages could live in one of these communities for a time. Apart from Planchak's own charisma and the fame of the monastery as a highly spiritual place, the attractive point for other monks was the monastery's open-mindedness and the feeling of individual freedom they could achieve within the community. Brother Arseny said, in relation to this:

> I think that each person who couldn't find something in his own community came here. I see now that Kolodiivka was the symbol of a dream come true. Something like the Promised Land . . . And each hoped that here in Kolodiivka, he could finally find something, everything that was, until now, impossible. And here things were boundless; people could search for what best fit them . . . [You] want to live in the desert, go to the mountains! Feel like being a parish priest? You have a parish, go and try! . . . Many of us dreamt about complete seclusion, that there would be possibilities like this [in Kolodiivka]. We read books about monasticism, about those saints, deserts, caves . . . Then, after some time, it came out clearly that this [seclusion] is like a step. . . Caves, deserts can come only after [living in] a community. Without that, people become savage.

Kolodiivka tried to find the right balance between seclusion and social involvement, and its position was ideal for this. Visiting monks attracted by seclusion could remain in Kolodiivka without having to pass through the

[221] In Catholicism and eastern Christianity, religious vows are promises made by members of monastic orders to follow certain values that form the core of monasticism. After completing a novitiate of usually one to two years, a monk can take minor vows, which are temporary and must be renewed. Permanent vows are taken after several more years to confirm the monk's full commitment to the order.

novitiate and after a time would return to their own monasteries. There was no official *rite de passage* for departing from the monastery; a discussion with the abbot sufficed to let one go. These clarifying discussions could be postponed for months, given that Planchak was rarely in Kolodiivka. The monastery retained an institutional flexibility, open to novel opportunities and new religious experiences, which to a certain extent repeatedly reshaped the community.[222]

The Kolodiivka community was a heterogeneous mixture, affected by the fluctuation of people and the community's openness towards newcomers. Together with monks who hoped to achieve a spiritual ideal in Kolodiivka were some who chose monastic life for more pragmatic reasons. For some young novices the monastery was a good alternative to daily struggle and social obligations. For others who were social outcasts it was an opportunity to reintegrate into society, and being a monk was a highly respectable social role in western Ukraine. People who were not accepted into other monasteries because of their pasts were welcomed in Kolodiivka and given a second chance. In these cases Kolodiivka acted in the first instance as a place of 'levelling' and 'stripping away' of the former social person, giving him a new, respected identity.[223]

One of the monks, Brother Jaroslav, had converted while in jail and decided to become a monk after long discussions with Brother Arseny, a missionary monk from Kolodiivka who was visiting prisons for pastoral care. After being released from jail, Jaroslav tried to enter various monasteries but was refused because of his previous conviction. He sought out Arseny, who suggested he come to Kolodiivka, where he would be accepted. 'In one monastery,' said Brother Jaroslav, 'they didn't accept me; they said, [You are a] convict! In the second one I would have had to wait for the superior to come . . . [They were] Redemptorists and Basilians . . . So Arseny told me: There is one which accepts everybody. There is one father,

---

[222] At some point, a small group of monks from the monastery left for Canada, having been invited by a local bishop to take over a monastery there. They resided in an abandoned Cistercian monastery for three years, under a rule of seclusion. Financial constraints made it difficult to get by, and although the small local community contributed what little support it could afford to the monastery, costs were too high to maintain the building. After three years it was closed down. The monks tallied their experience in Canada as an experiment, albeit an 'unsuccessful' one, as one of the brothers put it.

[223] Erving Goffman (quoted in Turner 1995: 108) described this process as a characteristic of total institutions, those social systems that encompass and undercut their members' individuality. The norms that govern institutionalized relations are transgressed and social distinctions dissolved upon one's entrance into a monastery. After this first phase, often described as liminal, a second one follows in which novices reintegrate into the structures of monastic hierarchy.

Planchak, who takes everybody . . . You [should] go and ask, he will take you in.'

The initial ideal pursued by the founders of the monastery, linked to the rediscovery of eastern Christian spirituality, became altered through the social processes that brought the monastery to fruition. As the community grew in size, so it grew in terms of wishes and dreams as each new member brought in his own views of monastic life and spirituality. There were various voices in the community, but they gathered around one vision, which could then be pursued individually. In the beginning, Planchak's ideas and charismatic teachings provided guiding principles and a cohesive force for the community. As the monastery expanded, it became more difficult to maintain the bonds that the original group had forged.

Rather than follow the path of institutionalization, which would have involved stricter rules and formalized relations and led to the formation of a centralized, hierarchical authority, the monks in Kolodiivka sought a third way. They tried to preserve the initial feeling of communitas and thus avoid more rigorous organization and the strict pursuit of a doctrinal mode of religiosity. Following the abbot's inspiration, they did so by cultivating an imagistic ritual, which, through its compelling emotional content, maintained the cohesion and increased the motivation of the group. Exorcism, brought to the monastery by Planchak, shaped both the practice and the beliefs of the community, to such a degree that it became the monastery's focal point. In a way, exorcism created Kolodiivka, and the monastery sustained itself through the exorcist ritual.

6.2 Exorcism in the Eastern Christian Tradition

The modes theory distinguishes between rituals by differentiating the modalities through which the religious message is transmitted. In Whitehouse's ethnographic examples, taken mostly from male initiation rituals in Papua New Guinea (Whitehouse 1996; see also Barth 1975), imagistic rituals are linked to terror and violence experienced by participants. Their primary characteristic, however, is not violence but emotional intensity, which is triggered by the ritual performance and the potential revelation. Exorcism, too, with its violent enacting of a symbolic fight, its possession trance, and its powerful imagery, falls into the category of imagistic religiosity. Yet the ritual has a venerable doctrinal tradition in Christianity, having been standardized and controlled by church authorities since the third century, when it became a permanent liturgical service.

The form and content of exorcism changed little during centuries of Christian practice.[224] The first written cases of demon exorcism appear in the Gospels among the miracles of Jesus. These biblical examples constitute the basis for the religious imagery surrounding the exorcism ritual up to present times. With the development of church tradition, exorcism prayers were incorporated into the baptismal service, which remains today the basic form of exorcism in Christianity (Stewart 1991: 207). The early church fathers wrote their own prayers as means to heal ailments of the bodies and souls of both humans and animals, protecting them from further afflictions.[225] Most of these exorcism prayers remained in the Orthodox tradition as part of the *Great Book of Needs* (*Velyki Trebnik*), the most comprehensive liturgical guide available for priests and still in use in Ukraine.[226]

Over the centuries, eastern and western Christianity developed distinct forms of the exorcism rite and different mechanisms of control over its practitioners. The main differences emerged when eastern and western theological conceptions of the devil began to differ, and the two attitudes towards exorcism were endorsed by the divergent modes of authority and dogma of the two traditions. Nevertheless, both traditions continue to share a common view of exorcism as a prayer to God to restrain the power of the devil or demons over mankind. Churches tried to contain the practice of exorcism by standardizing the ritual and integrating it into orthodox practice.[227] With the rationalization of etiologies of illnesses in the medical sciences, churches partially accepted the psychopathological aspects of previously defined 'evil afflictions'. Belief in evil forces was condemned as

---

[224] The exorcism ritual exists in many religions in various forms, but I refer here to the Orthodox Christian doctrine and practice of exorcism. See the website of the Greek Orthodox Archdiocese of America, http://goarch.org/en/ourfaith/articles/article7078.asp (accessed 2 March 2006). See also Stewart 1991.

[225] The early church fathers of the desert lived an ascetic life which revolved around their struggle with demons. Their stories of exorcisms were transmitted through the hagiographical tradition of the church and supply models for exorcism rituals down to the present day (H. Goltz, personal communication). St Basil and St John Chrysostom, two of the most important fathers in the Orthodox liturgical tradition, wrote the most widely used exorcist prayers for the expulsion of evil spirits from afflicted persons in the name of Christ (see Stewart 1991).

[226] 'The Mohyla *Trebnik,* made in the seventeenth century by Metropolitan Petro Mohyla, includes a standardized service of exorcism: Psalms 142, 22, and 27; a series of prayers to God, the Mother of God, and saints; Psalm 91; a canon of prayer to Our Lord Jesus Christ; . . . a reading from Mark 26: 14–17; a prayer to Christ; Psalm 67; and a series of psalms, prayers, incantations, and readings from the Gospels' (Worobec 2001: 228 n. 49). *Paisie Velichkovskii,* a great inspiration for Ukrainian Orthodox spirituality and the Kolodiivka monks, also recommended the 'Jesus prayer'.

[227] In recent years, fear of abuse has led to strong regulations and to the medicalization of the ritual. The Catholic Church enacted new guidelines for exorcists in 1999, as did the Anglican Church in the 1990s (Milner 2000).

mere superstition, and exorcist practices started to be seen as primitive actions connected to these beliefs. However, by representing collective anxieties, the devil and demons remain important actors in the cosmological views of many religions.[228]

In his book on Greek Orthodoxy, Charles Stewart (1991) provided a comprehensive overview of the role of the devil and evil spirits in Orthodox tradition and theology. He showed how the devil remained part of modern Greek cosmology as an Orthodox theological construction and also as a body of popular beliefs in evil spirits (exotica). Stewart contended that it was difficult to draw clear distinctions between the two constructions and that they actually reinforced each other's presence in the Orthodox tradition. His conclusion, that Orthodoxy 'has remained flexible and constantly assimilated new representations as long as they did not contradict basic principles' (1991: 141), underscores my assumptions regarding the specificity of the Orthodox tradition. This mechanism of renewal made possible the continuous updating of the devil's presence in modern Greece, as it does today in Ukraine.

The persistence of the devil in the modern social imaginary caused exorcism to remain part of the religious tradition as the church's most suitable response to the devil's presence. The ritual is to be used only in cases where the influence of the devil can be recognized, and so the main difficulty lies in properly identifying evil as the source of an affliction, indicating a case of possession.[229] In the first stage, an exorcist identifies the possession and then chooses the best means of intervention from among the available church rituals. The monks in Kolodiivka follow the common pattern provided by the Orthodox tradition for identifying the possessed. Brother Roman told me: 'The proof that people have a spiritual problem is that they are afraid of religious objects. Mentally ill people should not be afraid of crosses, holy water . . . The first criterion is that the person reacts strangely in the presence of religious objects. He has a fear of icons, crosses, water. The second is that he is conscious that there is someone else living in his body.'

The moment of identification is simultaneous and relational: the priest, the afflicted, and those around him – usually the family – act to-

---

[228] A large anthropological literature deals with modernity and representations of evil in various parts of the world (Parkin 1986; Stewart 1991; Clough and Mitchell 2001; Kapferer 2003).

[229] Possession by evil spirits as the cause of a personal affliction is one among many etiological systems present in society. A discussion of alternative explanatory frames and of possession as social construct is beyond the purpose of this chapter.

gether.[230] The anticipation of this moment came earlier, when the family decided to present the afflicted to a priest, but all details and discrepancies that affected the victim's social life are brought together in this moment to support the diagnosis. If the possessed is incapable of speaking to the priest, then a brief interrogation of his relatives serves instead. This usually includes a question about whether other authorities, such as other priests, medical doctors, or alternative practitioners, have already recognized the person as 'having a problem'. Sometimes it is enough for the family to say that the relative they are bringing has 'problems with nerves' (*problemy z nervami*). The cultural symptom of 'nerves' is popular in Ukraine, and as Setha Low (1994) remarked in a more general context, it represents an idiom for emotional and social distress.[231]

The first meeting between the person believed to be possessed and the exorcist is important for discerning the problem and choosing the right treatment: an exorcism (*ekzortsyzm; vychytka*) or a healing prayer (*molytva za ozdorovlennia*), depending on the gravity of the case.[232] Only a few monks in Kolodiivka have the special gift of discerning the spirits, an issue with a long past in the history of possession cases in Christianity (Caciola 2000).[233] They use the gift in this critical context of discerning which spirit bothers the afflicted, gaining information through divinely inspired intuition. The gift of seeing involves recognizing the signs and deciding whether a religious experience, an unexpected event, or an affliction is divinely or demonically inspired. Those without the gift pursue the disputable path of questioning before establishing which agent is responsible.

The monastery is in constant need of such judgement because it is a site of intense, highly animated imagistic activity. Monks are constantly confronted by evil forces and often 'see' demons or discern their presence in certain signs. For the ordinary monks, demonic presence is harder to bear because of the uncertainty around it, and they need to check their personal experiences continually with the more experienced monks. This usually

---

230 An extended review of the literature on spirit possession and its anthropological interpretations can be found in Boddy 1994. Her definition (1994: 407) is also broad enough to encompass the Orthodox form of involuntary possession, in which an evil spirit takes over the body of a person usually without the knowledge of that person.

231 'Nerves' have much in common with possession (Grey 2005: 62). Low (1994) argued that the cultural construction of nerves as an illness derives from factors related to social suffering.

232 People often confound the two and refer to both as 'exorcism'. *Vychytka* is the popular term for exorcism, but people also use *ekzortsyzm;* the priest who performs it is called an exorcist (*ekzortsyzt*).

233 In the Orthodox tradition the monk is a bearer of the Holy Spirit (*pneumatophoros*) and thus has the charisma which allows him to know a person's heart (*kardiognosia*) and to expel demons (H. Goltz, personal communication).

happens during confession, a practice that develops into a spiritual relationship that enhances the authority of charismatic monks. In Kolodiivka, imagery related to the devil is reinforced by the regular practice of exorcism. As one of the younger monks, brother Roman, said: 'You watch the exorcism and it reminds you how close the devil is!'

The monks, following the Orthodox tradition, make a distinction between healing prayers, which can be read by anybody – even alone at home from a prayer book – and exorcisms, which require special preparations and can be performed only by an authorized exorcist priest. Being related to controversial beliefs in demons and the devil, exorcism has been kept separate from the routinized practice to which most people have access. In the larger frame of the eastern Christian tradition, exorcism lies between standardized forms of the Orthodox rite as proposed by the church and creative, highly personal forms of devotion as practised by mystics. Its practice has been restricted to specialized priests and to particular places – monasteries, in Orthodoxy – where the ritual also includes an exegetic aspect.

Exorcists interpret a large variety of phenomena as possible cases of possession, including some that have been taken over by the medical sciences in Western cultures. Diagnosis is often based on the performative aspects of the afflicted when facing religious symbols. Whereas exorcists work in only one etiological system, which is provided by the religious imaginary of the exorcism, persons in search of a cure may switch between alternative explanatory frames that propose different diagnoses and respective cures. Monks are aware of the pragmatic approach of the ill, for whom exorcism is just one available therapy, and of their role in relation to the pilgrims' needs. When talking about it, Brother Arseny remarked realistically:

> Today there are many spiritual problems because people don't know what spiritual life, what Christianity is. For them it is the same to go to witches [*vorozhky*] or to a priest. This is why [exorcism] is practised in the monastery and not in churches, [so that] with the occasion of those [exorcist] prayers we can teach people the basic truths of Christian faith and tell them: 'Spiritual problems exist and we all have them. They come from the fact that human nature is corrupted by sin. To cure it, you should do this and that.' This has always been the role of the monastery, like a bank where money gathers. Those who need money go to the cash machine. We have to live our spirituality, otherwise we don't have [enough] and we cannot give to others . . . like an empty bank.

6.3 Exploring the Exorcist Ritual

There are only a few exorcist priests in western Ukraine today, and most of the popular ones actually perform healing prayers, not exorcisms. In Soviet times the practice remained confined to the few extant monasteries and was seldom used in the underground. Even in the monasteries its form underwent some changes because of the practical demands of adapting to harsh conditions. Always associated with the devil, the practice of exorcism had an exacerbated anti-Soviet connotation, because the devil often represented the Soviet state in the religious imaginary. The transmission of this religious practice was extremely difficult in the underground church. Father Vasyl Voronovsky, well known as an exorcist in L'viv, had been the apprentice of another exorcist priest in the underground and had learned the ritual from him: 'I started to read [healing] prayers immediately after they ordained me [as a priest],' he told me. 'In the beginning I didn't know what to read . . . Father Bohdan Repetylo taught me how to read prayers for ill people. He told me [to take] that prayer from the Small Vespers and the Great Blessing of Water . . . and that's what I did. First confession, then communion, and afterwards these prayers.'

After the death of an elderly exorcist in 1977, one of the underground bishops allowed Voronovsky to perform exorcisms in critical cases. Because of a lack of prayer books, he somehow re-created the ritual from memory and developed a sequence of prayers that formed his personal style of exorcism. In 1990, when he started to celebrate the liturgy openly in Sykhiv, many people came to the church there because of the spectacular character of his services, especially the inclusion of exorcist prayers. At the time of my fieldwork Voronovsky performed such prayers daily in the Studite monastery in L'viv, as well as on his journeys throughout western Ukraine.

Like Voronovsky, the monks in Kolodiivka had their own understanding of the exorcist ritual based on their understanding of spirituality and monasticism. The abbot, Hryhoryi Planchak, became interested in exorcism after meeting some exorcists in Rome, but he was unable to develop his skills in the Basilian monastery in Krekhiv. Immediately after the community moved to Kolodiivka he decided to perform exorcisms for pilgrims. He argued to the few brothers who were reluctant in the beginning that exorcisms were part of the early church tradition, and the monastic ideal they were following obligated them to rediscover the ritual. In this way he mobilized the entire monastery to support his activity, and the imaginary of the community was gradually shaped around the cosmological world of the exorcist ritual: the fight between God and the devil. Father Artemie recalled, referring to Planchak: 'And then he said, 'I don't do it through my own will, it is the power which has been in the church from the beginning . . . and if here we pray together, if there is one, a second, and a third priest [exorcist], and we all pray together, then all this work is efficient.'

The monks who followed his example soon became both priests and exorcists, for the boundaries between the two slowly disappeared. 'It is the duty of each priest to be an exorcist!' the community declared, and it was the first to provide an example.[234] To the Kolodiivka community, being an exorcist was like accepting the spiritual gift that a priest obtains at his ordination. In 2004 there were seven exorcists in the community who had discovered and nurtured their 'gifts' and two deacons who exercised their 'potential gifts' during services held on the last Tuesdays of certain months. The parallel the monks drew between exorcism as a spiritual gift received at a priest's ordination and baptism as a spiritual gift received automatically after the baptism ritual gave every priest a chance to become an exorcist. It thus challenged both the authority of the church to appoint exorcists and the marginalization that the church and monastic tradition had imposed on this special practice.[235]

The manner in which the ritual is usually performed, with a direct and controlled interaction between the priest and the victim, is reversed in Kolodiivka. Exorcism in the community's understanding has opened up, becoming accessible to both practitioner and patient. Cultivating 'the gift of exorcism' (*dar ekzortsyzmu*) thus becomes a legitimate quest that all priests have the duty to undertake. Father Artemie, himself an exorcist who discovered and cultivated his gift, explained: 'The gift can grow . . . Every person when baptized receives all the gifts of the Holy Spirit and afterwards he can cultivate certain gifts and not develop others. So if you talk about those prayers [exorcisms], each priest has this gift to pray for the spiritual and physical healing of every person. And you can call this many things: exorcism or healing prayer or something else.'

Among the visitors to Kolodiivka are priests from Ukraine and Poland who come to attend the ritual and try their spiritual gifts. Sometimes they take part in the service and perform exorcisms themselves, with the abbot's blessing. For this and for popularizing the ritual, Planchak is criticized both inside and outside the monastery. Because of the cult of exorcism, the image of the monastery is that of a privileged place for accessing the ritual. Ac-

---

[234] The quotation was the title of an extensive interview published in the local newspaper: 'Oboviazok kozhnoho sviashchennyka buty ekzortsystom: Rozmova z ottsem Myhaylom Hrytsaiem' (The duty of each priest is to be an exorcist: Talk with Father Myhail Hryts), *L'vivska Hazeta,* 178, no. 254, 23 September 2003.

[235] Exorcism always challenges clerical authority. Its possible manipulation comes from the ambiguous status of the ritual and its practitioners. In both Latin and eastern traditions there was always the possibility for laypeople to take over and practise exorcisms outside the church (Condie n.d.; Grey 2005).

cording to Brother Roman, people say that 'Kolodiivka is a nursery for exorcists [*rozsadnyk ekzortsystiv*]'. The form of the exorcism ritual is a matter of contention among exorcists in particular. Even when the ritual form is prescribed by the liturgical tradition, it is less standardized than in the Latin rite. Therefore each exorcist develops his own style, which, as in Kolodiivka, can sometimes diverge significantly from the written forms in church tradition. Planchak and the other exorcist priests in Kolodiivka have been accused by other exorcists of practising the ritual too freely. Confronted with this issue, Brother Arseny remarked:

> There are certain people, not many, who are allowed [to exorcise]. But it seems to me that they can at least count on those books published by the Orthodox [Church], which write about it [exorcism] in a clear, beautiful way. [Exorcists are] mostly educated people . . . And some of them [say] that you cannot improvise. This was precisely one of the accusations against Father Planchak, [that] he improvises. Because, they say, you are not supposed to chat at any moment with those from whom you expel [evil spirits]. There is the prayer, which you have to read calmly and slowly, and that's it; you shouldn't ask anything [of the possessed].

In most monasteries where exorcisms are practised, they take place in a relatively intimate setting and involve just a few people. The audience is usually composed of the exorcist, the possessed, and his family, who together constitute a 'healing triangle'. Sometimes another monk or priest helps with other parts of the ritual, but the exorcism prayers are performed by only one priest, the main exorcist. In Kolodiivka, however, the exorcism ritual is the central aspect of monastic life, and the entire community mobilizes around it.

In 1999, facing increasing number of pilgrims, the monastery decided to set special days for pilgrims to visit: the last Tuesday of each month between Easter and autumn (before Advent).[236] During each last Tuesday (*ostanniy vivtorok*), large numbers of pilgrims come to the monastery early in the morning and stay until late at night. It is also one of the rare occasions when the entire monastic community comes together, with nuns and monks

[236] The chosen date has no liturgical meaning, but it resonates with popular beliefs. Some pilgrims use a special calendar to guide them in their spiritual endeavours. The calendar marks certain days as 'blessed days', which favour the reception of spiritual gifts and blessings, and others as 'evil days', on which evil forces are potentially stronger and able to do more harm. According to this spiritual calendar, the twenty-ninth day of the month is an evil day, and the setting of the last Tuesday as a pilgrimage day may counteract the work of demons.

from other monasteries and hermitages also in attendance.[237] The monks set the program of the day according to a succession of rituals familiar to pilgrims. Both monks and pilgrims prepare intensely for this day. The monastic program consists of prayer and fasting, concentrating on spiritual fortification. Preparations are made with the idea that the community becomes spiritually strong enough to incorporate and process all the problems to which they are exposed and thus to 'fight evil forces' brought by pilgrims.

Plate 19. Pilgrims from L'viv travelling to Kolodiivka for a last Tuesday service, 2004.

During the day pilgrims continuously move between the monastery gate, the interior and exterior of the church, and the nearby building used as a guest house. They stray from this small spiritual triangle only to go to their cars and buses, which are parked all around the church, to the cemetery, and to the holy spring outside the village. In the winter of 2003 a small chapel of the Mother of God was built on the spot where a spring surfaced just outside

[237] There are other events that gather pilgrims and thus create the possibility for performing exorcisms. The night before a religious holiday (*sviata*), monks organize a vigil of prayer starting at midnight and ending in the morning. Local villagers attend these kinds of events rather than last Tuesdays, which are perceived to be for outsiders. Depending on the number of pilgrims, these smaller celebrations take place in the church or in the monastery's chapel. For both pilgrims and monks, last Tuesday represents the most significant moment of the 'gathering of the exorcist community.'

the village, close to the fields belonging to villagers. One wealthy pilgrim and friend of the monastery sponsored the construction, but monks provided the labour themselves. Since the chapel's construction, the holy spring has gained an important role in the functioning of the monastic community.

Pilgrims' main expectations are focused on the exorcism prayers, though not all stay until the end of the day. They see the journey and religious services of the day as preparations for attending the exorcism prayers. Some pilgrims fast the entire day before travelling. Most pray the rosary during the journey and listen to Planchak's sermons, which are available on tape. Apart from its collective dimension, the last Tuesday pilgrimage is also a private spiritual quest. Exorcism catalyzes individual fears, and deep problems find their way out, expressed during the ritual in accepted cultural forms. The practice of last Tuesday creates a routine out of an extraordinary ritual and at the same time regulates the needs of those who come to the monastery.

Pilgrims have some knowledge of what is expected of them during the rituals, and this information is shared during the trip and in between rituals as an initiation for newcomers. Those who are experienced teach the others how to perform rituals properly in order to gain the maximum of spiritual benefits from Kolodiivka. In this sense one can talk of a socialization into exorcism, since newcomers become aware of the ritual process through intensive communication with other pilgrims even before attending the exorcism. This creates a predisposition towards accepting the workings of the exorcism, including healing, and an easier integration into the ritual context, similar to what Thomas Csordas (1993, 2001) called 'somatic modes of attention' in his attempt to explain healing among charismatic Catholics.

The sequence of ritual actions on last Tuesdays carries pilgrims from morning till night, determining a particular devotional rhythm. The day starts at 7.00 with Great Vespers, followed by the Morning Prayer (*Utrenia*). At 10.00 there is a special prayer to the Mother of God (*Akatist*). At noon the abbot preaches a sermon, which is followed by a lengthy liturgy and a general blessing. The unction (*miruvania*) of pilgrims takes place at 4.00 p.m., and from 6.00 onwards exorcism prayers continue until late into the night. Throughout the day more familiar, routinized practices are interspersed with moments of intense emotion, and the religious fervor reaches its climax during the exorcism prayers.

Unlike pilgrimages to other devotional sites, such as the new places of apparition discussed in the following chapter, during visits to Kolodiivka pilgrims are not accompanied by priests. Their own priests prefer not join the trip to the 'exorcist monastery' because of its controversial status, and pilgrims come precisely because they expect to find 'better priests' there than they would at home.

Many of the pilgrims stand in queues outside the church, waiting to confess; from five to nine lines usually form along the church walls, in front of the priests. People kneel in front of the sitting priest, confess, and enter the church to pray. The queues for confession go on until 6.00 p.m., when healing prayers start. One or two priests stand in the courtyard, laying their hands on people's heads and whispering prayers. A small group of pilgrims is always gathered around these priests, and this event can go on for hours.[238] Monks and nuns circulate between the monastery and the church and are often stopped and asked for blessings or advice.

Plate 20. Pilgrims waiting at the monastery door, 2004. Last Tuesdays are the best times to have a good confession with a priest-exorcist.

The 'regulars' among the pilgrims search for the monks they already know, or they gather and wait at the monastery gate, looking for their usual confessor. Some pilgrims come for a day or two and wait for the abbot or another priest to see them. Among these are the 'old clients' of the monastery – those who come regularly, announcing themselves in advance. Most of these old clients are from the region, but some come from distant places in central and

[238] These are simple healing prayers that the priests make over each pilgrim unconditionally. On the last Tuesday in April 2004, Father Artemie prayed like this from 11.00 a.m. to 4.00 p.m. for several hundred pilgrims.

eastern Ukraine. Pilgrims have little interaction with the villagers of Kolodiivka, who tend to avoid them. Some villagers profit by selling food to the steady flow of people, but most prefer not to offer accommodations to pilgrims, because most of those looking for accommodations have serious health problems and are seen as mentally or physically 'weak' (*slabyi*) and thus difficult to deal with.

Plate 21. Priests listen to hundreds of confessions during a last Tuesday; almost all pilgrims confess. Kolodiivka, 2004.

Near the temporary guest house for pilgrims in the courtyard of the village church, a tent is raised the day before the pilgrimage. There, novices sell candles, baked rolls, and blessed oil to pilgrims. Other religious objects such as icons, books, and rosaries are sold outside the courtyard, next to the village houses, by a few people from Ternopil. The monastery has its own small shop where its sells all kinds of things, including the abbot's tapes and icons the monks themselves produce. This is where requests for prayers and offerings for the monastery are also made.[239]

One of the monastery priests conducts morning services, and the abbot usually appears for the sermon at noon. Each homily has a theme, which he announces in the beginning: 'My dearest, today we will speak about Christian love' or 'about the gifts of the Holy Spirit'. In the summer of 2004 his

[239] These offerings constitute an important source of income for the monastery.

sermons began to include a 'message from the Mother of God to the children of Ukraine', similar to those read in Lishnia and Dzhublyk that I describe in the next chapter. Abbot Planchak's sermons employ an emotional and appealing rhetoric that creates an interaction between himself and the pilgrims. His style, reminiscent of the preaching used in charismatic communities, invokes strong emotions, electrifying the audience and making it part of the ritual performance. In the middle of the homily he introduces expressions that raise the intensity of the moment, as in this example from 29 June 2004:

> Abbot: [Do you] hear me!? Say it!
> Congregation: We hear!
> – Say: Love is power!
> – Love is power!
> – Repeat after me: Love is power!
> – Love is power! . . .
> – Do you hear?
> – We do!
> – And what do you hear? Do you hear how the Holy Spirit works in you?

The liturgy starts soon after the sermon is over and lasts for about an hour and a half, as long as a typical Sunday mass in any Greek Catholic church. Monks insist on two special moments during the liturgy: the homily and the communion. Two or three priests emerge from the church to administer communion to pilgrims who are outside, while others remain in the church giving it to those inside. The entire process takes at least half an hour, owing to the large number of pilgrims. Nuns sing throughout the course of the ceremony.

At the end of the liturgy the abbot comes out of the church to bless objects pilgrims have purchased during their visit or brought from home. For this people form two rows in front of the church and hold all the objects (icons, rosaries, family pictures, books, posters) they want to be blessed, making them as visible as possible. Many of the pilgrims hold pictures of their relatives for whom they came to pray or ask for healing. The priest moves through the group and sprinkles holy water on people and objects. It is at this moment that the first manifestations of possession appear. From contact with the holy water, some pilgrims start to shout and shiver.

At around 4.00 p.m. the unction ritual (*miruvania*) begins inside the church.[240] A priest stands in front of the altar, and one by one pilgrims come and are anointed with blessed oil on their foreheads. Some also ask for other parts of their body (such as the eyes, ears, hands, or nape of the neck) to be

[240] The unction is an act of anointing someone with blessed or exorcised oil, a sacrament generally used for the ill or moribund.

anointed. During this hour a monk recites the rosary or nuns sing the 'Jesus prayer', the prayer of the Orthodox mystics, repeating it continuously with the same rhythm and intonation: 'Jesus, son of God, have mercy upon us!'[241]

Plate 22. In spite of the large number of pilgrims, confession remains an intimate moment.

Once the anointing has been completed, the monks propose a longer break as preparation for the exorcism prayers. Sometimes at this time the abbot informs the pilgrims that exorcism prayers are reserved for the severely ill and asks those who are healthy to leave.[242] The actions most pilgrims have undertaken up to this point are confession, being blessed by one of the priests, communion, a second blessing, and the unction. These are all common rituals with which most participants are already familiar. They are now prepared for healing, but first a visit must be paid to the holy spring.

Some consider the prayer at the spring a must in the sequence of ritual acts to be performed in Kolodiivka. Most pilgrims walk or drive to the

[241] '*Isuse, Isuse, synu Bodzyi, pomylui nas*!' Sometimes they also sing a Marian prayer: 'Most Blessed Mother of God, save us!' (*Presviataia Bohorodytse, spasyi nas*!)

[242] In this he follows the church's distinction between exorcisms, which are already part of standard rituals (effective for the general spiritual well-being of pilgrims, keeping away the devil), and exorcism prayers addressed to those possessed by evil spirits. Stewart (1991) described the same structure in the case of Greek monasteries.

spring to obtain holy water to take home with them. While there they make a short prayer in front of an icon of the Virgin Mary framed in a stone heart. As part of the religious imagery related to springs, there are rumours in Kolodiivka that the Mother of God actually appears at the spring. Her reassuring presence pleases most pilgrims, who bring their own little miracles into the story.[243] Unlike at other apparition sites, here it is unclear who had the visions of the Mother of God, even if some monks talk discreetly about someone in the monastery who saw the holy figure. Brother Roman was sceptical of the apparition but acknowledged the role the spring played in his devotion and for the religious practice of the monastery: 'I don't know if this apparition is true,' he said, 'but for me it is important that I can go there and pray. When I pray, the Mother of God is with me. People say many things – [that they] saw the Mother of God; as for how much of this is true, I don't know.'

While some pilgrims visit the spring, others remain in the church and, together with the nuns, continue to sing the songs started earlier. People advance towards the altar in a slow procession during this long moment of waiting. One or two possessed persons shriek loudly from time to time and struggle violently to escape their relatives' hands. When the exorcism prayers begin, people are crammed into the church. Priests gather at the altar, and the possessed persons are brought to the space in front of it. Some stand; others sit in chairs or wheelchairs, agitated or completely numb. There are young girls brought by their parents or friends, middle-age women with their husbands, some older women and men, a few mentally and physically handicapped children, and teenagers with their parents.[244]

The exorcists start the exorcism prayers at the same time, placing their hands on the head of each possessed person. Some hold a cross; others use only their hands to bless while praying in silence or whispering prayers. When the person in front of them reacts by starting to shiver, scream, and shout, the exorcists touch the cross on certain parts of the person's body: the head, neck, chest, abdomen, back, or palms. As they place the cross on these spots, responses of anger and aggression are provoked from their temporary

[243] Pilgrims tell various stories about personal miracles related to the spring. Some describe a particularly disturbing pain of unknown cause that disappeared when they drank water from the spring. Others talk about help received from the Mother of God of the spring in a difficult moment.

[244] Those possessed were of different ages and backgrounds, and although women predominated, the use of exorcism as a means of expression was not exclusive to them, as it was in Ioan Lewis's (1990) peripheral possession cults. For Lewis, exorcism was a cultural idiom in which marginalized or underrepresented people could express their anxieties or frustrations. This is not the case in Ukraine, where exorcism is a mode of religious expression consistent with the mainstream religious tradition.

victims. Some priests blow air over the exorcised person, which has the same effect. One exorcist can pray for two people at the same time.

Plate 23. Children are brought to the monastery to receive the powerful blessing that will protect them from evil. Kolodiivka, 2005.

The priests also walk around, selecting any of the pilgrims to pray for briefly in the same manner. Thus each person in the church may potentially reveal a hidden 'affliction', and the exorcists 'discover' the presence of evil through something akin to an act of divination. Here again the ritual in Kolodiivka differs from other exorcisms in the way it reveals the possession and uncovers the evil spirits behind it. Two monks continuously pass through the crowd, across the entire church, one carrying an incense censer and the other sprinkling holy water on people. Those who react to the water are identified as possessed, and exorcists move towards them and start to pray. The possessed all display similar reactions: shrieking and shivering with their eyes closed. They are held firmly by those around them and at times try to attack the others with their hands, groaning, growling, and spitting all the while. The groans become deep, guttural sounds, and some of the possessed burst into voices that sound unlike their own. Eventually they fall to the floor, wracked by waves of convulsions.[245]

When an exorcised person becomes violent, one priest may ask another for help. Then two exorcists pray over one person, who is either subdued by a relative or crawls on the floor. Exorcists may also become more aggressive in response to the aggression of the possessed, in which they see the devil opposing them. The exorcists do not cease until the possessed gives signs of fatigue, at which point the priests move on to another of the possessed. After such an intense session the possessed, still not fully exorcised, breathe deeply and slowly, become numb, and barely react to holy water or the people around them. Often they spit and vomit into plastic bags.

A second part soon follows when the priest returns to interrogate the possessing spirit. This time a sort of dialogue takes place between the priest and the possessed, who speaks in a modified voice. This does not occur during the first exorcism, and sometimes it takes several performances until the possessed learns to speak with the voice of the evil spirit. The aim is to identify the spirit and thus determine how difficult it will be to exorcise it. Only one exorcist in Kolodiivka has the gift of recognizing evil spirits as soon as the inflicted person is brought to him. By looking at the person in front of him he 'sees' what is beyond the affliction and can thus propose a cure. The other exorcists must discover demons by asking the possessed person questions about his or her past and behaviour. This is a joint effort to create meaning from a person's life experience and suffering by setting them within the network of meaning proposed by the religious idiom (Obeyesekere 1981: 106).

Identifying the demon and calling it by name are the most important and difficult parts of the exorcism ritual.[246] By using the name of the demon, the exorcist can directly ask it to leave the person's body. There are hierarchies of demons, and sometimes several demons might possess a single person. Usually the demons exorcised in Kolodiivka reflect attributes of the person who is possessed: an older man from Transcarpathia might be possessed by the demon of the Carpathians, while a teenage girl brought by her parents because of her hypercritical attitude towards everyone, has the demon of criticism. A demon's name can also indicate the specific place of affliction – for example, the demon of the womb or demon of the throat.

---

[245] In the anthropological literature on possession, this is identified as a possession trance, and it can be found in many religious traditions (Bourguignon 1973).

[246] In a chapter entitled 'The Power of Names', Stewart (1991: 214) talked about the symbolic importance of naming and names in Orthodoxy and their role in the exorcism ritual: 'The drama of exorcism lies in forcing the demon to reveal its name, thus surrendering itself to the control of the exorcist.'

Once the demon has been discovered, it is a matter of persuasion to make him leave. A dramatic dialogue, according to the style of each exorcist, follows:

> Exorcist: Let me introduce you to God!
> Demon: Ah, you shouldn't!
> Exorcist: Come out in the name of God!
> Demon: I don't want to! No! No! No!
> Exorcist: Irineus [the name of her spirit], depart from her, go away from her!

The priest directly addresses the evil spirit, who responds through the voice of the possessed. When addressing the spirit, the priest uses a series of expressions, continuously repeating them: Leave! Rid yourself! Breathe out! Go away! Come out!

During exorcisms the church is extremely crowded, lacking air and light. Those who are not possessed or exorcised continue to sing and pray in a repetitive, reassuring way, gathered around the spots where exorcisms are being performed. Loud cries and screaming induce fear in those in the back of the church, who cannot see. Few try to help the possessed, and most of the audience looks on in terror. Many persons hold pictures of their children or relatives and point them out to the exorcists.[247] Towards evening, people begin to emerge from the church in order to rest or leave the village. The exorcisms continue until late at night, with fewer pilgrims and priests in attendance.

The exorcism ritual in Kolodiivka takes a compound form (Kapferer 1991: 110) as it systematically incorporates into its performance a collection of major and minor rites directly connected with common religious practice. Both monks and pilgrims see the Tuesday ritual as an entirety, a continuous prayer for healing of the soul, the spirit, and the body. The exorcists demand of all those subject to the exorcism prayers that they complete all the stages of the ritual: confession, communion, blessing, unction, and, at the end, exorcism prayer. The vast majority of pilgrims also follow all the stages, including the exorcism prayers, even if they are not possessed. The abbot's homilies, at the same time, constitute introductions to the cosmology and exegesis of the ritual.

Some of the smaller rituals that make up the last Tuesday ceremony are practised regularly as elements of other rites or as rites in themselves: the blessing of water, the blessing of people and objects with water, the unction,

---

[247] It is extremely important for pilgrims who take part in the exorcism to symbolically bring the family and the afflicted to the monastery. This accounts for the reach of symbolic healing outside the monastery walls and shows how the religious imaginary functions in a larger social context, involving more people than those directly participating in the ritual.

and the liturgy. Most of what happens in the church is already familiar to many of the participants because these are standard forms of church ritual. The feeling of being accustomed to the ritual is an important factor for the pilgrims who take part. The novelty and, for some, shock come only with the final part of the Tuesday ritual, the exorcism. Thus, over the course of the day, one is first involved in a series of common rituals that are already familiar from everyday religious practice, only to later be startled by the exorcisms at the end. The performative aspects of the ritual are extremely important: the repeated singing, the pungent aromas, the almost imperceptible movement of the crowd in the church, the initially sporadic cries that later become unbearable shouting, and the dramatic struggles between exorcists and afflicted. These aspects form the aesthetics of the ritual (Kapferer 1991) and create the drama that underscores the cosmology of the exorcism.

Pilgrims expect to witness such performances, and the enactment of the exorcism ritual reinforces the religious imaginary proposed by the community in Kolodiivka. The audience measures the gravity of a possession and the success of the exorcism by evaluating the degree of performativity of the ritual. The stories one hears from pilgrims and exorcists always describe the spectacular way in which the exorcism took place. The actual violence of the ritual comes from the aggressive enactment of the symbolic fight between the two actors. This elicits strong emotional responses and sometimes disorientation from the audience. Because of the intensity of the moment and the circumstances of the performance, it is rare for audience members to remain outside the exorcism and thus not to share in the imaginary created around the ritual. Exorcism generates its own imaginal world composed through its cosmological practice within the space of the ritual performance (Kapferer 2003: 118). In this sense the ritual creates its own reality, which is reinforced with each performance in Kolodiivka.

There is an anticipation of the drama among the participants, yet its actual enactment violates their expectations every time. The ritual generates high levels of emotional arousal, both collective and individual, that challenge participants' rational expectations. The exorcism ritual is set in the language of metaphor, which, through 'analogic imagery' (Barth 1987), triggers multiple connotations that have a strong emotional or sensual character. The medium of exorcism offers a specific set of multivocal symbols and acts that generate public and private interpretations. Each act or word is interpreted within the imaginary of the ritual (at least by the exorcist) but is individually reflected upon by all the other participants. Their subjective interpretations, which can be equated to the spontaneous exegetical reflection of the modes theory, are then adjusted and framed to correspond to the collective imaginary.

The special religiosity of exorcism at Kolodiivka belongs to the wide range of 'particular rituals' that includes the ecstatic practices Gananath Obeyesekere (1981) studied in Kataragama and the exorcist rituals studied by Bruce Kapferer (1991, 2003) in Sri Lanka. Such powerful rituals create a 'dynamic field of force in whose virtual space human psychological, cognitive, and social realities are forged anew, so that the ritual participants are both reoriented to their ordinary realities and embodied with potencies to restore and reconstruct their lived worlds' (Kapferer 2005: 51).

The emotional intensity of the imagistic rituals provokes unique and vivid memories that, later recalled, can trigger the same emotions. In this sense one can conceive of a successful transmission taking place in the ritual. Leaving aside the contents of the transmission, I would stress that the medium of the ritual is as much responsible for the effective transmission as it is the means of codification. Exorcism, an imagistic ritual by default, builds on metaphor and thus on the vagueness and multivocality of symbols. Yet it does so in a specific context that brings together familiar and routinized practice and intense emotions and thus accounts for the successful propagation of the message. It is the counterintuitive context of ritual communication (Severi 2004) that accounts for the persistence in time of the representations related to the exorcist imaginary among monks and pilgrims.[248] Looking at the strength of the imaginal field surrounding exorcism, as I do in the next section, shows how disbelief and estrangement appear only later, when these representations are disconnected from the ritual performance and the 'ritual virtuality' (Kapferer 2005) is challenged by the outside world.

6.4 Shaping Kolodiivka: The Power of Imagistic Practice

The exorcism ritual practised in Kolodiivka is now the central aspect of the monastery, around which the dynamics and cohesion of the community are maintained. Exorcism creates its own virtual world, which substantiates the religious imaginary of the community. The monks' cosmological views develop around the continuous struggle between God and the devil, and to a certain extent such views determine the monks' reactions to the changing world. Evil spirits attack not only people who are spiritually weak but also those who aspire to higher spirituality, and the monks of Kolodiivka are favourite targets. As their spiritual strength increases, they are assaulted ever more by evil, and so they must pray more often to gain the spiritual power

[248] As Carlo Severi (2004: 817) has argued, 'the persistence in time, and success, of notions of this kind are not explained by their 'counterintuitive' content, but rather by their insertion within very precisely defined, and yet counterintuitive, contexts of ritual communication'.

necessary to overcome evil. Evil spirits are believed to cause a great deal of harm in the monastery, and the life of the community is seen as a continuous attempt to overcome these forces. The general interpretation for many common events in the everyday life of the monastery is that they are 'manifestations of evil' or, on the contrary, 'gifts of God'. Monks cultivate imagistic practices as a support for their belief, and this reverberates in their daily lives.

Taras, a nineteen-year-old novice in the monastery in 2004, enjoyed painting icons, although he had no prior experience or training in this craft. His work was highly valued by the other monks, whose activity involved only the mechanical reproduction of icons in the monastery's workshop.[249] His talent was explained as a result of 'divine intervention' as in the old tradition of Orthodox icon painters. While painting, in the middle of intense concentration, he occasionally began to shiver, eventually falling to the floor, unconscious. During such episodes he had at times destroyed the icon on which he was working, but upon waking he remembered nothing. Losing consciousness is seen in the monastery as a sign of being touched by the Holy Spirit; during the exorcism ritual, younger nuns and monks often faint briefly. The others leave them alone, on the shared understanding that it is the Holy Spirit who 'took them over'.[250]

This young novice, however, had recently had a minor accident that affected his hand, which sometimes began to tremble uncontrollably. The accident was explained in the community as having been caused by evil, in the same way Taras's temporary losses of consciousness were seen as gifts from God. Both were understood as necessary steps in the spiritual life of any monk, part of the individual struggle to overcome evil. The source of evil is usually believed to lie in a sinful act by the victim or one of his family members, and the confessor has a duty to investigate the origins of the sin. In Taras's case the abbot determined that his older brother, also a monk in the monastery, was the source of sin, and thus he shared some of the blame for the demon attack.[251]

In many cases the source of both sin and salvation lies in family genealogies. Physical and psychic afflictions can result from sins committed by previous generations or close kin, and moral fault is transmitted intergenera-

[249] Making and selling icons is one of the profitable activities of the monastery. Monks buy printed pictures of icons that they glue on a wooden frame and stain, after which they bless the completed object. The result resembles a painted icon.

[250] This is another striking resemblance to charismatic Christians, who practise the gifts of the Holy Spirit, leading to similar physical manifestations (Cox 1996).

[251] The brother was one of the monks who later left the monastery because of conflicts of 'interpretation'.

tionally. When recognizing the possession, the priest restores the social status of the afflicted, and the family reintegrates him or her by accepting the interpretation and thus the past faults of both themselves and the afflicted. The exorcism ritual attempts to heal the person by reinstating and re-enforcing social bonds. By restoring the person's wholeness, the ritual acts symbolically over his or her family and the larger community. Thus the religious imaginary of the community extends beyond the world of the monastery into pilgrims' lived reality.

It passes by the village of Kolodiivka, however, with little effect. Villagers completely avoid the exorcism prayers and thus stay away from the main source of conviction. The use they make of the monastery is limited to simple religious functions. Instead it is pilgrims who carry the messages of the monastery into the world. Transformed by the experience of the exorcism, some pilgrims become transmitters of the monastery's cosmology, taking over its message and practices and thus feeling empowered to change their immediate reality accordingly.

Plate 24. Father Hryhoryi Planchak (centre), founder of the community in Kolodiivka, is a charismatic figure sought continually by pilgrims. Kolodiivka, 2005.

One example is Volodea, who began coming to the monastery in 1999, when he was a boy of thirteen. He was brought by his mother, who was searching for a cure for his convulsions and asked Father Planchak to pray for him. The boy was extremely tired after that day but felt better, so the mother decided to bring him again the next time.[252] The two continued to attend almost every last Tuesday for the next five years, and the priests prayed for Volodea each time. Eventually he was completely healed, as mother and son attested during our meeting.

The day I met Volodea and his mother in 2004 he was eighteen, and the two were waiting at the monastery gate to talk to Planchak. This time they had come because Volodea wanted to join the monastery. Over the years he had learned to pray like the Kolodiivka monks and, according to his mother, had even absorbed some of the abbot's spiritual power. He now prayed for other people in the neighbourhood who were ill, and his efforts were said to be helpful. The power of his prayers and the spiritual strength he and his mother had received at the monastery had recently, they believed, saved them from a car accident. This miraculous event convinced them that Volodea must join the monastery. His mother said that Volodea was not adapting well to school and put all his energy into religious matters, so the choice of the monastery for him seemed evident. He was not accepted into it during my stay there, however.

Most of the pilgrims who visit the monastery hope to find a cure for their unexplained suffering; it is sometimes their last hope after a stay in a psychiatric hospital. Popular belief is that problems related to the nerves should be treated by the church, and people usually try the healing prayers of the church as a first resort and exorcism as a last one. Exorcists in Kolodiivka are aware that some of those in need who visit them have mental problems, being 'psychoneurotic' (*psykhonevrotychnyi*). Yet in their view a problem of the body or mind is first of all a spiritual imperfection. Their role is to heal 'the whole person' through their prayers, and so they assume that mentally ill persons belong first to their sphere of healing. In Kolodiivka a monk does not send people to psychiatrists, although psychiatrists from the nearby town sometimes send patients to the monastery as the last of a series of attempts to be healed. For an afflicted person, exorcism is usually a last hope, following unsuccessful attempts ranging from medical approaches to paranormal treatments and witchcraft. A successful healing confirms the cosmology of the exorcism ritual, whereas repeated failure produces mistrust.

With distance from the ritual context, the meaning of the exorcism and consequently the effect of the symbolic healing can weaken or disappear. One example is the case of the nineteen-year-old daughter of a university professor in L'viv. She began to behave strangely at home, so her mother took her to a psychiatrist friend for a check-up. The doctor diagnosed her as

---

[252] This family was from Ternopil and so could attend regularly. Many pilgrims seldom get to Kolodiivka or give up because of the distance, costs, and difficulty of travel in Ukraine.

having an incurable, advanced form of schizophrenia and prescribed medicine to slow the progression of the illness. The expensive medicine did not improve the young woman's condition. The mother had doubts about the diagnosis; she thought her daughter's problem was more an illness of the soul (*dushevna balnoi*) than a psychological illness (*psykhichna balnoi*). Her suspicion, deriving from the daughter's excessive interest in spiritual literature, already placed the girl's affliction in the realm of possibility for spiritual healing.

The parents began to seek alternative ways to challenge the diagnosis and find a cure for their daughter. When they learned about Kolodiivka, they decided to try it out. The monks prayed for the young woman the first time the family came, and her condition improved. Encouraged, the family visited Kolodiivka twice more. After each visit the daughter felt better for a short time but later re-entered deep crisis. For her parents it required great effort just to come to the monastery, and the exorcism prayers seemed to improve the young woman's health only temporarily. Eventually, they had to give up the exorcism, doubtful that it would completely heal her, and they began looking for yet another alternative form of healing.

Healing and exorcism are strongly linked in Kolodiivka. The ritual itself seems to be the cause of healing; 'the rite is the cure', as Stewart (1991: 221) remarked about exorcism in Greek Orthodoxy. Exorcism has always been one curative procedure among others, its cosmological view giving meaning to people's afflictions. In every society alternative explanatory frameworks are at work at any one time, and exorcism is one among many. While its ritual form varies significantly, the cosmology of exorcism has been remarkably constant over time, regardless of historical period (Goodman 1988; Levi 1988; Worobec 2001; Grey 2005). In this sense exorcism always remains modern because the ritual first destroys social meaning and then creates a new meaning following its own cosmology (Kapferer 2003). James Dow (1986: 56) suggested that the symbolic healing that takes place in a successful exorcism happens because 'the culture establishes a general model of the mythic world believed in by healers and potential patients'. The acceptance of possession before entering the ritual creates a symbolic dissociation in the afflicted person: he is no longer one but two, himself and the evil spirit. The exorcism ritual proposes a symbolic reintegration of the self in which one has to get rid of the evil identified during the ritual.[253] To understand the role of healing in the terms proposed here, one must take into

---

[253] Dow (1986) tried to develop a universal structure of symbolic healing by looking for the deep structure of the ritual in different cultural models of healing. He was later criticized because his schema of symbolic healing put the patient in a passive role, and the healer structured the entire event according to his own worldview (Shaara and Strathern 1992).

consideration the subjective imagery of both the afflicted and the healer within the imaginary generated through the ritual. In a hierarchical view of the transformation, the exorcism ritual becomes a transition rite (Kapferer 1991: 246). If successful, it takes one from a lower state, one of illness or disturbance (physical, psychic, or social), to a higher state in which one is integrated into the cosmological order of the ritual.

Religious practice in Kolodiivka, concentrated on exorcism, draws extensively on the imagistic mode of religiosity. The exorcism rituals performed in the monastery play a role similar to that of the imagistic practices developed at the sites of Marian apparition discussed in the next chapter. Visions are a significant part of the imagistic activity at work in the community and commonly take the form of dreams and private visions of the Mother of God and other spiritual benefactors. The monks cultivate this religious imagery as a mode of orientation in domains such as prayer, prophecy, and healing, but it reaches beyond the monastery. Spiritual agents give guidance, support certain intuitions and behaviours, and warn against dangers, but such experiences are always checked with the priest-confessor. It is he who has the gift of discernment, the ability to distinguish between divine message and the believer's own ideas. Both visions and exorcisms draw on the metaphorical language provided by the imagistic mode, becoming places of mediation between individual and collective imageries. Kolodiivka appears on the western Ukrainian map of sites of alternative, imagistic religiosity as a discrete place, but it is firmly connected to other sites of imagistic practice.

Father Artemie, one of the exorcist priests, joined Planchak's community in Kolodiivka soon after its establishment. Artemie came from an extremely religious Roman Catholic family. His three sisters were nuns in Byrki, the female branch of the monastery, and his brother was a Roman Catholic priest. He began by studying theology with Franciscans in Poland but after four years switched to the eastern rite and entered the Basilian order, doing his novitiate in Przemyśl. In search of a way to get closer to the Orthodox tradition, he became interested in Planchak's community as soon as the news spread in the Basilian order that a group was splitting off to start a new community. 'I heard two things about [Planchak],' said Father Artemie: 'that he prays a lot and he is of Orthodox spirituality. So I understood that he respects the tradition of the church fathers, he loves them, he loves tradition, and loves inner life; he loves prayer. So I felt that I should be there because this was the orientation of my heart.'

In Kolodiivka Artemie found the environment he was looking for. Sharing the abbot's ideas, he followed in Planchak's footsteps and became a priest and later an exorcist. For a short time in 2001 he left Kolodiivka to become abbot of an emerging monastery in Dzhublyk (see chapter 7). There, the Mother of God had appeared to two girls, and the place had become an important apparition site. In one of the visions the Mother of God asked the local community to support the construction of a monastery dedicated to the holy family. With Planchak's blessing, Artemie moved to Dzhublyk and started a small community of nuns and monks that was to be the basis for two future monasteries. Artemie believed in the verity of the apparition and supported the visionaries, but he found himself involved in a conflict between the local priest and the church hierarchy. He had to abandon the project and return to Kolodiivka, waiting for things to calm down in Dzhublyk.

Plate 25. Nuns from the nearby convent join the monks during last Tuesdays. Nuns play an important role in the imagistic practice in the monastery. Kolodiivka, 2004.

After his return, the Mother of God made her presence felt in Kolodiivka, too, in an event that is revealed to pilgrims only indirectly, through the messages Planchak reads to pilgrims on last Tuesdays. One of the younger nuns in Byrki, the associated convent, began to have visions of the Virgin in 2001. Her private visions were first tested by the abbot and then accepted and even encouraged by him. She was asked to accept her gift, and while her influence on the abbot grew, her visions also became increasingly important to the monastery. The community's inclination towards imagistic practices and the overwhelming presence of the Marian cult in the local religious tradition facilitated the acceptance of the visions by most monks and nuns. Visions and dreams are favourite means of transmitting religious messages, but these avenues are cultivated primarily in other religions (Stephen and Suryani 2000), and one might not expect them to occupy a central place in a traditional branch of Christianity. Such practices, however, play an important role in both western and eastern Christianity as part of the mechanism of revelation and renewal of religious traditions (see Christian 1996; Csordas 1997, 2001).

The two modes – the imagistic, as represented by visions and exorcisms, and the doctrinal, as represented by the monks' daily devotional routine – were able to coexist in the community as long as one mode was not accorded a higher normative authority. But the visionary nun and the group around her began to impose imagistic practice as the most authentic form of knowledge and guidance for the monastery. Her visions became the primary guides for interpreting monastic reality. The community found itself split between those who believed in the visions and followed an imagistic mode of religiosity, fully expressed in the practice of exorcism, and those who questioned the authenticity and religious efficacy of such practices. With Planchak's support, the imagistic mode became the norm in the community, which led to major conflicts and, in the end, to the departure of several monks from Kolodiivka during 2004–2005.

6.5 Conclusion

The development of the Kolodiivka monastery illustrates both the 'making of churches' and the interaction between the different modes of religiosity cultivated within the monastery. By interpreting the eastern Christian religious tradition according to its own philosophy and beliefs, the community in Kolodiivka became yet another splinter group within the Greek Catholic Church. The case bears certain similarities to that of the Basilians who became 'traditionalists', as described in chapter 4. Both groups insisted on following a particular mode of religiosity by cultivating imagistic practices in opposition to mainstream, institutional religion. The community that formed around Father Planchak had the characteristics of a spontaneous communitas brought together around an ideal initially expressed by the founder. The establishment of a community in Kolodiivka, however, undermined the natural, ideologically based cohesion of the group, which was to be replaced by the structure of a normative communitas. But the turn towards the doctrinal went only halfway: the community increasingly took the shape of the imagistic ritual it was practising.

The monks remained together for several years not because of successful institutionalization but because they placed an imagistic ritual at the core of their community. Exorcism and the imaginary generated by it became the cohesive force for the monastery and legitimated its singularity. The monks in Kolodiivka rediscovered and re-created the exorcism ritual, making it a cultural idiom available to many. By cultivating the empowering discourse of 'gifts', the community opened the ritual to pilgrims and priests, making them aware of its potential. Much as in charismatic movements that preach a theology of spiritual gifts (Cox 1996), the monks in Kolodiivka experienced God through different gifts, the external measure of personal charisma. Monks proved their charisma through unusual displays of spontaneous thoughts and intuitions and a reputation for devout, ascetic living. Discerning spirits and exorcising them through the ritual performance was both an enactment of the monks' gifts and the means for counteracting demonic presence in the monastery. 'Seeing' was a spiritual gift of the few – the more experienced, charismatic monks – who were the main sources of authority within the community.

The revelatory potential of exorcism represents a sign of divine presence for the Kolodiivka monks. It is also part of the struggle to combat evil forces with the same imagistic means. Identifying demons and exorcising them are enactments of the monks' gift and the means for counteracting demonic presence in the monastery. 'Seeing' is a spiritual gift of the few, the more experienced, charismatic monks, who also gain and maintain authority within the community through it. Other visions manifested among participants (pilgrims and monks), separate from the actual exorcism, involve trance (fainting), hallucinations (seeing or hearing), and sensorial experiences (turning numb, cold, warm, suffocating). Monks regularly undergo such experiences, which become meaningful with the help of their confessors and enter into an 'economy of spiritual welfare' that increases and sometimes decreases their charisma.

In Kolodiivka, imagery related to the devil is continually reinforced by the practice of exorcism. The religious message is successfully transmitted because of the counterintuitive context of the ritual, which combines imagistic practices with standardized ritual forms. The powerful imagery triggered by the exorcism ritual forces new meanings into previous interpretations of illness and distress. Exorcism acts at the same time as symbolic healing and reorientation in the world for participants (Kapferer 2005: 51). At the monastery the healing aspect of the ritual eventually became more important than its sacrality, which had been carefully preserved by the church over the centuries. Exorcism in Kolodiivka became more accessible, beyond the authority of the church and even of the exorcists themselves.

The drama of the ritual performance takes in the entire monastic community and most of the pilgrims, but through the religious imaginary it is directed towards a much larger audience. The strength of the imaginary derives from the fact that the ritual performance permeates the lived reality of monks and pilgrims in concrete ways. The successful incorporation of participants into the exorcism ritual derives from the context and the unexpected dramatism of the performance; the aesthetic and performative aspects are essential for engaging participants in the sequence of ritual acts. During this process participants tend to find individual interpretations of the acts and symbols transmitted through the ritual. The ritual generates its own 'reality', which is accessed by pilgrims and monks. Rather than simply accepting the cosmology of the exorcism, pilgrims negotiate their subjective imagery with the religious imaginaries at hand. The interaction facilitated through the 'ritual virtuality' can produce symbolic healing and transformations of both the individual and social realities.

In Kolodiivka, contestation appeared when one mode of religiosity was imposed as the sole normative form of religious practice in a community where the two had previously coexisted. The monks who left Kolodiivka feared that the imagistic mode of religiosity would become the rule in their community, governing their lives. They opposed the imposition of the imagistic mode, yet in doing so, they denied the religious imaginary of the monastery, which was shaped by the exorcism ritual. Thus they found themselves outside the world of meaning of their own community, and the community splintered.

Chapter 7
The Religious Imaginaries of Western Ukraine

In previous chapters I have explored the connections between religion and social change in western Ukraine by looking at transformations of social organization and of the modes of religious transmission in the local tradition. The connections can also be explored through an investigation of the religious imaginaries at work in the local tradition. I focus here on variations in the contents of religious imaginaries in relation to specific social transformations. With the fall of the socialist regimes, religion became a prominent feature of all the former Soviet bloc countries, and people all over the region rediscovered faith and spirituality. Yet in western Ukraine, religious practice had been preserved in a modified form throughout the Soviet era. Its remarkable re-entry into the public sphere, starting in the 1980s, was not an overnight phenomenon but the result of a strong commitment and a long struggle for religious beliefs and practices in the face of waves of repression. The re-establishment of religious institutions and the emergence of a plurality of faiths in western Ukraine were also marked by troubling moments in the early 1990s when people fought each other for churches. Nevertheless, a high level of religiosity remained a continuous attribute of the region, and even today, in comparison with other Ukrainians, 'Galicians' (Halychyany) are thought to be very religious.

The confluence of eastern and western Christianity in western Ukraine shaped local practices and beliefs into an original synthesis incorporating aspects of both traditions in modified forms. This inclusive sphere of practice and belief was able to accommodate the frequent changes this historically peripheral region faced. The survival of the Ukrainian religious tradition during Soviet times relied on lay believers who, forced to improvise in order to survive, opted for 'practical adaptability' (Shlikhta 2004a) instead of fidelity to orthodoxy. Modifications to both life-cycle and sacramental rituals throughout the Soviet period were made by laypeople who took over the 'relationship with the divine' of traditional, institutional churches and tailored it to local circumstances.

For these reasons it makes little sense for an anthropologist to work with top-down approaches to Ukrainian religion, focusing on institutions and collective identities. Rather, one gains a clearer view of the religious tradition by focusing on the nuanced and fragmented expressions of local religiosity. The local tradition is a 'cosmology in the making', a living tradition of knowledge undergoing reproduction and change, not just a set of ideas fixed in collective representations promoted by religious institutions (Barth 1994: 84). On the one hand, the written, doctrinal basis of church teaching and the uniformity and standardization of ritual practice binds the imagined community of Orthodoxy, including Greek Catholics, together. On the other hand, practices and beliefs vary substantially because of the localization of eastern Christianity, which results in various orthodoxies. The evolution of these local orthodoxies takes place from the bottom up as popular exegesis and common practices produce and shape theological knowledge.

One step in understanding the functioning of this complex process is to observe variation in the contents of local religious knowledge in relation to specific social transformations. For this purpose I turn to religious imaginaries emerging around imagistic practices, particularly the visionary activities of the socialist and postsocialist periods. These types of imagistic practices are not part of the daily routine of religious life in the Orthodox and Greek Catholic Churches. They are to be found in movements such as the underground church during Soviet times and in the religious fervour in the last days of the Soviet Union.

Today, in spite of the institutionalization of mainstream orthodoxy that led to the increasing marginalization of imagistic practices, such practices remain the main means of people's adjustment to postsocialist transformations. Individual responses to such transformations that are expressed in religious idioms can reach the religious imaginary and become shared knowledge within a community of practice. Such is the case with visionary activity, the example I use to illustrate this process. Apparition sites are usually spaces of unmediated interaction between believers and the sphere of the divine, spaces in which the religious imaginary takes shape. In this chapter I look at two cases of apparitions of the Mother of God in western Ukraine and describe the local cosmologies formulated around the apparition sites.[254] Each vision came during a period of rapid social changes brought by, respectively, collectivization and the anti-religion policies of the Soviet regime and, later, postsocialist transformations, both equal sources of distress and general anxiety.

[254] The Virgin Mary is addressed as 'Mother of God' (Bohorodytsia) in eastern Christianity, and I use this term in relation to the Ukrainian apparitions.

Map 2. Apparition sites and the Way of the Cross between L'viv and Dzhublyk.

7.1 Soviet Apparitions: Seredne

When I went to Ukraine for the first time, it was with a group of colleagues from my Ukrainian language course. We travelled to a village close to Transcarpathia, wanting to practise our conversational skills by conducting interviews and speaking to the locals. Having heard of my interest in religious issues, the village teacher introduced me to an old woman whom she called 'sectarian' (*sektanty*). I went with some colleagues to talk to the woman, Anna, and we steered the discussion towards her beliefs by asking about religious life during Soviet times. Anna's story, like those of many other practising believers in Ukraine, was dramatic, illustrating the hardships believers faced under the atheist regime.

I did not return to this village during my following months of fieldwork, but Anna's story remained with me, and I decided to pursue it as an aside to my main research project. I later learned that Anna belonged to a religious group calling itself the Penitents (*Pokutnyky*). The group appeared in western Ukraine during Soviet times, prompted by an apparition of the Mother of God in the small village of Seredne (also known as Serednia), in Kalush *raion,* Ivano-Frankivsk oblast. The 'miracle of Seredne', as it was then known, received publicity during the years immediately following the event, and Soviet authorities launched a vigorous campaign against the Penitents. Two historians whose work deals with religion in Soviet Ukraine have discussed the case briefly. For Vasyl Markus (1989) and Bohdan Bociurkiw (1977), the Penitents represented an extreme version of the larger phenomenon of the underground church and was the best illustration of the strong connection between religion and nationalism in Soviet Ukraine.

On 22 December 1954, a villager named Hanna Kuzminska had a vision on a hill in the vicinity of Seredne. The woman was said to have received repeated visions with messages from the Mother of God (Bociurkiw 1977: 86). The apparitions urged people to repent of their sins in order to escape Soviet domination and gave precise instructions for proper personal penitence.

In spite of a general fear of repression by Soviet authorities, large crowds of pilgrims began to visit the site of the apparition. Three Greek Catholic underground priests supported the visionary and organized religious services for the pilgrims gathering in Seredne. One of the priests, Father Ihnatii Soltys, was the former Greek Catholic priest of Seredne; he had refused to become Orthodox in 1948 and had to hide to avoid imprisonment. The other two were also itinerant Greek Catholic priests who were hiding from the Soviet authorities and performing illegal religious services in the region. They promoted the 'vision of Seredne', which became the core conviction for the community of believers that gathered around the 'holy mountain' and 'holy spring' on the hill.

The religious practices of the movement were similar to those of any other underground Greek Catholic community: night-time celebrations in private houses, home prayers in small groups, and strict observance of individual devotional obligations. Forced to practise at home, people were encouraged to follow a strict daily program in which they prayed the rosary, the Way of the Cross, and other private prayers. The culmination of private practice was the pilgrimage to the hill in Seredne. Such sojourns took place on special nights announced through the group's informal network. In order to avoid informants and the secret police, pilgrimages to Seredne were not held on Sundays or during religious holidays but rather on weeknights. The liturgical service was celebrated on the hill, beginning at midnight and ending by 5.00 a.m.

The movement that developed around the miracle of Seredne combined eschatological views with a strongly nationalist stance and total rejection of the Soviet system. It began in a context of Stalinist repression and the systematic destruction of church structures in western Ukraine. Between the late 1940s and early 1950s, state authorities managed to annihilate the Greek Catholic Church in western Ukraine: most of the bishops and clergy who refused reunification with Orthodoxy were imprisoned or killed, active lay members were sent the way of the Gulag, and by 1952 the last surviving Greek Catholic monasteries were closed down.[255] In its campaign to control and eventually eliminate public forms of religiosity, the state's first targets were 'holy places', the most popular sites of mass religious practice. Hundreds of holy springs, miraculous icons, and visionary sites, which had appeared all over the country as a result of these sudden, disruptive political and social changes, were destroyed and erased in the crackdown on pilgrimages and popular devotion. The anti-religious campaign triggered, in response, more miracles and visions, both remarkable means of religious mobilization and anti-Soviet resistance.

Visions in Seredne became more radical between 1954 and 1958, portraying Ukraine and the world to be at the end of days, which was predicted for 1962. According to the Mother of God's messages, salvation would be possible only for those who came as pilgrims to the 'Holy Mountain, the new Mount Sinai', as one apparition named the hill. Even before the death of Pope Pius XII in 1958, apparitions in Seredne were becoming increasingly judgemental towards the Vatican and the head of the universal Catholic Church: 'Rome is in danger of being destroyed and the pope killed,' the Mother of God announced in one of her messages in 1956 (Emanuil 2001).

Although the reaction of the Penitents to changes in the Catholic Church was in line with that of the larger traditionalist movement within the church, the coherent reinterpretation of world politics through this local vision was nonetheless remarkable.[256] People were looking for an explanation that would make sense of the visible abandonment of the Ukrainian Greek Catholic Church by its protector in Rome and the disarray in which both laity and clergy found themselves. Seredne offered Ukrainian Greek Catholics a response and a means by which to carry on their beliefs and

[255] The last to be closed were the Basilian monastery in Hoshiv (1950) and the Studite and Basilian convents in Yachtoriv (1949) and Suchowolya (1952).

[256] The term 'traditionalist Catholics' covers a variety of groups and movements that chose to preserve the pre–Vatican II tradition of the Catholic Church. Several groups considered Pius XII to have been the last 'true' pope and refused to recognize his successors.

practices. In the view of the visionary, Seredne would eventually become the 'new Rome', where the Basilica Mundi would be built, the new centre of spirituality for Ukraine and the world. The movement claimed that with the death of Pius XII, an acknowledged anti-communist, the spiritual authority of the pope had been inherited by their leader, Emanuil, the 'Emperor of Christ' (Emanuil, Hrysta Tsaria), from Seredne. Pius's successor, Pope John XXIII, because of his reconciliation with the Moscow Patriarchate and the Soviet regime, became in their eyes an 'anti-pope', the Antichrist. According to the Penitents, the real successor to Pius XII was Arkhyierei Emanuil, the pope from Seredne.[257] The apparition site became the only place where complete absolution could be obtained. The group developed a special nine-day ritual for penitence, the *deviatnytsia,* and created its own icons, songs, and prayers separate from the Greek Catholic ones.

The 'neo-Uniates', as they were called in Soviet propaganda (Markus 1989: 156), repudiated any contact with the Soviet state or collaborationist churches. They refused to send their children to state schools, join collective farms, work in state enterprises, or undertake military service. New visions enforcing clear-cut attitudes were received each time local authorities put pressure on Greek Catholic priests to convert to Orthodoxy. One of the apparition's messages, reprinted in a book by Tsar Emanuil, the movement's leader, condemned reunited Greek Catholic priests as well as underground Greek Catholic priests who had denounced the group as heretical:

> In the times of Jesus Christ, Pharisees, Sadducees, legislators, theologians, and orthodox Jews believed they were the best, but instead it was proven that they were God's traitors, because they crucified Him. Nowadays those who consider themselves to be good are the worst; Catholic priests are Satan's people. They brought a lot of trouble to the church, more than those who have subscribed to Satan, because they betrayed God and the Holy Gifts (Emanuil 2001: 68).

The radical character of the visions provoked some underground priests to question the veracity of the apparition and to strongly oppose the content of the Seredne messages. The Penitents perceived their detractors to be enemies to the degree that reunited priests were held to be traitors. Regarding the Soviet state as a personification of the devil was a common theme of the religious imaginary at the time. Atheistic campaigns and the general repression of religion were perceived as signs of an evil presence against which Christians had to fight in order to remain strong in faith. The stakes were high for those who were part of the underground, and their position required

[257] In his book Emanuil explained how spiritual authority had been transferred by Pope Pius XII to him in Seredne between 1954 and Pius's death in 1958. Emanuil's explanation combined historical facts and visionary arguments.

moral severity and firm convictions – unlike the position of the reunited priests, who opted for compliance and joined the Orthodox church, which was a Bolshevik church and thus evil, according to underground believers.

The radical accents of the visions were a reflection of the times and the lack of choice. In 1958, when the KGB sought out underground priests in order to make them sign a statement that they would refrain from all religious activity, the message of the visionary incriminated in no uncertain terms those priests who chose to sign the agreement. At the same time it provided a moral model to follow: martyrdom.

> Priests committed a sin: they signed the warning about religious activity . . . This sin is bigger than the first one [reunion with Orthodoxy]. The first [sinners] undersigned openly, and these ones in secret, and they believe this is no sin . . . The true shepherd gives his soul for the flock; the true shepherd does not cover the eyes of the wolf: 'he either kills the wolf, or he dies by the wolf' (Emanuil 2001: 68).

The development of such an extreme religious movement, combining apocalyptic imagery, suffering, and salvation, all couched in terms of Galician traditions and Ukrainian nationalism, triggered a brutal Soviet reprisal. The Soviet media initiated an intense campaign against the 'sect' in the 1950s and produced a film about the 'fake' apparition. The group reached a crisis in 1962 with the imprisonment of its leader, Father Ihnatii Soltys, and the failure of the initial prophecy about the end of the world. The movement, known until then as the Ihnatiivstsi, after its first leader, was reorganized and renamed itself Pokutnyky (Penitents) under the new leadership of another underground Greek Catholic priest, Anton Potochniak. State repression resumed in 1968 when Potochniak was arrested and his group subjected to severe persecution. The adult members of the group were sent to Siberia or locked in psychiatric hospitals, while their children were put into state orphanages. Authorities repeatedly bulldozed the apparition site and cemented over the spring.

In spite of the repression, the group partially survived, and its remaining members continued to witness apparitions and to meet in Seredne on the 'Holy Mountain'. Their visions and dreams sustained and updated the original vision according to new challenges, thus providing guidance to group members and reinforcing their crusade against communism. According to Emanuil's book, visions and dreams continued to be experienced by more than one visionary until 1978.

Plate 26. The chapel of the Penitents, Seredne, 2003.

On a trip to Seredne in 2003, I tried to meet Pope Emanuil in order to learn more about the recent history of his community. On the famous hill near the village stood a wooden church serving the local community. A Greek Catholic parish had occupied the church since 1990, attended by a priest from the nearby village. The apparition site was on the opposite side of the hill, hidden behind trees. There I saw a small open chapel and 'three springs of holy water' – exactly as portended by the first of the Penitent visions. The only presence testifying to the existence of the community surrounding the miracle was a big house built on the road to the church. Two women lived there, but they scarcely mentioned the life of the Pokutnyky, remaining as secretive as before. The Penitents group still functioned in the same secretive way it did during Soviet times. The villagers whom I met were not part of the group and recognized neither the apparition nor the movement.

The few existing historical references on the subject mention that the group was composed mostly of peasant women and that its membership had decreased significantly since the 1970s. Nonetheless, there exists no realistic evaluation of the amplitude of the movement up to present times, although plenty of rumours circulate. Villagers occasionally witness the arrival and departure of people who walk to the hill, attend services, and then leave. As in Soviet times, there is no centre to the group, apart from the actual hill. There, young people, priests, and nuns come on certain dates to perform religious services. According to villagers' recollections, around a hundred people attend such services.

However, people do know about the Pokutnyky, usually referring to them as a sect, and in nearby villages it is easy to find someone who can guide you to a *sektanty,* a member of the movement. The apparent absence of a leadership structure and the shrinking of the group are reflected in the complete absence of Penitents from the postsocialist religious scene. Unlike other splinter groups that emerged after the legalization of the Greek Catholic Church in the early 1990s, the Pokutnyky remained silent on matters related to the institutionalization of the Greek Catholic Church. And unlike many other sites of holy apparitions and imagistic devotion, Seredne lies on no pilgrimage circuit for mainstream religious practice. Because of its extreme response to the political and social transformations of the Soviet era, the miracle of Seredne did not succeed in remaining part of the local religious imaginary. In this case, the universal Christian message typically promoted through Marian apparitions became too radical to appeal to a large mass of believers.[258]

In the 1980s several other apparition sites emerged in western Ukraine, attracting people to visit and triggering religious fervour. Believers heard about new apparitions and searched them out individually or in small groups. It was still dangerous to visit sites of devotion, for they were still considered anti-Soviet and were kept under surveillance by the secret police. Pilgrims taking the trouble to visit such places often arrived only to find the object of their pilgrimage destroyed. Agafia Mykhailovna, now a pilgrimage organizer, went on such trips during Soviet times as well. She recalled a trip she took in 1986 with a friend from L'viv to look for a new apparition site:

> Under the Russians it was not as simple . . . When I went to Bylychi [an apparition site] . . . I found out in the church, people were coming out of the church talking: 'In Samir there is a village and the Mother of God appears there, and the water there heals the eyes.' That's what people were saying to each other. It was 1986 and I decided to go with another woman . . . but it was hard, everything was hidden . . . you had to pretend that you were going there on some other business. Now one can find out [about new sites] through the church, the priest, and people.

---

[258] As I learned later, the Ukrainian pope, Emanuil, had died a few years earlier. Lacking a leader and the possibility of updating the group's message through new visions, the Pokutnyky seem to have faded away.

Increased visionary activity led to the appearance of new devotional sites all over western Ukraine during the late Soviet years, and some of them gained immediate popularity. Like the hill near Seredne, these sites became channels for collective expressions of religious feeling and engendered popular mobilization around religious symbols against the Soviet state. Personal visions and dreams emerging from such mystical encounters motivated courageous actions and individual initiatives that soon turned into a mass movement. One visionary, Iosyf Terelya, became a celebrated figure in Ukraine and abroad because of his relentless efforts to resurrect the Greek Catholic Church and spread the divine messages to which he was witness.[259] In 1982 Terelya founded the Initiative Group for the Defence of the Rights of Believers and the Church in Ukraine (also known as the Helsinki Group for the Protection of the Ukrainian Catholic Church in the Soviet Union), the first group to actively promote religious freedom in the Soviet Union, not only for Catholics but for all believers.

Terelya was also one of the visionaries of a famous apparition site in western Ukraine that announced the impending fall of the Soviet Union. In 1987 a twelve-year-old girl from Hrushiv, an obscure village south of L'viv, had a vision of the Mother of God near the local church. The news spread through the informal networks of the underground church, and people began to come to Hrushiv from all over the Soviet Union. The village became one of the most important pilgrimage sites in the USSR, almost on the scale of Medjugorje, a famous apparition site in Bosnia.[260]

In the late 1980s, similar visionary activity appeared in places throughout western Ukraine, at both new and old Marian sites: Spivoche Pole, Ozerna, Berezhany, Kamianka-Buzka, Buchach, Hoshiv, Zarvanytsia, and Ternopil. The 'miracle of the sun', an apparition originating in Fatima, Portugal, in the early 1900s was seen in each of these places, first by a visionary, usually a young girl, and later by large crowds of people, among whom many experienced visions and dreams.[261] The apparition in Fatima

---

[259] His stories are described in an autobiographical book, *Witness to Apparitions and Persecution in the USSR* (Terelya and Brown 1991).

[260] Local media estimated that 50,000 pilgrims arrived in the village daily (Markus 1989: 11). Medjugorje has acquired great fame, becoming one of the most visited apparition sites in the Catholic world. Since 1981, when six children first saw the Virgin Mary there, they have continued to receive and transmit her messages, gathering large crowds of pilgrims at the apparition site (see Bax 1995).

[261] In an apparition at Fatima, Portugal, the Virgin Mary promised to the visionaries that she would perform a miracle that everyone could see. On 17 October 1917, the Catholic pilgrims gathered there witnessed the transformation of the sun into a multicoloured, shining disk in which different saintly figures could be seen. This 'miracle of the sun' was repeated afterwards in many other apparition places inspired by the phenomenon in Fatima. The last

and the Virgin Mary's message there asking for the conversion of Russia clearly lent inspiration to the wave of apparitions in Ukraine. The state made several attempts to stop and discredit such visions, but it was overwhelmed by the scale of the phenomenon. Apart from such public apparitions, a multitude of private visions and small miracles were also taking place at the time, few of which could be documented or controlled by church or state officials. This increase in imagistic practices was a catalyst for religious revival in Ukraine. It provided believers with evidence of divine intervention and motivated them to strengthen their religious activism and increase their devotional activity.

7.2 Postsocialist Apparitions: Lishnia

The phenomenon of Marian apparitions did not end with the creation of the independent Ukrainian state in 1991 and the opening up of the religious sphere. Nor did apparition sites and visionaries fall under the control of newly established churches. In addition to previous sites still in use, several new sites have emerged in western Ukraine in recent years.[262] They are continuations of the Soviet-era apparition phenomenon, and both pre- and post-Soviet phenomena were inspired by twentieth-century Catholic imagery of Marian apparitions.[263] However, there are differences in the contents of the newer messages that reflect the changing circumstances of contemporary Ukraine. Nowadays, such miraculous apparitions are sometimes controversial, and local communities do not always support them. Their main bases of support are the large numbers of pilgrims who travel from all over Ukraine to see them and a certain category of priest that frequents the sites. In addition to numerous devotional sites that represent an alternative to mainstream religious practice, established religious places such as monasteries function in a similar way. Since the 1990s, monasteries have opened all over western Ukraine, producing a recurrent pattern: a miraculous spring appears nearby, followed by reports of healing and rumours of apparitions near the spring, which attract more pilgrims to the monastery.

---

message the Virgin Mary transmitted to the visionaries in Fatima, in October 1917, requested the consecration of Russia.

[262] These are Dzhublyk (Zacarpathia), where an apparition was seen in 2002; Lishnia (Drohobich), 2003; Vysoki Zamok (L'viv), 2003; and Nyjankovych (Starosambirski *raion*), January 2005.

[263] This imagery has been described in the anthropological literature by, among others, Christian (1989), Zimdars-Swartz (1991), Bax (1995), and Matter (2001). Each site can be compared to a specific model of apparition, such as Lourdes for healing and Fatima and La Salette for apocalyptic messages.

Among the more recent sites, the apparition of the Mother of God in Lishnia is known to pilgrims as 'the new Fatima'. Lishnia is a small village about ninety kilometres south-west of L'viv. There, in the summer of 2003, two ten-year-old village girls, Iulia and Nastia, were purportedly spoken to by the Mother of God. The local priest, Father Mykhail, was the first to question the girls about the apparition. Mykhail had been one of the first graduates of the Greek Catholic seminary after 1990, and when the event took place he had been priest of the village's Greek Catholic parish church for five years. He lived with his family in the village and so was well acquainted with the families of the two girls, all practising Greek Catholics and members of his parish.

Before informing his bishop, Father Mykhail questioned the girls about their vision and decided that they had not spoken to the Mother of God. Apparently, they could not even answer basic theological questions, and the message from the Mother of God they had transcribed contained a prayer that Mykhail was able to find in an old prayer book. His belief was that modern apparitions were usually generated by an evil force, as was written in the apocalypse of John in the Bible, and such visions should not be publicized by the church.

Under pressure from his parishioners, however, Mykhail enlisted a church committee to investigate the case. When I spoke with him, the committee had not yet completed its enquiry, but the priest was already convinced that the apparition was mere 'foolishness'. His worry about and vehemence against the apparition were motivated by the competition he felt emanating from priests who were regularly visiting the site to assist pilgrims. These travelling priests, or missionaries, are usually regular priests (monks) who go to serve communities lacking in priests. Priests who undertake such missions continue a mode of activity specific to the underground period and the early days of the religious revival.[264] Then, Greek Catholic priests in hiding travelled around the countryside to hold 'illegal' services in people's houses, in forests, and in abandoned churches. Now they visit apparition sites such as the one in Lishnia.

---

[264] This missionary phenomenon should not be confused with the missionary activity of the church in eastern Ukraine and elsewhere, where priests are sent to establish new parishes and build up Greek Catholic communities. The missions in western Ukraine are often connected to religious activities that parallel church practices, usually holdovers of the underground period and its mode of religiosity.

Plate 27. Pilgrims attending a liturgy in Lishnia celebrated by a travelling priest who is also Basilian monk, 2004.

The apparition site is near the river, in a field behind some houses. Despite the priest's discouragement, villagers support the verity of the apparition and the visionaries, and they have built a small chapel at the site. Local religious practice gravitates between the village church and the apparition site. People attend church on Sunday morning, and in the evening they gather at the apparition site to pray the rosary. The prayer takes place daily, at around 6.00 p.m. on weekdays, a time for villagers to visit the site in the absence of pilgrims. Pilgrims come during the weekend, and larger groups bring their own priest to perform the liturgy. On certain dates, travelling priests visit the site for special celebrations that include healing prayers and sometimes exorcisms. Both locals and pilgrims are aware of a site's 'schedule' and plan to be in attendance when the priests stop by. In Lishnia this happens on the twenty-second of every month, which does not coincide with the 'day' of any other apparition site. The two girls have visions on this day and write down short messages from the Mother of God to pilgrims. They also receive messages intended 'for the entire nation' (*za Ukrainski narod*) and sometimes 'for the entire world' (*za tsilyi svit*).

Among the pilgrims are some who see the Mother of God in a tree or in the sun and others who only feel the warmth of the place where she once appeared on a broken tree branch, which still lies on the ground. Many experience neither vision nor physical sensation, but participating in the ritual gives them the feeling that they have made an appropriate devotion. The liturgical service is less important than the reading of the message, which is the most intense moment. Afterwards, anyone can ask questions and receive a reply from the Mother of God through the mediation of the priest and one of the two girls. Most questions are related to personal and family problems, although there are also requests for further explanation of the earlier divine message, followed by an impromptu collective exegesis. The priest's authority is limited, and his social role is reduced to performing the liturgy and reading the message aloud.

Plate 28. Leaflet about the apparition in Lishnia, 2004. The pictures show the miraculous branch, the statue of the Mother of God, and the two visionaries holding icons of Bishop Charnetskyi, a famous underground figure and UGCC martyr.

Both questions and answers are concrete, and often pilgrims cross-check the answers of the Mother of God with those they have heard at other apparition sites. One person asks when the pope will die and is told, 'In four years'.[265]

[265] This was in February 2004, before John Paul II died. The person asked the question to cross-check the answer given by the Mother of God in Dzhublyk. She provided the same answer in both places, but this does not always happen. The content of the answer seems to

Another person is not accepted for confession and communion in her village church because she is not married to the man she lives with. She asks the Mother of God for absolution and receives a positive response, followed by a series of rituals she must perform in order to gain absolution. People often ask about relatives who are ill and receive spiritual recipes for healing or a prayer performed by the priest over the person who asks. Such specific answers are taken as guidelines by pilgrims and are not necessarily performed afterwards.

In one of her apocalyptic messages the Mother of God announced a series of cataclysms that would shake the world over the following thirteen years, among them the sinking of the American continent. Such messages create anxiety for pilgrims whose families are abroad, and they ask what will happen to their relatives in the United States. The Mother of God's answer, through the mouth of the visionary, is that they should return to Ukraine. In Lishnia the Mother of God's messages decry the separation of families, an important social problem today in Ukraine.

The same messages are transmitted in Dzhublyk, another apparition site in Zacarpathia. There, in September 2002, two girls had a vision of the Mother of God, and the site has since developed into an important pilgrimage destination, though still unrecognized by the Greek Catholic Church. In Dzhublyk the local bishop supported the visions and promoted them in the church.[266] The apparition of the Mother of God (*obiavlennia Bohorodytsi*) in Dzhublyk became the apparition of the Holy Family (*obiavlennia Presviatoi Rodyny*) once pilgrims also began to see Jesus and Joseph next to Mary. One of the visions asked for the erection of a monastery 'of the Holy Family' in Dzhublyk, prompting construction to begin in the summer of 2003.[267]

Dzhublyk and Lishnia are first of all places of unity. Recurring messages implore pilgrims to pray for the unity of the Ukrainian people, Christians, and churches (*zednaty tserkvy*). In Dzhublyk the Mother of God's first message to the girls was, 'I want to help to renew the authority of priests among the people, to unite this divided nation, and to unite the church.' Apart from typical requests for prayer, her messages contain precise instructions for bringing about this desired unity. She asks priests not to mention the word 'Orthodox' during the liturgy but to replace it with 'Christian', and

matter less than the act of asking and being answered, which is why inconsistencies in answers are often overlooked.

[266] Ivan Margytych, the late local bishop, together with the two visionaries and a group of other people, visited the pope in December 2002 to ask for his blessing and for the initiation of a commission to investigate the apparition.

[267] The construction stopped soon afterwards because of a conflict between locals and clergy that caused the head of the monastery, Father Artemie, to leave Dzhublyk and move to Kolodiivka, where he resided in 2004.

she makes special reference to one prayer in the liturgy called 'the prayer of the faithful'. This plea for unity is obvious in common discussions in which people complain about 'fragmented Orthodoxy'.

In Lishnia people are asked to pray the rosary for the conversion of souls, after the Fatima model, but the explicit focus is on eastern Ukraine, the part of the country perceived to be atheist. People pray with the idea of bringing God to a certain part of Ukraine and beyond it, for the conversion of souls and the purification of cities (*pochystyty mista*). This is an attempt to create a meaningful relation between west and east, one of the unsolved problems of the new Ukrainian state.[268] The intense missionary activity of priests and laypersons and the opening of new communities by all religious groups present in Ukraine show that a real effort is under way to 'convert the east'. This activity is closely accompanied and justified by an increased preoccupation with eastern Ukraine in the local religious imaginary. The Mother of God is the privileged means for this activity, not only because of her role as intercessor but also because of the images of purity and innocence she carries. The multiple meanings this symbol bears makes her the best tool for such an enterprise to be effective in both regions. Yet apart from these collective imaginings, as translated into concrete practice, each participant contextualizes the holy message according to his or her personal understanding. The religious act of praying for someone unknown takes place with an awareness of its social use and the concomitant integration of the 'other' into the religious imaginary.

Visions are not restricted to any specific location or person; the Mother of God appears not only in Lishnia and not only through the mediation of visionaries. Most pilgrims who have seen her or participated in such rituals feel empowered to communicate with the divine themselves. They continue to have visions at home or, more commonly, to have dreams related to the visions. These are held to be true because their content draws on the religious imaginary related to apparitions, and later confirmations are provided by Marian messages heard at the apparition site. This offers to a number of people the means to act in their lives in a particular way inspired by the lived experience of imagistic rituals, as was the case in Kolodiivka.[269]

Tereza is a person who has had such intense religious experiences. She comes from a highly educated religious family, and both her grandfather

[268] Yet even the difference between eastern and western Ukraine is more imagined than real, as is shown in an excellent article based on a comparison between two emblematic cities, L'viv and Donetsk (Hrytsak 2000).

[269] This is of course a limited phenomenon, and the number of 'enchanted' people is small. This has always been the case, and today their role as agents of change is reduced relative to what it was during Soviet times.

and father were Greek Catholic priests. The family suffered under the Soviet regime. Because her father did not want to sign the reunification agreement, the whole family was arrested and sent to Siberia. Tereza now lives in Sykhiv and frequents the Church of the Nativity there at least once a week, on Friday or Sunday. For her, however, the religious service at the Nativity church is too strict, so she tends also to visit other churches in L'viv where the practice is closer to her views. She does not feel linked to any single church or priest, and her devotional routine involves visits to several church services and a series of carefully selected private prayers. She is part of a group of continuous prayer similar to the prayer chain in Shchirets; it prays thematically according to the most urgent spiritual needs. At the time of my fieldwork the group was praying for the conversion of souls in eastern Ukraine because the Mother of God, in her appearance in Lishnia, requested such prayers. Tereza's obligation was to pray the rosary for the Holy Family between 1.00 and 2.00 a.m., ten days out of each month, for the entire year.

Together with her older sister, and often joined by other family members and acquaintances, Tereza travels to apparition sites and monasteries in western Ukraine, usually through organized pilgrimages. In the two years since the first apparition in Dzhublyk she had visited Dzhublyk nine times, and Lishnia, a more recent apparition, just four. Both she and her sister have experienced visions in Lishnia and Dzhublyk. In their encounters they see the Mother of God bearing certain features that are not common to the usual Marian representations. Both continue to have visions at home while in prayer or upon waking in the night, as well as dreams in which different religious figures appear and communicate. After several of these dreams and visions Tereza developed a special relationship with a few of the saints who appeared to her more often, and she appeals to them when there is a particular problem to be solved. She finds it difficult to confess her visionary activity to either priests or her family, because she believes neither is prepared to understand. She considers that it is a matter of 'understanding' (*rozumyty*) first of all, and then of 'believing' (*viryty*) in visions:

> Not all priests [can] understand . . . what for example the abbot in Univ [monastery] understands . . . Not all of them practise [deal with spirits], do they? Not all priests perform exorcisms. They don't understand, [they] might even say that it's not true, but actually it is!. . . And such miracles! . . . But why the church didn't recognize it until now, I don't know . . . Still people go, are cured, and understand.

The more recent apparition sites are connected not only by the similarity of the messages emanating from them but also literally by the pilgrims, priests, and objects that travel between them – a regular traffic of people, songs, prayers, pictures of the Mother of God, and travelling icons. Pilgrims who visit a site have usually visited at least one other beforehand. The travelling priests also tour the apparition sites, celebrating liturgies for pilgrims. Instead of competition, there is mutual support among the sites, and the divine messages emphasize the spiritual connections between them. This is how pilgrims start mapping the landscape, by symbolically connecting several sacred places.

The most visible result of symbolic mapping is the recently built Way of the Cross (Hresna Doroha).[270] During the autumn and winter of 2003, 15 crosses, each 6 metres tall, were placed across a 300-kilometre area, in small villages, on the sides of roads, on distant hills, and at the borders between oblasts (see map 3). The erection of every cross was attended by three to four priests, who blessed the cross during a short service. The priests, among whom was Vasyl Voronovsky, the exorcist, were always accompanied by the travelling icon of the Mother of God called the Chair of Wisdom (Prestil Premudrosti), which the pope blessed in 2001 in Sykhiv. The religious journey along the Way of the Cross, symbolizing a penitent pre-Pascal prayer, starts in L'viv, the centre of western Ukraine, and goes to Dzhublyk, the new spiritual centre in Zacarpathia. The first cross in L'viv was placed on Vysokii Zamok, the hill overlooking the city. Recently the hill became a site of devotion when the Mother of God was reported to have appeared there. The entire Way of the Cross project was initiated and supported by a lay community from L'viv called the Missionary Fellowship Thanking God's Cross (Podiachnoho Khresta Hospodnoho). Its mission was to create spiritual unity between L'viv and the apparition site in Dzhublyk. En route to Dzhublyk, pilgrims from L'viv stop to perform the stations of the cross as part of their preparation for their divine encounter with the Mother of God. In their actions one sees a process of symbolic appropriation and connection between distant places through symbolic mapping.

---

[270] The Way of the Cross is a Catholic prayer, usually recited during Lent and important penitential celebrations, that commemorates the last moments of Jesus's life, from his arrest to his burial.

Plate 29. The travelling icon of the Mother of God that, together with her carrier, witnesses all major Greek Catholic events and sites of popular devotion. L'viv, 2004.

7.3 Conclusion

Recent years have seen an increased number of apparitions, visions, and pilgrimages to shrines and holy places throughout the postsocialist region. The proliferation of imagistic practices is neither a new phenomenon nor unique to the post-Soviet setting. In a book discussing religious imagery in Malta, Paul Clough and J. P. Mitchell drew the conclusion that as a reaction to modernity, Maltese Catholic society had produced an imaginative excess of religious belief and practice: 'Social fluidity empowers the religious imagination' (Clough and Mitchell 2001: 244). These creative responses were continuously shaped by collective imagery and often corrected by religious institutions and their representatives.

But religion is also a field of action with the power to transform social reality through individual agency (Taussig 1987: 447). Religious rituals, particularly those of the imagistic type, allow individuals to become agents of social change. In Catholicism, imagistic activity remains at the margins of institutional religion, rarely entering mainstream practice and never making its way into doctrine. Still, it serves a definite function in the preservation and renewal of the religious tradition. As in any religious tradition, in Catholicism revelation is the mechanism through which innovation takes place, providing new motivations and hopes (Christian 1996: 399). Believers have little input into the official doctrine and practice of the Catholic Church. Yet 'by praying at new places, by venerating uncanonized holy persons, and by joining groups not yet approved, Catholics make statements about the way heaven ought to be' (Christian 1996: 400), their only avenue for amending a doctrinal religion. In contrast, such imagistic practices seem better integrated into mainstream Orthodoxy and act as catalysts of social change.

In the Christian world, Marian apparitions have long been regarded by scholars as believers' favourite means of expressing ambivalence about social and political tensions. Scholars of modern Christianity, notably Sandra Zimdars-Swartz (1991) and William Christian Jr. (1984, 1996), have explained the twentieth-century rise in apparitions of the Virgin Mary as part of a broader response to social and political tensions. During the most difficult periods of the Soviet regime, an increase in apparitions in western Ukraine mobilized national and religious feelings around visionaries and apparition sites. Visions became a means of empowerment for activists opposing the regime (Markus 1989; Bociurkiw 1993). This shift in ritual practice towards more imagistic modes of religiosity deepened the breach between the community of believers and the official church.

The new apparitions carry with them a message of revolt against modernity and secularization, together with a concern for contemporary social problems. Comparing the 'miracle of Seredne' and the resulting Pokutnyky movement of Soviet times with the postsocialist visions at Lishnia and Dzhublyk shows that the imagistic response present in each case represents a pattern of accommodating social change in the local religious tradition. These cases also show that rather than being motivated by psychological factors such as boredom and apathy, as in Whitehouse's modes of religiosity model, the imagistic mode serves to channel individual creativity into religious imaginaries, freshening doctrine and ritual.

Marian apparitions take place all the time in western Ukraine, and new places emerge to replace forgotten ones. The mechanisms for keeping an apparition site functioning can be of two types: imagistic, when the message is updated by permanent visionary activity and dreams, and doctrinal, when the church institutionalizes the apparition site, standardizing ritual practice and devotion. In both cases there is a political dimension involving religious experts who either uphold the visionaries as alternatives to church hierarchy by promoting their message as a critique of doctrine or else take over the vision and the site for the church (for an example in Poland, see Buzalka 2007: chapter 5). Irrespective of politics, people continue to visit these sites and sometimes, as I would argue for the cases presented here, actually 'create' the apparition to satisfy their needs for an alternative expression of religiosity.

Local communities in western Ukraine benefit to a limited extent from apparition sites, although sometimes they oppose such apparitions. The Basilian order supports the sites and thus promotes the imagistic trend within the Greek Catholic Church against the line of doctrine proposed by church hierarchs. In this sense Basilians are a classic example of the kind of competition and power struggle between monastic orders and church organization that Mart Bax (1995) showed for Medjugorje. Yet Lishnia and Dzhublyk are not just means of instrumentalizing religious politics. The imagistic activity related to apparition sites is part of the variety of local religious expression and should be seen as one modality of transmission in a continuum of modalities encompassed in the local tradition. Apparitions thus can be understood as a means through which religion is adjusted. Such small but cumulative changes can reshape vast collective institutions, and this dynamic of change is embedded in the eastern Christian tradition. The imagistic rituals surrounding visionary activity draw on the religious imaginary, which is at the same time shaped by individual creativity active in the ritual process. By investigating religious imaginaries and the variety of religious expressions within a particular religious tradition, one can better understand the workings of religion in the postsocialist context.

Chapter 8
Conclusion

Exploring the religious dynamics of western Ukraine in the context of post-socialist transformations reveals the mechanisms of reproduction and change at work in an eastern Christian religious tradition. To a certain extent Harvey Whitehouse's modes of religiosity theory provides a useful frame for this exploration, because of the explanatory potential of the modes' interaction. As I carried out this exploration, attempting to move beyond the apparent plurality of faiths emerging in Ukraine since the 1990s, the focus of my research turned out to be religious practices more than religious institutions or identities. Because of the emphasis on orthopraxy in Orthodox theology, such an approach corresponded to the church's own conception of itself. The Orthodox church is a community of practice, in the sense of practising the sacraments (Lossky 1985; Badone 1990), and so it creates and reproduces tradition through practice rather than through doctrinal interpretation.

In order to research a religious tradition such as eastern Christianity, which has a long tradition of literacy, one needs to work with its theological products and historical accounts alongside ethnographic materials. Orthodox theologians have extensively engaged the question of tradition and generated a considerable body of literature. They have tried to explain how such a variety of churches and local traditions could be united under one commonly acknowledged label, Orthodoxy. The answer, coming especially from the work of Vladimir Lossky (1985), is based on a model of 'Tradition' as a 'living tradition of faith' that preserves all past and particular forms of religious expression, renewing itself directly through revelation. This theological idea contradicts the common image of Orthodoxy as a conservative tradition, resistant to change, a view that is largely maintained in anthropological treatments of the topic.

An ethnography of the local religious tradition of western Ukraine not only challenges widespread images of Orthodoxy but also helps further the understanding of mechanisms of change in a religious tradition. To frame it in Whitehouse's terms, I believe change occurs in eastern Christianity as the outcome of a particular alternation between the doctrinal and imagistic modes of religiosity. Through expressions of religiosity belonging to the imagistic mode, minor but cumulative changes reshape local tradition in western Ukraine. The precise manner in which imagistic rituals channel such changes has been discussed in the literature, predominantly in relation to phenomena such as possession trance, exorcism, and visions. What the case of western Ukraine contributes to these discussions is a better comprehension of the function and role of imagistic rituals in eastern Christianity. When seen through the filter of the modes theory, eastern Christianity appears to have found an equilibrium in which both modes are equally effective means of religious expression.

In studying religion in western Ukraine, both diachronic and synchronic perspectives are useful. The evolution of the local (Galician) tradition involved a synthesis of influences from eastern and western Christianity. Because Greek Catholics are products of the interaction between the two great traditions, they offer a valuable window into features of eastern Christianity as a whole. Because of the nature of Orthodoxy, which forms a unified imagined community despite all its particular traditions, one can discuss a local tradition and eventually make claims about eastern Christianity at large.[271] In the religious tradition of western Ukraine, Greek Catholic and Orthodox are conjectural identities, for both communities are ultimately rooted in the same local tradition. People connect to an Orthodox imaginary that encompasses the four eastern Christian churches present in western Ukraine. This, I believe, rather than the models advocated by sociologists and uncritically accepted by anthropologists, is what constitutes the tolerance of plurality and the basis for practising religious pluralism in this region. As a result, people move beyond confessional borders and transport their practices between churches, leaving aside those aspects of their practice that would appear too different and thus represent otherness.

The existence of the Orthodox imaginary calls into question the specificity of Greek Catholic identity. The identity markers used in the few previous anthropological works dealing with Greek Catholics were ethnicity, language, and rite. But such markers fail to effectively differentiate the Greek Catholic Church from other Orthodox churches in Ukraine. In Greek Catholicism, eastern and western Christianity are embedded to such an extent that they and their influences cannot be separated. The continued existence of Greek Catholicism is a matter of balancing the two tendencies.

---

[271] Charles Stewart (1991) took a similar approach in his work on Greek Orthodoxy, in which he was sensitive to the particularities of the Orthodox tradition as shaped by interaction with local culture.

The position of Greek Catholics at the peripheries of these great Christian traditions has been a source of both conflict and growth.

The Greek Catholic Church draws on two models of authority that derive from its western and eastern influences, respectively: church hierarchy and the diffuse authority of tradition. Both models work in practice, producing the dissimilar trajectories of the two splinter groups discussed in chapters 4 and 6. 'Traditionalists' emerged as a splinter group because of their 'purification of rite', a transformation of the mode of religiosity from the imagistic mode of the underground period to the doctrinal mode of the normal functioning of the church. Traditionalists chose to operate according to Catholic authority, thus challenging the authority and orthodoxy of the church until they were expelled from it. The monastic community in Kolodiivka, on the other hand, exploited the Orthodox roots of the church. The monks looked for their own expression of religiosity within the limits of the religious tradition, thus remaining within the tradition's basic doctrine, its salvation idiom. The monks found exorcism, an imagistic ritual well maintained in the church, and placed it at the core of their community. Their case shows that changing forms of religiosity alter the patterns of social organization.

To a certain extent, looking at the monks' practice, one can speak of the 'Pentecostalization' of this Orthodox community. This development could be part of a more general change in patterns of religious expression that also accounts for the rapid spread of Pentecostalism worldwide (Robbins 2004). With the imagistic ritual at the core of their community, the monks in Kolodiivka developed a religious practice similar to that of charismatic churches, centred on an unmediated relationship with divinity manifested through 'gifts', visions, and dreams. Their experiment in creating an ideal community can be seen as a solitary example, but in the future it might also inject a more substantial innovation into local tradition. In eastern Christianity, monasteries have always been defenders and, at the same time, innovators of religious tradition.

In order to grasp the variety of religious forms in western Ukraine, I have attempted to cover a wide range of religious practices and expressions of local tradition. Each ritual can be seen against the background of everyday religious practice, moving between the two ideal poles, the imagistic and doctrinal modes of religiosity. Each of the three communities I have described – Sykhiv, Shchirets, and Kolodiivka – draws on a specific set of practices and represents a different type of community of practice. In a comparison of rural and urban religiosity, interesting similarities emerge, revealing that a continuity of practice exists between the two. Under socialism, rural religiosity served as a storehouse of rituals and beliefs and formed the core of church tradition. The underground experience shows that religious tradition has the capacity and mechanisms to adapt to extremely hostile conditions. The church's situation during the underground years generated unexpected problems that were solved with the available means. The practical adaptability adopted by priests and the laity altered religious practices, and these modifications called into question and eventually modified official doctrine. At the time, religious institutions had no means of enforcing doctrine on underground practitioners, and religious authorities had little opportunity to perform regular checkups on practice, as the doctrinal mode would require.[272]

The underground experience was tremendously important for the Greek Catholic Church and its local religious tradition. Fortunately for scholars, an impressive documentation of the underground church exists in the oral history archive of the Institute for Church History in L'viv, although this archive has been underutilized.[273] The church's oral history project is, however, somewhat one-sided, focusing on issues that support the 'making of the Greek Catholic church' and obscuring most of its failures. The catacomb church and its martyrs, as presently perceived, are products of this explicit project related to the recovery of memory, a project in which individual memories have been transformed into the standardized memory that constitutes the 'official' history of the church. The uses of memory discussed in chapter 4 have been part of a process of institutionalization that meant, first of all, a distancing of the mainstream from the practices of the underground. I have differentiated between two stages in the postsocialist religious life of western Ukraine: first, the making of churches, accompanied by social reorganization and unrest, and second, the institutionalization of the church, starting in the mid-1990s.

The fit between the modes model and my analysis of the religious tradition in western Ukraine exposes not only the theoretical benefits but also the limits of the cognitive approach. Whereas Whitehouse's main finding was the connection between cognitive and social processes, a relationship anthropologists have only recently begun to appreciate, I have used his theory to analyse social reality almost independently of psychological factors. My observation is that often the psychological explanations Whitehouse proposed to account for social dynamics can be replaced by explanations related to social context instead. In the modes model, the dynamics of

[272] Priests maintained their role as observers of orthodoxy, but because of the restricted conditions in which they found themselves, they also had to adapt creatively rather than adhere to doctrine.

[273] The doctoral work of Natalia Shlikhta (2004a) is still the only substantial publication in English that makes extensive use of the ICH's oral history archive.

change depend on a psychological factor called the 'tedium effect', that is, boredom. The church, long preoccupied with combating boredom (acedia), which theologians perceived as a sinful condition, found the means to integrate it into its doctrine as a necessary part of the religious experience (Raposa 1999). Thus boredom, which suggests the 'dark night of the soul' described by Saint John of the Cross, a sixteenth-century Catholic mystic, came to be seen as a necessary stage in the spiritual journey, a stage that announces an imaginative eruption. But this psychological cause and the proposed interaction of the modes of religiosity are seldom found in reality, and Orthodoxy does not require boredom to renew itself. In eastern Christianity and presumably elsewhere, splinter groups rarely arise, because the imagistic mode sits at the core of the religious tradition. Even when one witnesses an intensification of imagistic activity, it appears as a normal adaptive feature of the religious tradition, an attempt to react to change by either accommodating or rejecting it. In eastern Christianity the doctrinal religious structure possesses the flexibility to accommodate such changes, and so splinter groups do not have to arise continually to modify the norm.

Because the two modes are constructed as ideal types, it is common to find a mixture of rituals combining them. Especially in pluralistic communities such as those in western Ukraine, people tend to participate in all kinds of rituals and do not adhere to an exclusively doctrinal or imagistic set of rituals. It would indeed be efficient if religious institutions were to encourage both modes equally, but this rarely happens. What does happen is that religious traditions include all kinds of rituals drawing on both modes, and people alternate whenever it suits them, irrespective of the church's opinion.

The breaking apart of the monastic community in Kolodiivka that I mentioned in chapter 6 reveals another factor absent from the modes theory. In this case, conflict, and thus splintering, appeared when a group attempted to impose one mode as the norm of religious practice in a community. A similar situation appeared in the case of the traditionalists in western Ukraine. These examples show that opposition between the two modes is a matter of religious politics, not just of personal expression, and that power appears as a major factor in the dynamic interaction of the two modes of religiosity.

One of my goals in this book has been to illustrate the role religion plays as an agent in transforming social reality. One approach to this end was to examine the contents of religious imaginaries in relation to specific social transformations, because religious imaginaries encompass individual reactions to such changes, expressed in the religious idiom. Visionary activity, my example, emerged in various settings in western Ukraine during both the socialist and postsocialist periods. Apparitions are particularly related to times of unrest and social instability, which generate a surplus of imaginative activity channelled through imagistic practices. This offers an interesting comparison with postcolonial contexts in which religion has a similar function and offers the same means for accommodating change. My aim, however, has been to reposition imagistic activity in the western Ukrainian religious tradition against a background of doctrinal church practice. Seen through the lens of the modes theory, imagistic rituals, by channelling small and not necessarily spectacular changes into the mainstream tradition, appear to function as the means of innovation and change in religion.

My emphasis on religion, to the neglect of other social factors, reflects my wish to bring postsocialist reality into the anthropology of religion and to analyse religion through this approach. I have discussed Greek Catholicism as part of the larger eastern Christian tradition, to which Orthodoxy also belongs, in the hope of reframing such discussions in terms of praxis and forms of religiosity. I recognize, though, that the first shortcomings of such an approach stem from tackling big issues related to patterns of evolution in religious traditions on the basis of one ethnographic case, that of the western Ukrainian tradition. In order to engage with one of the great religious traditions, eastern Christianity, I have drawn on several different disciplines, the surfaces of which I have barely scratched. To follow the path I have suggested more fully, historians and theologians could exploit a larger base of materials than the one I have used.

Underpinning my argument in this book is the belief that society permeates individual consciousness and that individuals have the means to change social reality. Religion remains a major field for studying interactions between individuals and society, and recent theories in cognitive studies of religion have expanded our understanding of the interrelatedness of psychological and sociological processes. In restating the role of psychological processes in social dynamics, however, they overlook the role of social and historical dimensions in shaping individual cognition.

Bibliography

Anderson, B. 1991. *Imagined Communities: Reflections on the Origin and Spread of Nationalism*. London: Verso.

Asad, T. 1993. *Genealogies of Religion: Discipline and Reasons of Power in Christianity and Islam*. Baltimore, MD: Johns Hopkins University Press.

Babiak, A. 2004. *Legitymnist' ukrainskoho patriarkhatu*. L'viv: Missioner.

Badone, E. 1990. *Religious Orthodoxy and Popular Faith in European Society*. Princeton, NJ: Princeton University Press.

Barker, E. 1997. But Who's Going to Win? National and Minority Religions in Post-Communist Society. In I. Borowik and G. Babinski (eds.), *New Religious Phenomena in Central and Eastern Europe,* pp. 25–62. Kraków: Nomos.

Barth, F. 1987. *Cosmologies in the Making: A Generative Approach to Cultural Variation in Inner New Guinea*. Cambridge: Cambridge University Press.

Bax, M. 1995. *Medjugorje: Religion, Politics, and Violence in Rural Bosnia.* Amsterdam: VU University Press.

Bellah R. N. 1980. *Varieties of Civil Religion*. San Francisco: Harper and Row.

Berger, P. 2001. Reflections on the Sociology of Religion Today. *Sociology of Religion* 62 (4): 443–454.

Bociurkiw, B. 1977. Religion and Nationalism in the Contemporary Ukraine. In G. W. Simmonds (ed.), *Nationalism in the USSR and Eastern Europe in the Era of Brezhnev and Kosygin,* pp. 81–95. Detroit, MI: University of Detroit Press.

——. 1991. The Ukrainian Autocephalous Church. In G. A. Hosking (ed.), *Church, Nation and State in Russia and Ukraine,* pp. 228–249. Basingstoke, UK: Macmillan.

——. 1993. UGCC v katakombah. *Kovcheh* 1: 124–125.

——. 1995. Politics and Religion in Ukraine: The Orthodox and the Greek Catholics. In M. Bourdeaux (ed.), *The Politics of Religion in Russia and the New States of Eurasia,* vol. 3, *The International Politics of Eurasia,* pp. 131–162. Armonk, NY: M. E. Sharpe.

——. 1996. *The Ukrainian Greek-Catholic Church and the Soviet State, 1939–1950*. Edmonton: Canadian University Press.

Bociurkiw, B. R., W. John, and J. K. Laux (eds.). 1975. *Religion and Atheism in the USSR and Eastern Europe.* London: Macmillan.

Boddy, J. 1994. Spirit Possession Revisited: Beyond Instrumentality. *Annual Review of Anthropology* 23: 407–434.

Boeckh, K. 2003. Staat und Kirchen während der Transformation in der Ukraine. In T. Bremer (ed.), *Religion und Nation: Die Situation der Kirchen in der Ukraine*, pp. 67–86. Wiesbaden: Harrassowitz.

Borowik, I. 2002. Between Orthodoxy and Eclecticism: On the Religious Transformations of Russia, Belarus and Ukraine. *Social Compass* 49: 497–508.

——., and G. Babi'nski (eds.). 1997. *New Religious Phenomena in Central and Eastern Europe*. Kraków: Nomos.

Bourdeaux, M. 1995. *The Politics of Religion in Russia and the New States of Eurasia*. Armonk, NY: M. E. Sharpe.

Bourguignon, E. (ed.). 1973. *Religion, Altered States of Consciousness, and Social Change*. Columbus: Ohio State University Press.

Bowie, F. 2000. *The Anthropology of Religion: An Introduction*. Oxford: Blackwell.

Boyer, P. 1990. *Tradition as Truth and Communication: A Cognitive Description of Traditional Discourse*. Cambridge: Cambridge University Press.

Boyko, N. 2004. Religion(s) et identité(s) en Ukraine: Existe-t-il une 'identité des confins'? *Revue d'Etudes Comparatives Est-Ouest* 35: 37–74.

——., and K. Rousselet. 2004. Les Eglises ukrainiennes: Entre Rome, Moscou et Constantinople. *Courier des pays de L'Est* 1045: 39–50.

Bruce, S. 1999. Modernisation, Religious Diversity and Rational Choice in Eastern Europe. *Religion, State and Society* 27: 265–275.

Buzalka, J. 2007. *Nation and Religion: The Politics of Commemoration in South-East Poland*. Berlin: LIT Verlag.

Caciola, N. 2000. Mystics, Demoniacs, and the Physiology of Spirit Possession in Medieval Europe. *Comparative Studies in Society and History* 42: 268–306.

Caldwell, M. 2005. A New Role for Religion in Russia's New Consumer Age: The Case of Moscow. *Religion, State and Society* 33: 19–34.

Casanova, J. 1998. Ethno-Linguistic and Religious Pluralism and Democratic Constructions in Ukraine. In B. R. Rubin and J. Snyder (eds.), *Post-Soviet Political Order: Conflict and State Building*, pp. 81–103. London: Routledge.

Chernish, N. 2003. Odna, dvi chi dvjadtsjat dvi Ukraini [One, two, or twenty-two Ukraines]. *Dukh i litera* 11–12: 6–20.

Christian, W. A., Jr. 1984. Religious Apparitions and the Cold War in Southern Europe. In E. Wolf (ed.), *Religion, Power, and Protest in Local Communities: The Northern Shore of the Mediterranean*, pp. 239–265. Berlin: Mouton.

——. 1989. *Person and God in a Spanish Valley*. Princeton, NJ: Princeton University Press.

——. 1996. *Visionaries: The Spanish Republic and the Reign of Christ*. Berkeley: University of California Press.

Clough, P., and J. P. Mitchell. 2001. *Powers of Good and Evil: Social Transformation and Popular Belief*. Oxford: Berghahn.

Condie, L. n.d. *The Practice of Exorcism and the Challenge to Clerical Authority*. Unpublished paper, University of Queensland.

Congregation for the Eastern Churches. 1996. The Inalienable Value of the Particular Heritage of the Eastern Churches and the Urgency of Its Flourishing. In *Applying the Liturgical Prescriptions of the Code of Canons of the Eastern Churches,* chapter 2. Vatican: Libreria Editrice Vaticana.

Conquest, R. 2002. *The Harvest of Sorrow: Soviet Collectivization and the Terror-Famine*. London: Pimlico.

Cox, H. G. 1996. *Fire from Heaven: The Rise of Pentecostal Spirituality and the Reshaping of Religion in the Twenty-first Century*. London: Cassell.

Creed, G. 2002. Economic Crisis and Ritual Decline in Eastern Europe. In C. M. Hann (ed.), *Postsocialism: Ideals, Ideologies, and Practices in Eurasia*, pp. 57–73. London: Routledge.

Crowley, D., and S. E. Reid. 2002. *Socialist Spaces: Sites of Everyday Life in the Eastern Bloc*. Oxford: Berg.

Csordas, T. J. 1997. *The Sacred Self: A Cultural Phenomenology of Charismatic Healing*. Berkeley: University of California Press.

——. 2001. *Language, Charisma, and Creativity: Ritual Life in the Catholic Charismatic Renewal*. Basingstoke, UK: Palgrave.

Czaplicka, J. 2002. *Lviv: A City in the Crosscurrents of Culture*. Cambridge, Mass.: Ukrainian Research Institute, Harvard University.

D'Anieri, P. J., R. S. Kravchuk, and T. Kuzio. 1999. *Politics and Society in Ukraine*. Boulder, CO: Westview Press.

Derdziak, L. 2002. Uwiezienie, Katorga i Meczenska Smierc Ks. Hryhorija Lakoty Biskupa Pomocniczego Grecokatolickiej Diecezji Przemyskiej. *Biuletyn Ukrainoznawczy* 8: 130–145.

Dorondel, S. 2002. Orthodoxy, Nationalism, and Local Identities: A Romanian Case Study. *Ethnologia Balkanica* 6: 117–144.

Dow, J. 1986. Universal Aspects of Symbolic Healing: A Theoretical Synthesis. *American Anthropologist* 88: 56–69.

Dragadze, T. 1993. The Domestication of Religion under Soviet Communism. In C. M. Hann (ed.), *Socialism: Ideals, Ideologies and Local Practice*, pp. 148–156. London: Routledge.

Dumas, F. 2000. *Gest si Expresie in Liturghia Orthodoxa*. Iasi, Romania: Institutul European.

Dunn, E. 1971. The Importance of Religion in the Soviet Rural Community. In J. R. Millar (ed.), *The Soviet Rural Community: A Symposium,* pp. 346–375. Urbana: University of Illinois Press.

Emanuil. 2001. *Seredne: Realnist vichnosti.* L'viv: Ukrainian Press.

Evdokimov, M. 1999. *Pelerini rusi si vagabonzi mistici* [Russian pilgrims and wandering mystics]. Targoviste, Romania: Pandora.

Fagan, G., and A. Shchipkov. 2001. 'Rome Is Not Our Father, but Neither Is Moscow Our Mother': Will There Be a Local Ukrainian Orthodox Church? *Religion, State and Society* 29: 197–205.

Fairbairn, D. 2002. *Eastern Orthodoxy through Western Eyes*. London: Westminster John Knox Press.

Finke, R., and R. Stark. 1996. Religious Choice and Competition. *American Sociological Review* 63: 761–766.

Fletcher William, C. 1981. *Soviet Believers: The Religious Sector of the Population*. Lawrence: Regents Press of Kansas.

Forbess, A. I. 2005. *Miraculous Democracy: Political and Religious Power in a Convent and Village of South Central Romania*. PhD thesis, Department of Anthropology, London School of Economics and Political Science.

Froese, P. 2004. After Atheism: An Analysis of Religious Monopolies in the Post-Communist World. *Sociology of Religion* 65: 57–75.

Gal, S. 1989. *Ritual and Public Discourse in Socialist Hungary*. Paper presented at the 91st annual meeting of the American Anthropological Association, Washington, DC.

Geertz, A. W. 2004. Cognitive Approaches to the Study of Religion. In P. Antes, A. W. Geertz, and R. R. Warne (eds.), *New Approaches to the Study of Religion,* pp. 259–399. Berlin: Walter de Gruyter.

Geertz, C. 1966. Religion as a Cultural System. In M. Banton (ed.), *Anthropological Approaches to the Study of Religion*, pp. 1–46. London: Tavistock.

Gellner, E. 1981. *Muslim Society.* Cambridge: Cambridge University Press.

Goody, J. 1986. *The Logic of Writing and the Organization of Society.* Cambridge: Cambridge University Press.

Grey, C. 2005. Demoniacs, Dissent, and Disempowerment in the Late Roman West: Some Case Studies from the Hagiographical Literature. *Journal of Early Christian Studies* 13 (1): 39–69.

Gudziak, B. 1998. *Crisis and Reform: The Kyivan Metropolitanate, the Patriarchate of Constantinople, and the Genesis of the Union of Brest.* Cambridge, MA: Harvard University Press.

——. 2000. Raccontare la storia ucraina. *Regno-Documenti* 15: 520–528.

Hamnett, I. (ed.). 1990. *Religious Pluralism and Unbelief: Studies Critical and Comparative*. London: Routledge.

Hanganu, G. Forthcoming. Eastern Christians and Religious Objects: Entangling Materiality with Networks of Relations. In C. Hann and H. Goltz (eds.), *Eastern Christianities in Anthropological Perspective.*

Hann, C. 1985. *The Village without Solidarity: Polish Peasants in Years of Crisis*. New Haven, CT: Yale University Press.

——. 1993a. Introduction. In C. M. Hann (ed.), *Socialism: Ideals, Ideologies and Local Practice*, pp. 1–26. London: Routledge.

——. 1993b. Religion and Nationality in Central Europe: The Case of the Uniates. *Ethnic Studies* 10: 201–213.

——. 1998a. Postsocialist Nationalism: Rediscovering the Past in Southeastern Poland. *Slavic Review* 57: 840–863.

——. 1998b. Ukrainian Epiphany in Southeast Poland. *Ethnologia Europea* 28: 151–168.

——. 1999. Ecclesiastical Property and National Identity in Postcommunist Poland. *Frontier* 1: 8–10.

——. 2000a. Problems with the (De)Privatization of Religion. *Anthropology Today* 6: 14–20.

——. 2000b. Culture and Civilization in Central Europe: A Critique of Huntington's Theses. In W. Konitzer and K. Bosselmann-Cyran (eds.), *Ein erweitertes Europa verstehen. Understanding an Enlarged Europe: The Role of the Humanities, the Social Sciences and Economics,* pp. 99–119. Frankfurt: Peter Lang.

——. 2002a. The Development of Polish Civil Society and the Experience of the Greek Catholic Minority in Eastern Europe. In P. G. Danchin, and E. A. Cole (eds.), *Protecting the Human Rights of Religious Minorities in Eastern Europe,* pp. 437–456. New York: Columbia University Press.

——. (ed.). 2002b. *Postsocialism: Ideals, Ideologies and Practices in Eurasia*. London: Routledge.

——. 2003. Creeds, Cultures and the 'Witchery of Music'. *Journal of the Royal Anthropological Institute* 9: 223–240.

——. 2005. The Limits of Galician Syncretism: Pluralism, Multiculturalism and the Two Catholicisms. In C. Hann and P. R. Magocsi (eds.), *Galicia: A Multicultured Land,* pp. 210–237. Toronto: University of Toronto Press.

Hann, C. M., C. Humphrey, and K. Verdery. 2002. Introduction: Postsocialism as a Topic of Anthropological Investigation. In C. Hann (ed.), *Postsocialism: Ideals, Ideologies and Practices in Eurasia*, pp. 1–28. London: Routledge.

Himka, J.-P. 1986. *The Greek Catholic Church and Ukrainian Society in Austrian Galicia.* Cambridge, MA.: Ukrainian Studies Fund, Harvard University.

——. 1988. *Galician Villagers and the Ukrainian National Movement in the Nineteenth Century*. Basingstoke, UK: Macmillan.

——. 1991. The Greek Catholic Church in Nineteenth-Century Galicia. In G. Hosking (ed.), *Church, Nation and State in Russia and Ukraine*, pp. 52–64. Montreal: School of Slavonic and East European Studies.

——. 1999. *Religion and Nationality in Western Ukraine: The Greek Catholic Church and the Ruthenian National Movement in Galicia, 1867–1900*. Montreal: McGill-Queen's University Press.

——. 2005. Confessional Relations in Galicia. In C. Hann and P. R. Magocsi (eds.), *Galicia: A Multicultured Land,* pp. 22–35. Toronto: University of Toronto Press.

Hitsiak, V. 2003. Traditsiia yak kamin' spotykannia. *Patriyarkhat* 1 (January–February): 14–16.

Hosking, G. A. 1991. *Church, Nation and State in Russia and Ukraine*. Basingstoke, UK: Macmillan.

Hrytsak, Y. 2000. National Identities in Post-Soviet Ukraine: The Case of Lviv and Donetsk. In Z. Gitelman et al. (eds.), *Cultures and Nations of Central and Eastern Europe: Essays in Honor of Roman Szporluk,* pp. 263–282. Cambridge, MA: Harvard University Press.

Hurkina, S. 2002. *Popular Religion in Ukraine: 1944–1989*. MA thesis, Ukrainian Research Institute, Harvard University.

Husar, L. 1989. Sheptyts'kyi and Ecumenism. In P. R. Magocsi and A. Krawchuk (eds.), *Morality and Reality: The Life and Times of Andrei Sheptyts'kyi*, pp. 185–200. Edmonton: Canadian Institute of Ukrainian Studies, University of Alberta.

Hvat, I. 1984. *The Catacomb Ukrainian Church and Pope John Paul II*. Cambridge, MA: Cambridge University Press.

Iordachi, C. 1999. Politics and Inter-Confessional Strife in Post-1989 Romania: From Competition for Resources to the Redefinition of National Ideology. *Balkanologie* 3: 147–169.

Irwin-Zarecka, I. 1994. *Frames of Remembrance: The Dynamics of Collective Memory*. New Brunswick, NJ: Transaction.

James, W. 2003. *The Varieties of Religious Experience: A Study in Human Nature*. London: Routledge.

Jepsen, H. 2005. Orthodoxy and Autocephaly in Galicia. In C. Hann and P. R. Magocsi (eds.), *Galicia: A Multicultured Land,* pp. 71–81. Toronto: University of Toronto Press.

Kapferer, B. 1991 [1983]. *A Celebration of Demons: Exorcism and the Aesthetics of Healing in Sri Lanka.* Washington, DC: Smithsonian Institution Press.

-----. 2003. *Beyond Rationalism: Rethinking Magic, Witchcraft, and Sorcery*. Oxford: Berghahn.

-----. 2005. Ritual Dynamics and Virtual Practice: Beyond Representation and Meaning. In D. Handelman and G. Lindquist (eds.), *Ritual in Its Own Right: Exploring the Dynamics of Transformation,* pp. 35–54. Oxford: Berghahn.

Keleher, S. 1993. *Passion and Resurrection: The Greek Catholic Church in Soviet Ukraine, 1939–1989*. L'viv: Stauropegion.

Kideckel, D. 1983. Secular Ritual and Social Change: A Romanian Example. *Anthropological Quarterly* 56: 69–75.

Kligman, G. 1988. *The Wedding of the Dead: Ritual, Poetics, and Popular Culture in Transylvania*. Berkeley: University of California Press.

Kokosalakis, N. 1995. Icons and Non-Verbal Religion in the Orthodox Tradition. *Social Compass* 42: 433–449.

Kovpak, V. 2003. *Peresliduvana tradytsiia*. L'viv: Liga Press.

Krindatch, A. D. 2003. Religion in Postsoviet Ukraine as a Factor in Regional, Ethno-Cultural and Political Diversity. *Religion, State and Society* 31: 37–73.

Lane, C. 1981. *The Rites of Rulers: Ritual in Industrial Society. The Soviet Case*. Cambridge: Cambridge University Press.

Levi, G. 1988. *Inheriting Power: The Story of an Exorcist*. Chicago: University of Chicago Press.

Lewis, I. M. 1990. Exorcism and Male Control of Religious Experience. *Ethnos* 55: 26–40.

Lossky, V. 1985. Tradition and Traditions. In V. Lossky, J. H. Erickson, and T. E. Bird (eds.), *In the Image and Likeness of God,* pp. 141–167. New York: St Vladimir's Seminary Press.

Low, S. 1994. Embodied Metaphors: Nerves as Lived Experience. In T. Csordas (ed.), *Embodiment and Experience: The Existential Ground of Culture and Self*, pp. 139–162. Cambridge: Cambridge University Press.

Lührmann, S. 2005. Recycling Cultural Construction: Desecularisation in Postsoviet Mari El. *Religion, State and Society* 33: 35–56.

Magocsi, P. R. 1983. *Galicia: A Historical Survey and Bibliographic Guide*. Toronto: University of Toronto Press.

——. 1996. *A History of Ukraine.* Seattle: University of Washington Press.

——., and A. Krawchuk (eds.). 1989. *Morality and Reality: The Life and Times of Andrei Sheptyts'kyi.* Edmonton: Canadian Institute of Ukrainian Studies, University of Alberta.

Mahieu, S. 2003. *Pour une anthropologie des variations religieuses: La recréation de l'Eglise gréco-catolique de Roumanie après 1989.* Paris: École des Hautes Études en Sciences Sociales.

——. 2004. Legal Recognition and Recovery of Property: Contested Restitution of the Romanian Greek Catholic Church Patrimony. *MPISA Working Paper* 69. Halle/Saale, Germany: Max Planck Institute for Social Anthropology.

——. 2005. *Statues or Icons? The Greek Catholic Divine Liturgy in Hungary and Romania, between Renewal and/or Purification.* Paper presented at the conference 'Eastern Christianities in Anthropological Perspective', Max Planck Institute for Social Anthropology, Halle/Saale, Germany, September.

Markus, V. 1989. Religion and Nationalism in Ukraine. In P. Ramet (ed.), *Religion and Nationalism in Soviet and East European Politics*, pp. 138–170. Durham, NC: Duke University Press.

——. 1995. Politics and Religion in Ukraine: In Search of a New Pluralistic Dimension. In M. Bourdeaux (ed.), *The Politics of Religion in Russia and the New States of Eurasia*, pp. 163–181. Armonk, NY: M. E. Sharpe.

Matter, A. 2001. Apparitions of the Virgin Mary in the Late Twentieth Century: Apocalyptic, Representation, Politics. *Religion* 31: 125–153.

McCauley, R. N., and E. T. Lawson. 2002. *Bringing Ritual to Mind: Psychological Foundations of Cultural Forms.* Cambridge: Cambridge University Press.

Milner, N. 2000. Giving the Devil His Due Process: Exorcism in the Church of England. *Journal of Contemporary Religion* 15: 247–272.

Mitchell, J. P. 1997. A Moment with Christ: The Importance of Healing in the Analysis of Belief. *Journal of the Royal Anthropological Institute* 3: 79–94.

Mitrokhin, N. 2001. Aspects of the Religious Situation in Ukraine. *Religion, State and Society* 29: 173–196.

Morris, B. 1987. *Anthropological Studies of Religion: An Introductory Text.* Cambridge: Cambridge University Press.

Naumescu, V. 2004. Burying Two Bishops: Legitimating the Church through the Politics of the Past in Romania. In F. Pine, D. Kaneff, and H. Haukaness (eds.), *Memory, Politics and Religion: The Past Meets the Present in Europe,* pp. 137–157. Münster: LIT Verlag.

Obeyesekere, G. 1981. *Medusa's Hair: An Essay on Personal Symbols and Religious Experience*. Chicago: University of Chicago Press.

Ortner, S. 1999. *Life and Death on Mount Everest: Sherpas and Himalayan Mountaineering*. Princeton, NJ: Princeton University Press.

Pankhurst, J. G. 1994. Sociological Models of Religion in Post-Communist Societies. In N. C. Nielsen (ed.), *Christianity after Communism: Social, Political and Cultural Struggle in Russia*, pp. 75–84. Boulder, CO: Westview Press.

Parkin, D. 1986. *The Anthropology of Evil*. Oxford: Blackwell.

Peel, J. 2004. Divergent Modes of Religiosity in West Africa. In H. Whitehouse and J. Laidlaw (eds.), *Ritual and Memory: Toward a Comparative Anthropology of Religion*, pp. 11–30. Walnut Creek, CA: AltaMira Press.

Pelikan, J. 1974. *The Spirit of Eastern Christendom (600–1700)*. Chicago: University of Chicago Press.

——. 1989. *Christian Doctrine and Modern Culture (since 1700)*. Chicago: University of Chicago Press.

——. 1990. *Confessor between East and West: A Portrait of Ukrainian Cardinal Josyf Slipyj*. Grand Rapids, MI.: W. B. Eerdmans.

Pelkmans, M. 2006. Asymmetries on the 'Religious Market' in Kyrgyzstan. In C. Hann and the 'Civil Religion' Group, *The Postsocialist Religious Question: Faith and Power in Central Asia and East-Central Europe,* pp. 29–46. Münster: LIT Verlag.

Petryna, A. 2002. *Life Exposed: Biological Citizens after Chernobyl*. Princeton, NJ: Princeton University Press.

Pine, F., D. Kaneff, and H. Haukanes (eds.). 2004. *Memory, Politics and Religion: The Past Meets the Present in Europe*. Münster: LIT Verlag.

Plokhy, S. 1995. Between Moscow and Rome: Struggle for the Greek Catholic Patriarchate in Ukraine. *Journal of Church and State* 37: 849–867.

——. 2002. State Politics and Religious Pluralism in Russia and Ukraine: A Comparative Perspective. In P. G. Danchin and E. A. Cole (eds.), *Protecting the Human Rights of Religious Minorities in Eastern Europe,* pp. 297–315. New York: Columbia University Press.

Pustomytivschyna. 2003. *Pustomytivschyna: Istoryko-kraeznavchyi narys*. L'viv: Poligraphic House.

Ramet, S. P. 1987. *Cross and Commissar: The Politics of Religion in Eastern Europe and the USSR*. Bloomington: Indiana University Press.

Raposa, M. L. 1999. *Boredom and the Religious Imagination.* Charlottesville: University Press of Virginia.

Razumkov Centre. 2004. *National Security and Defence* 51 (3). Kiev: Razumkov Centre.

Richardson, T. 2000. *History Education and Transformation in Soviet and Independent Ukraine*. PhD thesis, Department of Anthropology, University of Cambridge.

Robbins, J. 2004. The Globalization of Pentecostal and Charismatic Christianity. *Annual Review of Anthropology* 33: 117–43.

Rogers, D. 2005. Introductory Essay: The Anthropology of Religion after Socialism. *Religion, State and Society* 33: 5–18.

Rudnytsky, I. L., and P. L. Rudnytsky. 1987. *Essays in Modern Ukrainian History*. Edmonton: Canadian Institute of Ukrainian Studies, University of Alberta.

Sarris, M., 2000. *Some Fundamental Organizing Concepts in a Greek Monastic Community on Mount Athos*. PhD thesis, Department of Anthropology, London School of Economics and Political Science.

Schmemann, A. 1977. *The Historical Road of Eastern Orthodoxy*. New York: St Vladimir's Seminary Press.

Senyk, S. 2002. The UGCC Today: Values versus Nationalist Doctrines. *Religion, State and Society* 30: 317–332.

Sevcenko, I. 1996. *Ukraine between East and West: Essays on Cultural History to the Early Eighteenth Century*. Edmonton: Canadian Institute of Ukrainian Studies, University of Alberta.

Severi, C. 2004. Capturing Imagination: A Cognitive Approach to Cultural Complexity. *Journal of the Royal Anthropological Institute* 10: 815–838.

Shaara, L., and A. Strathern. 1992. A Preliminary Analysis of the Relationship between Altered States of Consciousness, Healing, and Social Structure. *American Anthropologist* 94: 145–160.

Shlikhta, N. 2004a. *The Survival of the Church under Soviet Rule: A Study in the Life of the Ukrainian Exarchate of the Russian Orthodox Church, 1945–1971*. PhD thesis, Central European University, Budapest.

——. 2004b. 'Greek Catholic' – 'Orthodox' – 'Soviet': A Symbiosis or a Conflict of Identities? *Religion, State and Society* 32: 261–273.

Sperber, D. 1985. Anthropology and Psychology: Towards an Epidemiology of Representations. *Man* 20: 73–89.

Spiro, M. 1999. Religion: Problems of Definition and Explanation. In N. Frankenberry and H. H. Penner (eds.), *Language, Truth, and Religious Belief: Studies in Twentieth-Century Theory and Method in Religion,* pp. 137–175. Atlanta, GA: Scholars Press.

Stephen, M., and L. K. Suryani. 2000. Shamanism, Psychosis and Autonomous Imagination. *Culture, Medicine and Psychiatry* 24: 5–40.

Stewart, C. 1991. *Demons and the Devil: Moral Imagination in Modern Greek Culture*. Princeton, NJ: Princeton University Press.

------., and R. Shaw (eds.). 1994. *Syncretism/Anti-syncretism: The Politics of Religious Synthesis*. London: Routledge.

Stirrat, R. L. 1992. *Power and Religiosity in a Post-colonial Setting: Sinhala Catholics in Contemporary Sri Lanka*. Cambridge: Cambridge University Press.

Strauss, C. 2006. The Imaginary. *Anthropological Theory* 6 (3): 322–344.

Sysyn, F. 1990. The Formation of Modern Ukrainian Religious Culture: The Sixteenth and Seventeenth Centuries. In G. Hosking (ed.), *Church, Nation and State in Russia and Ukraine*, pp. 1–22. Edmonton: Canadian Institute of Ukrainian Studies, University of Alberta.

------. 1993. The Third Rebirth of the Ukrainian Autocephalous Orthodox Church and the Religious Situation in Ukraine, 1989–1991. In K. Batalden Stephen (ed.), *Seeking God: The Recovery of Religious Identity in Orthodox Russia, Ukraine, and Georgia*, pp. 191–219. DeKalb: Northern Illinois University Press.

Szelenyi, I. 1981. Urban Development and Regional Management in Eastern Europe. *Theory and Society* 10: 169–205.

Tataryn, M. 2001. Russia and Ukraine: Two Models of Religious Liberty and Two Models for Orthodoxy. *Religion, State and Society* 29: 155–172.

Taylor, C. 2002. *Varieties of Religion Today: William James Revisited.* Cambridge, MA: Harvard University Press.

------. 2004. *Modern Social Imaginaries.* Durham, NC: Duke University Press.

Terelya, J., and M. Brown. 1991. *Witness to Apparitions and Persecution in the USSR: An Autobiography*. Milford, Ohio: Faith Publishing Company.

Turner, V. 1967. *The Forest of Symbols: Aspects of Ndembu Ritual*. Ithaca, NY: Cornell University Press.

------. 1995. *The Ritual Process: Structure and Anti-structure*. New York: Aldine de Gruyter.

------. 1996. *Drama, Fields, and Metaphors: Symbolic Action in Human Society*. Ithaca, NY: Cornell University Press.

Uehling, G. L. 2004. *Beyond Memory: The Crimean Tatars' Deportation and Return*. New York: Palgrave Macmillan.

Ugolnik, A. 1989. *The Illuminating Icon*. Grand Rapids, MI: Eerdmans.

Valtchinova, G. 2004. Constructing the Bulgarian Pythia: Intersections of Religion, Memory and History in the Seer Vanga. In F. Pine, D. Kaneff, and H. Haukaness (eds.), *Memory, Politics and Religion: The Past Meets the Present in Europe,* pp. 179–198. Münster: LIT Verlag.

Verdery, K. 1991. *National Ideology under Socialism: Identity and Cultural Politics in Ceausescu's Romania*. Berkeley: University of California Press.

——. 1999. *The Political Lives of Dead Bodies: Reburial and Postsocialist Change*. New York: Columbia University Press.

——. 2002. Whither Postsocialism? In C. Hann (ed.), *Postsocialism: Ideals, Ideologies and Practices in Eurasia,* pp. 15–28. London: Routledge.

Vial, T. 2004. Modes of Religiosity and Changes in Popular Religious Practices at the Time of the Reformation. In H. Whitehouse and L. Martin (eds.), *Theorizing Religions Past: Archeology, History and Cognition,* pp. 143–156. Walnut Creek, CA: AltaMira Press.

Vogelsang, I. 1996. *Narratives of History in Ukraine*. PhD thesis, Department of Social Anthropology, University of Manchester.

——. 2004. Soviet Ideology and Religious Practices in Simferopol, Crimea. In F. Pine, D. Kaneff, and H. Haukaness (eds.), *Memory, Politics and Religion: The Past Meets the Present in Europe,* pp. 157–178. Münster: LIT Verlag.

Wanner, C. 1998. *Burden of Dreams: History and Identity in Post-Soviet Ukraine.* University Park: Pennsylvania State University Press.

——. 2003. Advocating New Moralities: Conversion to Evangelicalism in Ukraine. *Religion, State and Society* 31: 273–287.

——. 2004. Missionaries of Faith and Culture: Evangelical Encounters in Ukraine. *Slavic Review* 63: 732–755.

Weber, M. 1963. *The Sociology of Religion*. Boston: Beacon Press.

Whitehouse, H. 1995. *Inside the Cult: Religious Innovation and Transmission in Papua New Guinea*. Oxford: Oxford University Press.

——. 2000. *Arguments and Icons: Divergent Modes of Religiosity*. Oxford: Oxford University Press.

——. 2002. Book Review Forum: Arguments and Icons: Divergent Modes of Religiosity. *Journal of Ritual Studies* 16: 4–59.

——. 2004. *Modes of Religiosity: A Cognitive Theory of Religious Transmission*. Walnut Creek, CA: AltaMira Press.

Whitehouse, H., and J. Laidlaw (eds.). 2004. *Ritual and Memory: Toward a Comparative Anthropology of Religion.* Walnut Creek, CA: AltaMira Press.

Whitehouse, H., and L. Martin (eds.). 2004. *Theorizing Religions Past: Archeology, History and Cognition.* Walnut Creek, CA: AltaMira Press.

Wilson, A. 2000. *The Ukrainians: Unexpected Nation.* New Haven, CT: Yale University Press.

Worobec, C. D. 2001. *Possessed: Women, Witches, and Demons in Imperial Russia.* DeKalb: Northern Illinois University Press.

Wynot, J. 2002. Monasteries without Walls: Secret Monasticism in the Soviet Union, 1929–1939. *Church History* 71: 63–79.

Yelensky, V. 2005. Globalization, Nationalism, and Orthodoxy: The Case of Ukrainian Nation Building. In V. Roudometof, A. Agadjanian, and J. G. Pankhurst (eds.), *Eastern Orthodoxy in a Global Age: Tradition Faces the Twenty-first Century,* pp. 144–175. Walnut Creek, CA: AltaMira Press.

Yurash, A. 2005a. Orthodox–Greek Catholic Relations in Galicia and Their Influence on the Religious Situation in Ukraine. *Religion, State and Society* 33: 185–205.

——. 2005b. Orthodoxy and the 2004 Ukrainian Presidential Electoral Campaign. *Religion, State and Society* 33: 367–386.

Zerilli, F. 2002. Sentiments and/as Property Rights Restitution and Conflict in Post-socialist Romania. *Focaal* 39: 71–89.

Zimdars-Swartz, S. 1991. *Encountering Mary: From La Salette to Medjugorje*. Princeton, NJ: Princeton University Press.

Zucker, L. 1987. Institutional Theories of Organization. *Annual Review of Sociology* 13: 443–464.

Zugger, L. 2001. The Greek Catholic Church in Soviet Ukraine and Belorussia. In C. L. Zugger, *The Forgotten: Catholics of the Soviet Empire from Lenin through Stalin*, pp. 420–446. Syracuse, NY: Syracuse University Press.

Archival Sources

Archive of Univ Monastery [Arkhiv Svetouspenskoii Univskoii Lavry]. Interview with Vasyl Voronovski, L'viv, 1994. Fund no. 6.

ICH (Institute for Church History [Instytut Istorii Tserkve]), Ukrainian Catholic University, L'viv. Oral History Archive. Interview with Vitaly Dudkevych, L'viv, 6 February 1999. Fund no. 1549-51/P-1-1-946.

——. Interview with Yury Hrynchyshyn, L'viv, 18 November 1999. Fund no. 2032/3.

——. Interview with Orest Fredyna, L'viv, 26 November 1999. Fund no. 2102, 2180/P-1-1-1090.

——. Interview with Oleksander Prylip, L'viv, 5 February 2000. Fund no. 2104/ P-1-1-1262.

——. Interview with Maria Onysko, L'viv, 2 July 1994. Fund no. 693/P-1-1-436.

——. Interview with Kateryna Radkevych, L'viv, 29 September 2003. Fund no. 1933/P-1-1-222.

——. Interview with Kateryna Tytych, Riasne-Ruska, 2 July 2003. Fund no. 2605/P-1-1-1532.

——. Interview with Sofia Ventyk, L'viv, 2 July 1994. Fund no. 693/ P-1-1-4365.

——. Interview with Sofia Volianiuk, Riasne 1, 18 June 2003. Fund no. 2607/P-1-1-1534.

——. Interview with Vasyl Voronovski, L'viv, 3 January 1994. Fund no. 1469/P-1-1-903.

——. Interview with Vasyl Voronovski, L'viv, 3 January 1999. Fund no. 1796,7,1811/P-1-1-903.

Appendix
Frequency of Individual Participation in Ritual Practices

The following two tables tally participation in or performance of various rituals by people I surveyed in Sykhiv and Shchirets. The figures are percentages of the total number of persons in the sample, including non-respondents, the numbers of whom were insignificant.

Table A.1. Percentages of People Surveyed in Six Religious Communities in Sykhiv Who Participated in Rituals ($N = 312$)

Ritual	Daily	Weekly	Monthly	Occasionally	Annually/ Seldom	Never
Standard prayers from prayer book	46.8	9.9	2.9	21.8	5.1	12.8
Prayer in own words	68.6	7.1	1.9	12.5	2.2	6.7
Fasting	1.3	12.5	1.3	48.4	21.8	13.5
Confession	2.6	1.9	17.6	31.1	34.6	10.9
Reading the Bible	11.9	10.6	6.4	35.3	25.0	9.3
Reading religious literature	12.2	9.9	6.7	37.8	20.5	12.8
Reading horoscopes	0.3	10.3	2.6	20.2	13.8	51.6
Using holy water, icons, candles	5.1	3.8	2.9	60.3	13.5	13.1

Table A.1. (continued)

Ritual	Daily	Weekly	Monthly	Occasionally	Annually/ Seldom	Never
Visiting cemeteries	—	3.5	11.2	51.3	27.2	5.8
Participating in pilgrimages, visiting holy places	—	2.2	2.6	23.4	22.8	46.8
Participating in liturgy/ prayer meetings	2.6	55.4	10.3	15.1	5.8	10.3
Participating in other church services (e.g. vespers)	2.9	15.4	6.1	30.4	12.8	31.4
Celebrating religious holidays in the family	0.3	3.5	10.9	76.0	5.1	3.5
Visiting healers, fortune tellers, psychics	—	—	—	1.9	4.8	90.4

Table A.1. (continued)

Ritual	Daily	Weekly	Monthly	Occasionally	Annually/ Seldom	Never
Having revelations, visions	1.0	0.6	1.0	5.4	8.0	83.3
Having house, icons, religious objects blessed	0.3	0.3	1.3	47.1	35.3	14.4

Table A.2. Percentages of People Interviewed in Shchirets Who Participated in Rituals ($N = 51$).

Ritual	Daily	Weekly	Monthly	Occasionally	Annually/ Seldom	Never
Standard prayers from prayer book	51.0	5.8	2.0	21.5	4.0	11.7
Prayer in own words	70.6	5.8	—	—	—	19.6
Fasting	—	4.0	5.8	41.2	35.2	13.7
Confession	—	—	4.0	8.0	80.4	4.0
Reading the Bible	5.8	4.0	4.0	53.0	19.6	9.8
Reading religious literature	7.8	11.7	2.0	58.8	31.4	5.8
Reading horoscopes	2.0	15.7	7.8	5.8	4.0	64.7

Table A.2. (continued)

Ritual	Daily	Weekly	Monthly	Occasionally	Annually/ Seldom	Never
Using holy water, icons, candles	5.8	—	4.0	66.6	13.7	4.0
Visiting cemeteries	—	4.0	14.0	39.2	25.5	2.0
Participating in pilgrimages, visiting holy places	—	—	—	11.7	33.3	53.0
Participating in liturgy/prayer meetings	5.8	53.0	17.6	17.6	—	4.0
Participating in other church services (e.g. vespers)	—	4.0	5.8	15.0	5.8	51.0
Visiting healers, fortune tellers, psychics	—	—	—	—	7.8	90.1
Having revelations, visions	—	—	—	—	7.8	90.1

Index